SBS

The Inside Story of the Special Boat Service

Also by John Parker

Investigative:

The Killing Factory: The Secrets of Germ and Chemical Warfare
The Walking Dead: Judge Liliana Ferraro, Mafia Hunter
At the Heart of Darkness: The Myths and Truths of Satanic Ritual Abuse
King of Fools
The Trial of Rock Hudson
Elvis: The Secret Files

Royalty:

The Queen: The New Biography
The Princess Royal: Biography of Princess Anne
Prince Philip: A Critical Biography

Film:

Five for Hollywood
Sean Connery: A Biography
The Joker's Wild: The Biography of Jack Nicholson
Polanski
Warren Beatty: The Last Great Lover of Hollywood
Michael Douglas: Acting on Instinct
Richard Gere
De Niro
Bruce Willis

SBS

The Inside Story of the Special Boat Service

John Parker

HEADLINE

First published in 1997
by HEADLINE BOOK PUBLISHING

10 9 8 7 6 5 4

British Library Cataloguing in Publication Data

SBS : inside story of the Special Boat Service
1.Great Britain. Royal Marines. Special Boat Squadron
2.Special forces (Military science) - Great Britain
I.Title
359.9'6'0941

ISBN 0 7472 1976 1

Typeset by
Letterpart Limited, Reigate, Surrey

Printed and bound in Great Britain by
Mackays of Chatham plc, Chatham, Kent

HEADLINE BOOK PUBLISHING
A division of Hodder Headline PLC
338 Euston Road
London NW1 3BH

Contents

Acknowledgements

'Not By Strength, By Guile'

As will be evident from the text, the history of the Special Boat Service from its foundation onwards is comprehensively portrayed in these pages, with many of its major operations of the last half century recorded and recalled, often by those who were there. Their motto, Not By Strength, By Guile, underscores the low profile that the SBS prefers and the reasons will soon become apparent. Members of the SBS, which today forms part of the British Special Forces Group, are exceedingly security conscious, and for a number of reasons.

They are generally involved in operations which are surrounded by utmost secrecy and which are often politically sensitive. Their specialised role in numerous skills which are unique to the SBS, for example, in counter-terrorism or intelligence-gathering techniques ahead of a large-scale troop landing, also means they use equipment and tactical procedures which are classified, far more so than their counterparts in the SAS.

Apart from the interests of national security and their compliance with the terms of the Official Secrets Act, SBS members must also consider their own safety. In the diversity of tasks confronting them in this modern age, they are well aware that they themselves may become targets, a fact which the author acknowledged in setting out on this project.

Even so, former members of the Special Boat Service and its associated units of the Second World War assisted in the compilation of this work. Their first-hand recollections, reports and private memoirs form the basis for a running narrative from its beginnings in 1941. They have been quoted throughout the ensuing chapters, along with extracts from a vast collection of archive material, much of it previously classified but now accessible at the Public Records Office and published here for the first time, with permission of the Crown Copyright Office.

The author wishes to record his sincere thanks and appreciation to all those who participated and gave their time and hospitality so freely during the numerous interviews, meetings and telephone conversations. Responsibility for accuracy of this work, however, rests solely with the author.

PART ONE

Legends and Heroes

1940 to 1945

The modern Special Boat Service emerged from a number of now-famous groups and virtual private armies formed during the darkest days of the Second World War and which were wound up at the end of it. Skills, disciplines and traditions in the particular art of clandestine amphibious raiding, invented and learned in times of great need, came forth, sometimes through careful planning but often simply from the sheer courage and determination of individuals. Many of their swash-buckling tales have been told in voluminous accounts of those war-time activities. While it is not possible to cover them all, a recap is necessary to set the scene for all that was to follow in the remaining half of the twentieth century. Part One of this book focuses on stories that, even today, remain largely untold or incomplete through official secrecy or individuals shunning publicity.

It is with the benefit of much previously unpublished material and dramatic, if reluctant, first-hand accounts that those early days and some legendary figures are remembered. A few historical vignettes are recalled from a catalogue of hundreds that abound from that era of the founders, with apologies to those involved in the many operations whose acts of bravery have, for reasons of space or repetition, been omitted. The intent here is to signpost the development of principal wartime units whose equipment and traditions (though not necessarily personnel) were merged at the end of the war to form the basis of today's SBS. The units are described on the next page.

FORMER WW2 UNITS MERGED TO FORM TODAY'S SPECIAL BOAT SERVICE

ARMY	MARINES	NAVY
Special Boat Sections, attached to 8 Commando, founded by Roger ('Jumbo') Courtney: 1SBS, 1940; 2SBS, 1942; 'Z' SBS, 1943; 1SBS temporarily merged with SAS in 1942 as Special Boat Squadron under Captain (the Earl) George Jellicoe in 1943	Royal Marines Boom Patrol Detachment formed in July 1942, famous for Cockleshell Heroes led by Major H.G. Hasler; SBS today considers itself a direct descendant of the RMBPD Small Operations Group founded in 1944 by Lord Mountbatten, South-East Asia Command, with A, B, C Groups of (Army) SBS	Combined Operations Pilotage Parties formed in great secrecy in September 1942 specifically for harbour and beach reconnaissance prior to landings of Allied forces in virtually every theatre of the war. Sea Reconnaissance Unit, formed in 1942

Chapter One

Jumbo's army

The twenty-second of June 1996. The date was chosen as the one on which we were to make contact, but the quiet, unassuming voice of advancing years gave me no clue that he recognised its significance. If he did, he was not the one who was going to mention it. For Lieutenant-Colonel Robert Wilson, DSO and Bar – 'Tug' to his service comrades – the day was just another, like every other 22 June that has passed during his retirement in the relative calm and total anonymity of that Regency watering-place of Royal Leamington Spa. He says he is no different from 10,000 other servicemen and -women, who were just doing a job at the time. And that's right.

Their numbers are declining but, thankfully, as these words are being written there are still many like him: silver-haired heroes of that era, able to recall, when specifically asked, what exactly they got up to, in detail so graphic that it must be imprinted on their brain cells. Any one of dozens of their escapades could have been chosen to begin this account, and we will meet more of them as these pages progress to the present day. This escapade was historic; a pinprick in the panoply of wartime activity, sure enough, but historic none the less.

Tug Wilson and his former colleagues don't make a fuss about the past because in accord with SBS tradition they dislike exaggerated accounts of their exploits, preferring to this day to remain shadowy silhouettes compared with their upfront compatriots of the

SAS. Also, in the early days it was bows-and-arrows stuff compared with the operations of their successors in the Service today, who are as finely tuned fighting machines as the high-tech weaponry surrounding them. What cannot be taken away is that the original founding principles of the SBS still hold good.

Tug Wilson and others like him were the advance party. They wrote the guidebook and plotted the course. They were the forerunners of all those who followed in the derring-do traditions of Special Forces the world over and specifically in the terms of reference for this book, the SBS.

Wilson was a trailblazer in Special Operations. As novelist John Lodwick, a later volunteer to the service, wrote of him: 'As leader of the first successful raids . . . he occupies a position in our hierarchy not unlike that of St Peter in Holy Mother Church.' The date of his first mission, and the first ever successful sabotage strike in wartime Mediterranean – which became the model for so many in the future – was exactly 55 years before the present author made contact for this work: 22 June 1941.

UP PERISCOPE. Lieutenant-Commander Tommo Tompkinson gave the order as His Majesty's U-class submarine *Urge* hovered under a calm sea three miles off the east coast of Sicily between Taormina and Catania. On the surface, the Mediterranean was shimmering under the late-afternoon sun of that hot summer. Mount Etna was hugely visible, a dramatic rising backdrop to this particular theatre of war as the periscope cut a wide arc through the water.

Tompkinson was on his assigned patrol for what was known by submariners as a 'billet', roaming the Straits of Messina off the coast of southern Italy along the route used extensively by enemy shipping, and lately to supply Rommel's burgeoning presence in North Africa with the Afrika Korps.

Today, Tommo had a secret weapon aboard: two founding members of 1SBS, Lieutenant Tug Wilson and his partner, Marine W. G. Hughes, a lean, small man, but tough. Wilson himself was no tough guy – he was handsome, slender and middle-class – but he and Marine Hughes shared a common bond: they were canoe fanatics, and both were desperate for action.

Their first outing together as a partnership in sabotage had been a month or so earlier, when they sailed in HMS/M *Triumph* with the object of attacking shipping in enemy harbours with limpet mines. The mission had been aborted through rough weather, and their only action on that occasion had been to sink an Italian copper-bottomed schooner, named *Tugnin F*, loaded with macaroni. *Triumph* had dropped the pair off in Alexandria but, anxious for another mission, Wilson and Hughes had hitched a ride to Malta and the HQ of the 10th Submarine Flotilla in search of action.

Captain Shrimp Simpson, boss of the 10th, was among those yet to be persuaded as to the value of such clandestine missions by free-ranging saboteurs, of sending out two men in a flimsy little canoe on demolition and attacking tasks. *More bloody trouble than they're worth!* In the end, and more by way of getting them out of his office, Simpson had signed the docket that gave them permission to go to sea with HMS/M *Urge* when she came in to refuel in the third week of June; he entered their departure in his log.

The pair stowed their collapsible canvas canoe, known as a folboat (originally spelled 'folbot') deep in the bowels of the submarine along with their cache of explosives, tommy-guns and knives, and *Urge* set off on a hunting expedition towards the southern Italian coast. They had no particular target in mind. The plan was that they would scan the shore looking for something important to blow up.

That day, as *Urge* lay submerged off the coastline just short of Catania, Tompkinson called Tug Wilson to the periscope as he swung it slowly across his horizon. Almost at the foot of Mount Etna he had spotted what looked like a tunnel serving the main railway line, which was surely a key transport link for Sicily's hefty population of Axis troops and their civilian associates. They studied their charts and confirmed the sighting.

'Will that do you?' asked Tompkinson in a challenging tone.

'Just the job,' Tug replied. 'Just the job.'

'OK. I'll drop you off a mile or so from the coast.'

Wilson and Hughes went to the wardroom to eat some ham sandwiches, study their maps for a suitable landing-site and prepare for their attack as soon as darkness fell. Then they gathered together their gear, swallowed a couple of benzedrine tablets and brought their flimsy-looking boat towards the forehatch, ready to launch when the submarine surfaced. They unravelled the canoe from its canvas stowing-pack. It was 4 feet 7 inches (1.4 metres) by 1 foot (30 centimetres) by 1 foot (30 centimetres) and weighed just 48 pounds (22 kilogrammes). They assembled the jointed rods that slotted together to form the frame over which the canvas was stretched.

The frame, in turn, was kept solid with six cross-members of marine plywood to make it pretty sturdy whatever the weather; or at least that was the theory. Buoyancy aids were fitted in the bow and the stern and then a canvas sheet was fixed to the top by metal clips; the sheet fitted around the two canoeists supposedly to keep them and their cargo of explosives, weapons and stores relatively dry.

The risk of capsizing, especially when the canoe was floated off the submarine casing in heavy seas, was ever present. Everything that might float away – like the paddles, the waterproof map case and the two tin tea-mugs, used as bailers – was attached to the frame by a length of fishing-line.

The summer sun had given way to moonless sky and a light mist shrouding the sea as *Urge*'s captain prepared to surface later that night. Tompkinson took his craft to within a mile of the shore, as close as he dared. Wilson and Hughes were ready, the adrenalin running high as the effects of the bennies kicked in. With the water still surging over the casing, they moved their canoe through the forehatch and completed its construction, replacing the timber cross-members that had been removed so that the canoe could be squeezed through the hatch, and loaded the 110 pounds (50 kilogrammes) of explosives.

They positioned the canoe at the bow of the casing, clambered gingerly into their positions, faces blacked up, clothes greased, paddles in hand and tommy-guns slung over their shoulders. When they were ready, Wilson gave the signal and the submarine advanced slowly forwards and then dived, allowing the canoe to float off. Wilson and Hughes paddled in unison towards the shore.

Their somewhat minimalist training, plus make-do-and-mend equipment (which included no form of communications other than a torch for signalling, covered by an old sock or some such to dim the beam) for operations that had grudging approval from the wartime hierarchy, hardly prepared them for this moment. But as Wilson recalled, nothing could prepare the human psyche for the nervous excitement that welled up as they pressed on cautiously towards the Sicilian beach and the first mission of this skilful partnership which was to do the enemy a good deal of damage.

As they struck out towards the shore, *Urge* vanished from view. She would return at a given time to an agreed position and surface when the captain spotted the pre-arranged signal by torch that the two saboteurs were heading back. As ever, the disappearance of the mother vessel left a twinge of anguish: 'Will she be there when we get back? Will we find her in the dark?' One day, as Tug Wilson would discover to his cost, she would not be, and he would be left high and not very dry. That day lay in the future. This time, the first time, everything looked to be set fair.

But on the outward journey they hit trouble.

Hughes suddenly stopped paddling. 'Voices!' he hissed.

Tiny Sicilian fishing-craft, working in darkness and not visible through the mist were dotted along the coastline. Fishing-boats were to become the bane of many SBS operations in enemy waters, not least to Tug Wilson in his future missions. On this occasion, Wilson and Hughes manoeuvred their canoe around and past them, zigzagging towards the coast without being spotted.

They had no predetermined landing-spot but discovered an inviting deserted cove with a shingle beach and a few convenient rocks where they could unload their explosives and hide their canoe before they set off inland in search of their target. The embankment from the cove was steeper than it first looked, but once at the top they could see a row of telegraph poles which Wilson knew from his maps ran by the railway line. They were less than a quarter of a mile from the tunnel, which appeared to have no guard. Even so, they had to make a couple of trips to carry their gear and explosives from the beach.

Tug Wilson selected a point 30 metres or so inside the tunnel to lay the gelignite, which they buried out of sight under the sleepers. Hughes had brought a pick with him, but they decided that using it might attract attention, the sounds echoing through the tunnel, so they moved the shale with their bare hands. The fuses were to be laid to the underside of the rail line so that the raised studs on the casing would get pressed down by a train passing along the line, igniting the detonators attached to the gelignite the moment the train passed. The exercise was, in all honesty, a bit of a hit-and-miss affair, almost a trial run – only for real – in what would become an art form of the saboteurs which the SBS men learned to perfection.

They were an hour and a half making their way to the tunnel and setting the charges. Then Hughes tapped his partner on the shoulder. The rail signals in the distance had changed to green, which meant a train was heading in their direction. Wilson tenderly pulled the safety bar from the fuse while Hughes collected the rest of their gear. They made a rapid exit and moved back down the embankment to the beach and the canoe, still behind the rocks.

At that moment there were voices again. Hughes nodded towards a couple of fishing-boats, oil-lanterns glowing on their masts, swaying back and forth on the gentle waves directly in their path 500 metres out. Wilson pointed skywards. The moon was on the rise and would be breaking through very soon. The train heading towards them would, if all went to plan, blow up at any moment, and all hell would be let loose. They had to go now.

They launched the canoe into a few inches of water and paddled silently, using single paddles, until they reached the headland and were out of the way of the fishermen. Then they stopped to refit their double paddles and moved swiftly towards the pick-up point, where, hopefully, the submarine was lingering below the surface. *Urge* came up to their starboard, and in a short time the two men were hauling themselves on to the gun platform, dragging their canoe on to the casing behind them. They stood for a moment looking back at the coastline with exhilarated satisfaction tempered by concern that there had been no explosion. Had it failed to go off? Damp, perhaps, or wrongly connected?

Quickly, they collapsed the canoe and loaded it back through the forward torpedo loading hatch and headed below themselves as *Urge* glided towards deep water. As they went, the captain summoned Wilson and Hughes to the bridge on the conning tower. Through his binoculars, he had caught sight of dim lights on the shore. The train was just entering the tunnel when Tug saw it. He was counting the seconds . . . and then – boom! – the distant sky was lit by a flash of red.

To complete his report on the attack, Tommo Tompkinson hung around the area overnight, though in the safety of deeper waters. The following morning he turned *Urge* back towards Mount Etna and, with Wilson, scanned the attack site. Activity at the tunnel entrance confirmed the hit. Scores of workers were removing debris from the scene. His log for *Urge* that day recorded the satisfaction of all concerned, especially Wilson and Hughes.

What may in hindsight be viewed as a minuscule piece of wartime history at the time was in fact important. The mission marked the first successful raid for the Special Boat Section in the Mediterranean, but for Tug Wilson and Marine Hughes the Sicilian jaunt was not quite over. With the success of the raid confirmed, *Urge* resumed her billet patrol and moved on to the south of the Messina Straits, where a new target was spotted: a pair of 10,000-ton Italian cruisers surrounded by six destroyers. Tompkinson lost no time in selecting his target, the cruiser *Gorizia*. Within minutes she was sinking, with a couple of nasty gashes in her side sustained from his salvo of torpedoes. The Italian destroyers came looking for him and dropped a hundred or more depth-charges. The submarine shuddered and shook as if it were about to break into pieces, the noise deafening and frightening.

Tug Wilson had never experienced anything like it and immediately recalled the words of his SBS commanding officer, Roger Courtney: 'Those members of the SBS who have the privilege of being aboard one of HM submarines during a depth-charge attack should remain cool and calm, hide yourselves in some corner out of everyone's way, say nothing, do nothing and pretend to be reading a book.'

He didn't have a book, and the moment might have caused him to reflect: How in God's name was he, Robert Wilson, until recently quietly pursuing his rather staid career as a draughtsman in Bristol, harming no one, and with a new young wife at home with whom he should have been raising a family, now holed up in the corner of the control-room of a submarine somewhere deep under the Med, being bombed out of his mind by depth-charges, having just blown up a railway line and causing goodness knows what damage or loss of life and already thinking about his next mission?

He wanted action. He'd got it! And it was nothing like anything he had ever imagined when he volunteered for service in the Territorial Army just before the war began, or even contemplated when he was commissioned into the 5th Survey Regiment of the Royal Artillery when the balloon went up. His new wife, Marjorie, whom he had married in the early stages of the war at the local register office, honeymooning briefly in Bath, had kissed him goodbye and off he'd gone to his billet in a dirty, disused, eighteenth-century workhouse in Stroud, Gloucestershire.

Tug Wilson's story is not untypical of SBS personnel in the early years. They just appeared, as if from nowhere, to take up their duties with this strange new unit that conventional military men regarded with suspicion and generally dismissed as made up of a bunch of foolhardy, undisciplined eccentrics, often scruffily attired, paddling about in canoes and carrying backpacks full of curious gadgets.

It was a world away from Tug's original posting with the 5th Survey, a scratch regiment whose officers were mainly of First World War vintage and recruits, like himself, drawn locally to train as battlefield surveyors, using theodolites for gun placement and calculation of enemy positions.

Soon he was on the move, volunteering to join the British Expeditionary Force in France, posted to the 3rd Survey Regiment of the Royal Artillery near Amiens. Within a few weeks his sound-wave calculations pinpointing enemy fire were no longer necessary. The British Army was in retreat from a wide arc of Nazi heavy metal and hits from above by dive-bombers.

The desperate rearguard battle was in full swing as the British force made a humiliating dash for the coast and retreat. The Survey Regiment, carrying important equipment, was one of the earlier units to be evacuated from Dunkirk in comparative safety. But the scene of mayhem left its mark. Wilson was determined to get back into the fray as soon as possible, especially as he had been sent back to his old unit, now engaged on surveys. The work was important but dull, and Tug Wilson hankered for attacking missions after the disaster that had left so many British troops lying dead in northern France and God knows how many others transported to prisoner-of-war camps in Germany and Poland.

He wouldn't have to wait long. Dunkirk was the catalyst to rapid change. The old war managers from the last flare-up of 25 years earlier were swept away to take charge of the Home Guard. The War Office was shaken into an overhaul of its military thinking. New, younger men were appearing and being listened to as Britain reeled under nightly bombardment from the Luftwaffe.

Invasion of the British Isles seemed inevitable. The Channel Islands were already lost. In an atmosphere of retrenchment and little chance of any immediate large-scale re-entry into Europe, the enemy had to be attacked in any way possible. One obvious route was through the thousands of miles of unprotected coastline in enemy territory; the coast provided the gateways to raiders and saboteurs, both of whom could cause a good deal of trouble. New talent with new ideas came forth, almost from nowhere, ready to dive in and have a go.

Among them was a big-game hunter who had turned up out of the blue from Africa, attached himself to a recently formed commando unit in Scotland, and whose influence – during the war and beyond – would run through the whole network of small-party raiders and special operations groups.

His name was Roger 'Jumbo' Courtney, and his plan was to form a Folbot Squadron that would go into Europe, specifically the Mediterranean, and blow up enemy shipping inside its own harbours and mainland installations.

Courtney, from his background, might well have been dismissed as a crank, and the military hierarchy believed it had its fair share of such men already. Courtney certainly did not fit the conventional pattern of fighting men either. Naturally indifferent to authority, he was a wild, adventurous man of 40 who, between the wars, had been a professional big-game hunter and gold prospector in East Africa.

When he married at the age of 36, Courtney and his wife Dorrise spent their honeymoon paddling a collapsible German-built canoe named *Buttercup* down the Danube. Another of his own great adventures was to paddle the Nile from Lake Victoria to the delta with only a sack of potatoes and an elephant spear on board. The need to earn a living had led him to join the Palestine Police, where he reached the rank of sergeant. 'He was a big man in every way, though not very tall,' one of his wartime officers, Vere Holden-White, told me. 'He had a bashed-in kind of face and a blunt, no-nonsense manner that was intimidating on first meeting. Fortunately, that was soon dispelled by a great bellowing laugh . . . and the boast he could drink any bugger under the table. He enjoyed proving it. And a hoaxer. During the great "monster fever" of the 1930s, he discovered footprints on the muddy beach of Loch Ness, and the *Daily Express* made a great deal of his find. It wasn't until much later and many newspaper articles around the world that some bright spark discovered that the footprints were all from a left foot. Roger confessed . . . the footprint came from one of his own victims – it was from the sawn-off foot of a hippopotamus that he used as a doorstop.'

At the start of the war Courtney returned to England and joined the King's Royal Rifle Corps as a subaltern, and there he might well have remained. In the summer of 1940, however, Churchill launched the Special Operations Executive to 'set Europe ablaze'. The SOE was to spearhead sabotage, propaganda, subversion and clandestine attack missions across Europe while the conventional forces regrouped and prepared for re-invasion.

Almost immediately, swashbucklers and the adventurers in the tradition of British privateers sallied forth, along with a motley collection of madcap scientists and inventors. Volunteer groups began to take shape under mercurial figures who answered Churchill's call.

Among them would emerge David Stirling, a brilliant young Scots guardsman who had big ideas. In 1940 he had transferred to newly formed commando units under Lieutenant-Colonel Robert Laycock, in training at Inveraray and subsequently on the Isle of Arran. It was only much later that Stirling, having acquired 50 parachutes, set up his own band of pioneers under the heading of

Special Air Service, whose idea was to drop saboteurs behind enemy lines by parachute. It was a variation on the theme established by Jumbo Courtney for his amphibious raiders.

Courtney was there first, by at least a year. He put forward his plan to Laycock long before Stirling was even being noticed, theorising that from his own experience he was certain that a small force of men in canoes could carry out effective sabotage by secretly landing on enemy coasts and attacking enemy shipping. The men could also be used for recce missions ahead of larger troop landings and for a multitude of other tasks.

No one was particularly impressed; in fact senior officers made no secret of their views: the plan was positively foolhardy, bloody ridiculous. So Courtney set about proving his point. He took his canoe out into the Clyde Estuary, where the commando ship HMS *Glengyle* was moored. He slid out of the canoe into the water and pulled himself up the anchor chain, over the guard rail, slipped past the sentry and grabbed a souvenir.

He went back the way he came in, paddled to the banks of the Clyde and ran to a nearby hotel, where a conference of senior officers who controlled the commando units was in session. He burst in, still dripping wet, carrying with him the equally wet canvas gun cover from *Glengyle* and dropped it on the conference table.

Well, he might do it once . . .

Some remained unconvinced; others showed a glimmer of interest. Courtney persisted and volunteered to repeat the exercise as a pre-arranged mock attack. Admiral Sir Roger Keyes, a hero of Zeebrugge from the First World War, who was now in charge of Combined Operations, agreed. Courtney was to make a second raid on the ship and place chalkmarks on the hull to show where he might have planted limpet mines.

Wearing only bathing-trunks in the ice-cold sea, he paddled undetected to the ship's mooring, once again slipped over the side of his canoe alongside *Glengyle* and placed chalkmarks along the side. At that point he could have moved away and left the navy with egg on its face once again. But a length of rope hanging over the side was too tempting. He climbed aboard, intending to make a spectacular entrance on the deck of the ship – and fell into a trap the ship's captain, aware of his impending visit, had laid. He was captured.

But the demonstration was sufficient to convince Admiral Keyes. Within a month, Courtney was promoted to the rank of captain and given the task of forming the first Folboat Troop, which was to consist of just 12 men. He began to scout for suitable recruits.

A list was already being compiled of men who had answered the call by volunteering for 'special service of a hazardous nature' – totally unaware of what that might entail. Among them was Tug Wilson, the quiet subaltern with the 3rd Survey Regiment of the Royal Artillery, then languishing at Exeter.

He described to me that day in the autumn of 1940 when he received his secret orders. His understanding wife, fortunately born into a military family, kissed him goodbye and would barely see him again for another five years. 'I was instructed to travel at once to Scotland and report to the White House, which in spite of its grand name was actually a shooting-lodge on the estate of the Duke of Montrose on the Isle of Arran. I had no idea what was on, not a clue.'

A dozen men drawn from Horse Guards, Marines, Commandos and Royal Artillery assembled on the appointed day and were ushered into an introductory talk by Courtney. In his usual colourful language and persuasive words, he outlined his plans along with his assurance that he could drink any two men under the table.

The volunteers, Courtney said, should be prepared for excitement and danger, missions with impossible survival odds and constant high-risk operations. They were to become the foundation troop of the SBS, for which Courtney had obtained his 'fleet' of eight folboats, one of which was the *Buttercup*, in which he had paddled the Danube with his new bride.

That night, after the lecture, he and Tug Wilson began a conversation which lasted until dawn, and Wilson used a handily placed flowerpot to avoid disappearing under the table. He was mesmerised by Courtney's tales and by his plans for the small group of raiders. The whole concept captured his imagination. At the end of their conversation Courtney had appointed Wilson his second-in-command, and the next day they began mapping out their strategy.

They had less than three months to train in the skills that would be required of them. Few of them knew much about demolition explosives; others had never been in a canoe; some knew little about mapreading. An eccentric Scottish professor taught them how to survive on seaweed. Courtney and Tug Wilson, so totally unalike in everything they had ever done in life and in physical and personal demeanour, came together like two pieces of a jigsaw.

Wilson was everything that Courtney sought in his recruits. He preferred the alert, almost sensitive chaps who would work out the way of attack through a side window rather than go blasting their way in through the front. (This philosophy still holds good more than half a century later, and is still an approach that can be seen as distinctly different from that of another famous group of Special Forces who brag about daring and winning.)

Courtney swore by enthusiasm, skill and coolness under pressure, and that's what he and Wilson drummed into this tiny group of men now under his command and in training at Corrie, on the east coast of the Isle of Arran, near the northern end of the island. The landscape provided its own challenge. Goat Fell towered 2,867 feet (874 metres) behind them and Sannox Bay lay before them: the best, or worst, of both worlds, depending on your view of it, for training canoeists, swimmers, divers, mountaineers, survivalists, demolition experts and killers, descriptions that could be rolled up into one and applied to any member of 1SBS, as the unit was soon to be christened.

They had no special gear to speak of; training, as Tug Wilson recalls, was done in battledress. There was no such thing as a wetsuit, no breathing apparatus, no particular work had been done on waterproofing – always a problem – and standard-issue condoms would cover a multitude of sins.

Ten days' leave at Christmas was granted amid a buzz of rumours of forthcoming embarkation to foreign parts. The rumours proved correct. General Sir Archibald Wavell, who by the end of 1940 had amassed 300,000 men in what Churchill described as Our Army on the Nile, wanted more and had heard about the commandos in training in Scotland.

In spite of his successes in the Western Desert and the capture of

35,000 Italian prisoners of war, Churchill was repeatedly critical of Wavell's supposed reticence to attack on other fronts. 'What is he going to do with these great armies?' the Prime Minister demanded. Wavell replied that he was already committed to the capture of the Italian Dodecanese Islands and planned to move on to Rhodes early in the New Year to forestall a German base being established there. He was standing in defence of Egypt and planning to move against Rommel when the 'time was right'.

Thus, his request for the immediate dispatch of the commandos was granted, and Roger Courtney – a man well experienced in the Nile regions – would take his Folboat Section to the Nile. The group was attached to 8 Commando, which joined 7 and 11 Commandos under the command of Laycock; the group would, for the time being, be known as 'Layforce'. The convoy of commando ships left Scotland under heavy escort on 31 January 1941, heading out into the North Atlantic to stay out of range of long-distance bombers. The full force of the Atlantic swell gave them all a bad time before the convoy veered south around the tedious Cape route to arrive in Alexandria on 11 March.

Courtney was introduced immediately to Nigel Clogstoun Willmott, a 30-year-old senior Naval navigator for ships who was working on the ship-borne invasion of Rhodes. As a veteran of the Narvik disaster a year earlier, when the British suffered heavy losses as they foundered on rocks and hidden shoals off the Norwegian coast, Willmott, well aware that many ships' navigators had in the not-too-distant past been civilians and at best had only amateur navigational experience, put forward a strong case for a reconnaissance of the island. Lieutenant-Colonel Laycock agreed, and teamed him up with Courtney.

The two men were taken under cover of darkness to two miles or so off Rhodes aboard the submarine *Triumph*. They paddled away in Courtney's *Buttercup*, equipped with sub-machine-gun, tommy-gun, grenades and a thermos of coffee laced with brandy. They spent the night swimming around the beach areas that would make suitable landing-sites for the Layforce, noting data such as depths and rocks in chinagraph crayon on a slate-board. Finally, Willmott slipped ashore, dodging the sentries, to make a map of the terrain and nearby roads. He penetrated to within 60 metres of a large Axis headquarters at the Hôtel des Roses, apparently crawling about the lawn to get an idea of its troop population.

On the following night, he and Courtney made a recce of the main beach south of Rhodes town, with Willmott this time cutting through wire barricades to get on to the main highway. A third night was spent making a beach recce through *Triumph*'s periscope, and on the fourth and final night they set off again for the shore. Courtney swam to one beach, leaving Willmott to travel a little further down the coast. Willmott was to return and pick up Courtney, who would signal his position by dimmed torchlight.

Courtney, however, ran into triple trouble. He suffered severe cramp while swimming, and as he lay writhing on the beach he attracted the attention of a noisy dog, and then to cap it all his torch failed. Willmott managed to find him and brought him to safety only minutes before an enemy patrol appeared on the beach. Had Courtney been caught, he would undoubtedly have been shot, in accordance with Hitler's orders on dealing with saboteurs and non-uniformed commandos.

This was the first major beach reconnaissance of its kind. Both men were decorated for the mission – Willmott was awarded the Distinguished Service Order and Courtney the Military Cross – and promoted to captain. Their meticulous charting of potential assault beaches would later become one of the prime tasks of a most secret wartime organisation called Combined Operations Pilotage Parties, headed by Willmott himself, set up to guide major invasion forces in the latter stages of the war. COPPs, as they were called, was so secret that their very existence was not revealed until a dozen years after the war had ended.

COPPs' exploits (described in Chapter Seven) were to come later in the war, and its disciplines would become an integral part of the SBS throughout the second half of this century. Back then, this very first recorded beach recce was, in fact, to no avail. The Rhodes landing was cancelled in April. Rommel's Afrika Korps had succeeded in driving Wavell behind the port of Tobruk. Meanwhile, Hitler had ordered the invasion of Greece and the Germans were on the brink of taking Crete. The Layforce was now required as reinforcements elsewhere.

The Folboat Section suddenly found itself unattached and without masters. On 13 April Courtney's little army of canoeists was transferred to the depot ship of the 1st Submarine Flotilla of the Mediterranean Fleet, HMS *Medway*, in the port of Alexandria. Courtney and Wilson immediately began to plan their futures and commandeered enough supplies of limpets and explosives for what they had in mind – landing raiding-parties from submarines throughout the Mediterranean. The Folboat Section of 8 Commando was renamed 1SBS and at that moment the Special Boat Section was officially born.

CHAPTER TWO

Star of the show

Tug Wilson watched the Jolly Roger hoisted above the submarine *Urge* as she sailed into Malta under a cloudless sky after the Sicilian adventure and felt pangs of pride. On the corner of the flag, over the bar denoting the sinking of an enemy cruiser, the emblem of a dagger had been sewn in recognition of the first SBS attack. Shrimp Simpson, head of the 10th Submarine Flotilla, was waiting on the quayside to welcome them; when the full account of the raid by Wilson and Hughes was relayed, his early scepticism about the value of Tug and his colleagues vanished in an instant.

Simpson was soon requesting that Wilson and Hughes – and more like them, if possible – should join his command. He saw the opportunities for further raids, with SBS attacks on shoreline installations in addition to his submariners' general harassment of Italian and German shipping. Their base at Lazaretto Creek – known to the locals as X-base – on the sheltered side of Valletta in Marsamxett Harbour was a top priority for Axis bombers as they pounded the island daily. The strategic importance of Malta for the British fleet, lying midway between the two key Mediterranean bases of Gibraltar and Alexandria, was more vital now than at any time since the naval presence was first established in 1869. Lately, the Nazis were getting rather annoyed that the X-base subs were severely hampering the supply of men, stores and weapons to their star performer, Rommel, in his North African campaign and were in danger of stifling his spectacular advance, heading as he was towards Alexandria and Cairo. Goering ordered the Luftwaffe to blast the subs out of the island and the island out of existence. Shrimp Simpson and his 10th Flotilla, who had covered themselves with glory and won dozens of medals for sustained bravery, refused to budge – at least for the time being.

Simpson's request to hold on to Wilson and Hughes brought a swift response from Courtney in Alexandria: 'Carte blanche – and good hunting.' There was nothing Courtney would have liked better than to have had his whole team doing exactly the same. They had spent the summer training in limpet-mine attacks and other forms of sabotage and were raring to go. They were also aiding the Special Operations Executive, ferrying agents into various key Axis-held territory in the eastern Mediterranean. But the submarine fleet at Alexandria, No. 1 Flotilla operating under the general command of Combined Operations, was already hard pressed. It had fewer vessels available, and they could not be diverted from the main chance – attacking enemy shipping – to allow brief excursions ashore by SBS raiders.

In any event, Courtney's little gang had already been further diminished. One canoe team, Sergeant Allan and Marine Miles, having successfully sent an enemy ship to the bottom in Benghazi harbour with limpet mines, hit a jagged rock as they paddled their way to rendezvous with the mother sub and were captured.

Back in Malta, Simpson rapidly began to make use of his two new acquisitions, and his command was alerted to seek out suitable sites for attack. At the end of July 1941 Wilson and Hughes were assigned to the submarine *Utmost* commanded by Lieutenant-Commander Dick Cayley, a stocky man with whom Wilson struck an immediate rapport. In the following three months, the deadly duo, as they might well have been called, pulled off a series of raids that caused mayhem and disruption to the railway system of southern Italy. None of them was without incident.

The first was in the Gulf of Santa Eufemia. A main-line rail link to the north was in view, with no tunnel on the flattish terrain, and the link was obviously important enough to cause bother if disrupted. The pair made a daylight recce of the site through periscope surveillance and took to their canoe in the evening before the moon came up. They were floated off the sub casing in the usual way and paddled in to shore, carting enough explosives to blow the railway line sky-high. Everything went without a hitch. The explosives were laid under a hefty section of the track and set with instantaneous fuses, which gave them just sufficient time to take cover behind some rocks close to the beach. What they had not anticipated was that farm buildings nearby were filled with Italian soldiers, who spewed out shouting and screaming when the explosives blew. Tug and his partner kept their heads down, wondering how they were going to get out when a curious diversion came to their rescue.

A crowd of skinny-dipping bathers enjoying the late-evening warmth of the sea were spotted further up the beach and the soldiers dashed off to arrest them, certain that they were the saboteurs. During the commotion that followed, Wilson and Hughes found a route to their hidden canoe and paddled away unnoticed.

Their next raid was planned with more care to detail, and it would be their most spectacular yet. The target was a huge railway bridge over the River Seracino in the Gulf of Taranto. The bridge was so vital that the Italians, fearing it might be a target for saboteurs, had camouflaged the seaward side, hampering reconnaissance. A clear view of it was possible only by daylight scanning from the submarine's periscope.

As darkness fell on the evening of 27 August, Dick Cayley brought *Utmost* as close as he dared to the beach, as an extra-large load of explosives was required – eight charges of 'P-for-plenty' material, packed in bulletproof and waterproof bags weighing around 30 pounds (14 kilogrammes) apiece.

Wilson and Hughes were floated off the casing, and Cayley kept the submarine on the surface to watch them go; even though the sea was calm, the heavily laden canoe was low in the water. One false move and they could have capsized; there would be no second chance. A suitable landing-spot had already been pinpointed and the two beached without problems. They were hyped up with nervous excitement as they began unloading their packages. Then Wilson looked seawards and saw that *Utmost* had not submerged, its black hull clearly visible from the beach and too close for comfort. She could be hit by any shore batteries that might be around, and also might alert the Italians to their own landing.

In spite of the precision timing, and with brilliant coolness, he climbed back into his canoe and paddled back to the sub to suggest politely to Cayley that he should draw away to a safer distance. In other words: bugger off! Back on shore he and Hughes, with Thompson sub-machine-guns loaded and at the ready, began an initial sortie of the target, first climbing a steep incline of rocks and loose shale. Over the top, they saw the bridge looming before them.

Wilson scratched his head as he stood looking at the thing. It was bigger than they had anticipated: reinforced concrete pillars strung with steel girders spanning a deep gorge. Wilson concluded he would have to climb into the network of steel to set his charges.

They returned to the beach, where they had hidden the explosives. It took four trips to carry the packages to the bridge, and while Hughes unpacked and kept watch Wilson began his climb into the steel, carrying the lethal packs and swinging like a monkey between the girders and occasionally hanging one-handed from them while he set the charges and detonators in place. When it was done, Wilson made one last check of the connections, rolled out a long length of slow-burn fuse to hang over the bridge, and lit it.

'*Run like hell!*'

Wilson didn't need to say it; he was ticking off the seconds in his mind as he and Hughes dashed away, crashing their way through the undergrowth back towards the sea.

Boom!

The whole lot went up in a cloud of shattered concrete, twisted metal and dust, showering them with debris as they scurried, stumbling and falling, down the embankment to the beach. Fortunately, the canoe was safely hidden from the flying masonry, and the two pushed it into four inches (ten centimetres) of water and clambered inside to make their escape. *Utmost* had come to about 800 metres offshore. As Wilson and Hughes came aboard they were cheered by the crew, and one more dagger went into the corner of the Jolly Roger when the sub and its bold but modest bombers received another heroes' welcome in Malta.

By now their names were taking on the proportions of local

legend among the submariners and navy in Malta and Alexandria. News of their exploits brought interest and fascination from the war managers in war theatres and London. The Italians, whose own water-borne raids using frogmen and limpet mines were causing havoc in Gibraltar and elsewhere, realised that they were being hit by expert teams of saboteurs and began tightening security around rail and other coastal installations.

Wilson and Hughes were already being earmarked for further raids and were once again aboard *Utmost* when she resumed her patrol in September 1941. This time the target was another rail tunnel of the kind that could cause most disruption and chaos. It was south of Naples, and the job wasn't just an explosives one. They were to take with them propaganda leaflets to make sure the Italians knew exactly who was carrying out the wrecking missions and, secondly, to cause unrest and fear among the locals.

They made their attempt on the night of 22 September, this time using two canoes because of the weight of the leaflets and the explosives needed to blow the tunnel. They landed on a beach with a moderate incline behind it and, as usual, hid the canoes and their contents while they surveyed the scene to check for guards and likely obstacles. That done, they headed directly to the tunnel; seven trips were made to take the explosives and leaflets to the site.

Wilson and Hughes were busily laying the charges when out of the darkness came an enemy patrol. They took cover, but they were spotted. Wilson stood up, firing his Thompson sub-machine-gun, and the Italians dived for cover, back inside the tunnel. The patrol regrouped and could be heard coming back. Wilson and Hughes fired again and made tracks for the beach. Abandoning their gear and explosives, they paddled like fury back to *Utmost* and lived to fight another day – the next day, in fact. Overnight and the following day *Utmost* sped off down the west coast of Italy and on the night of 23 September was off the northern coast of Sicily, scanning the next target on Wilson's list, a three-span railway bridge over the River Oliva.

Once again they ran into trouble. The landing and locating the target went according to plan, but sentries were guarding the bridge with a group of workmen with lanterns. Out of the darkness, one of them challenged Wilson, who responded with the shout of 'Amico!' The guard was not convinced and raised his rifle. Wilson shot him. A hail of gunfire followed. Somewhere close by a Breda machine-gun crew was set up and ready. Wilson and Hughes dashed away in the dark and headed for their canoe and back to a safe return to *Utmost*.

The action was hotting up. The Italians had cottoned on and were evidently placing guards at likely sabotage targets – and that was in part the intent of the raids. The damage could always be repaired, usually within a week or so. The effect of the attacks was to divert Italian and German troops to deal with them; one more gun crew at a railway bridge meant one less on the battlefields. Even so, when Tug returned to Malta at the beginning of October, Shrimp Simpson told him that the top brass at Combined Operations were concerned that his operations were becoming too hazardous. His raids would have to stop.

Tug argued his point. Even if railway tunnels were attracting a regular protection squad, miles of track were still unprotected, and guarding it all was an impossible task for the Italians. And, anyway, he had been working on a new method of speeding up his operation, a ready-assembled device that he could leave beside the track to explode quickly when the train came by, rather than risking long periods ashore. Simpson was persuaded, and on 18 October Tug went aboard the latest T-class submarine, under Lieutenant-Commander Hugh Rider Haggard, grandson of the novelist Sir Henry Rider Haggard. *Truant* was on its way from the Barrow-in-Furness shipyard to join No. 1 Submarine Flotilla in Alexandria.

Haggard would pursue a route that would take him through the Strait of Otranto, between Italy and Albania, into the Adriatic. It was this that persuaded Simpson to allow Wilson to go along, by changing tack and hitting the east coast of Italy for the first time. In fact, it turned out to be one of the most hazardous submarine journeys Wilson had ever had. The last stage of the journey from Barrow-in-Furness provided the new vessel with a baptism of fire. *Truant* encountered a succession of high dramas and activity, including mortar attack from surface vessels and aircraft, depth-charges, torpedo action against enemy shipping and, for four hair-raising hours, being grounded on the ocean floor with only a bathtub of water over her periscope.

Even so, Tug was allowed ashore for one more attack to test his new explosives set-up. The target was the main Milan to Brindisi railway line near Ancona. The pre-prepared charges were attached to the rail in double-quick time just as a train was approaching, and his plan worked exactly as he had forecast, derailing the engine and 14 sleeping-cars, doubtless packed with Axis war executives, and causing a good deal of disruption to the line.

Wilson and Hughes spent a full three weeks on patrol with *Truant*, sailing into Alexandria on 17 November, almost seven months after leaving for Malta for what, at the time, was meant to be a brief sojourn. The date was Wilson's second wedding anniversary, though his young bride was far away in Bristol. Even correspondence between them had been at best spasmodic, although any particular news, such as Marjorie's survival of a blitz attack, had been radioed through to whichever submarines he had been aboard at the time.

Roger Courtney was in Alexandria to welcome Wilson back to the Special Boat Section based on HMS *Medway* with an anniversary present – he had been promoted to captain. Wilson noticed that the place was somewhat depleted in terms of personnel. By then the 1SBS had extended its particular repertoire of special operations, working largely from submarines. The range of tasks covered everything from beach recce for troop landings, sabotage operations on the lines of Wilson's own exploits, and rescuing Allied troops left behind after the fall of Crete in June 1941. In the month of August alone, one solitary SBS canoeist, Corporal G. C. Bremner, single-handedly rescued 125 British, Australian, New Zealand and Greek soldiers who had been hiding in the hills of Crete since it was overrun by the Germans. He brought them to safety via the submarine *Torbay* and on to Alexandria. He was eventually awarded a Distinguished Conduct Medal.

Another series of operations that became an SBS speciality during the latter half of 1941 was the insertion and evacuation of secret agents behind enemy lines across the whole of the Mediterranean theatre, and later in the Far East. These missions continued, often at great risk to canoeists, agents and the delivering submarines, throughout the remainder of the war. The situation became a familiar one: agents, often in smart civilian clothes and clutching a briefcase containing important papers and/or communications sets, would look in horror at the little canoe into which they were expected to climb to be ferried ashore; often, they ended up soaked to the skin in rough seas.

Alternatively, the SBS might be tasked to go into a particular region and bring out an agent who had been betrayed or lost. Courtney himself had to go in search of an important agent who had gone missing in Yugoslavia but failed to find him. On another occasion he sailed in HMS/M *Osins* to evacuate a group of agents from Albania who should have been waiting for him on the beach near Scutari, but who never arrived. They were not heard from again.

Betrayal was one of the worst aspects of these operations. In September that year, for example, SBS Lieutenant J. B. Sherwood and Corporal I. Booth had the task of repatriating eight Cretans back to their island at a pre-arranged place from HMS/M *Thunderbolt*. They were floated off in a canoe each, both of them taking one agent per trip, instructing the agents to wait in hiding on the beach until all were safely ashore. By the third trip to the beach, however, the four previously delivered agents had vanished. Sherwood took a severe dressing-down from those who remained, though the fault doubtless lay with a contact in Crete who had had the agents captured and probably tortured.

Tug Wilson's observation of the lack of personnel when he arrived back in Alexandria on 17 November 1941 was, therefore, understandable. Another reason was rather more hush-hush and was to remain so, certainly in its detail, for decades to come. The SBS had been tasked to provide their skills of beach recce and landings for a particular mission that was on at that very moment – a somewhat ambitious plan to destroy Rommel's intelligence centre at Appollonia, wreck communications systems further inland and finally attack Rommel's headquarters and eliminate or capture the man himself.

What went down in military history as a brave but ill-fated raid was placed in the hands of the remnants of Lieutenant-Colonel Robert Laycock's much-vaunted Layforce which had originally consisted of 7, 8 and 11 Commandos. The force had staged a heroic but costly stand against the Germans in Crete. Other operations had also taken a heavy toll, and by September Layforce was virtually wiped out; there remained only 53 men from the group that had sailed full of hope and bravado from Scotland 10 months earlier.

Those remaining members of the Layforce were now attached to the 8th Army as a special raiding-force, led by Laycock himself and Lieutenant-Colonel Geoffrey Keyes, son of Admiral Sir Roger Keyes, the first director of Combined Operations who had given such support to Layforce and the SBS foundation. They had now been earmarked to dispose of this rather pressing physical and psychological problem: Rommel, whose image reared up in front of the Allied North African campaign like a fiery dragon. An attempt would be made to eliminate him and to destroy his headquarters just ahead of General Cunningham's Libyan offensive.

There was obviously a good deal of high-level expectation of the commando raid and the main attack. Winston Churchill's son Randolph, who was in Cairo at the time, wrote to his father on 13 November: 'I hope you will soon have some news which will make it easier for you to make a speech than it is at the moment.'

The raid on Rommel's HQ, 200 miles inside enemy lines, would be made through a beach landing launched with the guiding arm of the SBS from HMS/Ms *Torbay* and *Talisman* through canoes and rubber dinghies. A British intelligence officer, Arab-speaking Captain J.E. Haselden, had found his way to the proposed landing-site via an inland journey, and three days before the assault he had met Lieutenant Ingles and Corporal Severn from the SBS on the very beach where the landing was to take place, they having been floated off *Torbay* for a final recce of the beach before the landing of the Rommel raiding-party.

The weather was already flaring up, and the SBS pointed out the dangers if it became worse – as it did. By the time of the landing on the night of 14 November, a storm was whipping up the surf. Two pairs of SBS men went ashore in their canoes to check the beaches prior to the main landing of the troops. When the all-clear was given, the landing was ordered to proceed in spite of the rough sea, with the SBS men guiding in the troops. As forecast by the SBS men, canoes and dinghies from *Torbay* were repeatedly swamped on their way to the beach. It took almost 7 hours to land the 36 men aboard *Torbay* instead of the 90 minutes estimated. By then it was deemed impossible to land the remaining 18 men aboard *Talisman*. Laycock and Keyes were among those who made it ashore.

The depleted group none the less decided to head off in the direction of Rommel's communications centre and then on to the villa that was used as headquarters for his Panzergruppe Afrika. Meanwhile, SBS Lieutenants Ingles and Allot, with their two partners, hid the rubber dinghies ready for the return of the raiding-party.

The disastrous start to the landing might have been an omen; the troubles kept on coming. The importance of the target buildings appeared to have been exaggerated and, as was eventually discovered, Rommel himself was not even there. He had gone to Rome. There were, however, sufficient German troops there to put up a fierce fight, in which the expedition leader, Lieutenant-Colonel Keyes, was among those killed (he was posthumously awarded the Victoria Cross). With Laycock at their head, the raiding-party retreated to the beach to rendezvous with *Torbay*. By the time they reached the coast, there were only 22 survivors of the original 36, and to make matters worse the weather was appalling and the sea hugely choppy, surf running in from the north-west straight at the beach.

Torbay came back to rendezvous at the appointed time to wait for the returning party, unaware of the shooting match that had ensued on shore. Soon after nightfall on 18 November (the first day of Operation Crusader, which was the 8th Army's offensive to relieve Tobruk), they arrived at the beach. The returning commandos, however, signalled that their rubber boats, previously hidden there, had disappeared. They were stranded.

SBS Lieutenant (later Major) Tommy Langton described the moment:

> We were relieved to see the arranged signal from the beach, but it was much too rough to launch a folboat. The [submarine]

> captain having decided to send Lieutenant Ingles and Corporal Severn on a spare rubber craft, this was attempted, but the boat was washed adrift by the swell before the crew could board it. Later, the party ashore reported they had found the boat with water and food . . . they also reported there were 22 of them. They did not know what had happened to the rubber boats which had been left on the beaches.

The submarine captain suggested in his signal to the shore that they should attempt at dawn to swim out to the submarine, which was hovering 800 metres from the beach. There were, however, a number of men who could not swim anything like that distance, and others who could not swim at all. The suggestion was declined on the basis of all or none. The submarine was in a risky position even under darkness, and, with no apparent way of rescuing them, the captain decided to put to sea and signalled he would return after dark the following day.

Langton continued:

> We put to sea again . . . and closed the beach very soon after dark the next night. The sea was considerably calmer . . . but we were dismayed to see no signals from the beach this time, so after waiting some time the captain decided to send myself and Corporal Freeberry in to reconnoitre. The beach was deserted . . . [then] we spotted a light which appeared on a hillside. It was the correct colour but not giving the correct [recognition] signal, so I was suspicious of it. We walked a little further and thought we saw a movement. We both heard a shout soon afterwards but found nothing, and, since we were by then some distance from our boat and liable to be cut off, I decided to return to it and wait.

Langton and Freeberry waited for several minutes but saw nothing further and decided to launch their folboat to paddle along the shore towards the location of the light. Langton flashed his torch, heard a shout but saw no signal in return. They beached again and were upturned as they did so, losing a paddle. Then Langton spotted the glow of a lighted cigarette in the undergrowth and realised the people ashore were the enemy. They clambered back into the folboat and headed back to the submarine, a feat completed with one paddle only through the brute strength of the 16-stone Corporal Freeberry. In fact, the 22 survivors of the raid had been attacked by German troops; some were killed, others were captured and at least four escaped into the hillside. Why the enemy troops had not killed Langton and Freeberry, too, remains to this day a mystery. Those who escaped included Lieutenant-Colonel Laycock himself; with Sergeant Terry he made an incredible 36-day trek on foot through hostile countryside and desert, reaching British lines on Christmas Day.

The operation was a costly failure in its execution but was regarded as a success from two aspects: first, it had brought pressure to the very heart of the Germans' desert campaign, and, secondly, the operation of beach landings became, for the SBS, a model from which lessons were learned and corrected for the future. Decades later, the landing of raiding-groups of the Special Forces, as in the Falklands War and the Gulf, benefited from the experience, and the standard final section of reports on all future operations would include a summary under the heading: LESSONS LEARNT.

Back at base, other matters of import for the future of the SBS were developing. Roger Courtney, in failing health, went back to England in November where immediately he began gathering suitable recruits to form 2SBS. The onshore sabotage operations of the indomitable Tug Wilson and 'Wally' Hughes had been vetoed from on high because of their increasing danger, although he and other remaining SBS personnel were now regularly aboard departing submarines in the 1st Submarine Flotilla.

Wilson himself was in fact in the process of preparing even more hazardous missions, and, when *Torbay* set off on her next billet in early December, Wilson and Hughes were aboard, specifically to try out a new triple-limpet-mine device Wilson had invented. They headed towards Navarino, the busy Greek port where enemy destroyers had been spotted from aerial reconnaissance. The plan was that Wilson and Hughes would be deposited outside the harbour, paddle in with their canoe loaded with their limpets, and hopefully blow up a couple of targets. Despite paddling almost 15 miles on the first night, Wilson and Hughes found no suitable vessels for the attack. A few nights later they returned to Navarino and through the periscope found an enemy destroyer moored at the pier.

They set off in their canoe, paddling to within 150 metres of the ship. At this point Wilson, wearing only greased-up long-johns to protect him from the cold, slid into the water to swim the remaining distance, cautiously pushing six limpet mines ahead of him on a buoy. The limpets consisted of two pounds (0.9 kilogrammes) of plastic explosives in a metal case that would be clamped to the ship's hull by magnets (see Appendix I). Each mine could blast a two-metre hole in the side of the destroyer. The hefty package needed careful manoeuvring, a slow task at the best of times, and the December waters were ice-cold.

Hughes could see that his partner was in trouble within 80 metres or so. He signalled on the line attached to Wilson that he was pulling him in. Tug was hauled, protesting, back into the boat, with numb hands and chattering teeth. It was a disappointing end to their partnership. Hughes and Wilson would never work together again.

At the beginning of January Tug was summoned back to Malta to undertake a number of vital missions landing agents on the Tunisian coast complete with stores and radios, a task increasingly in the hands of SBS personnel. It was there, too, that he learned that he had been awarded the Distinguished Service Order for his exploits – a fairly rare decoration for his rank. He was to be sent home on leave to England and take his decoration from the king at Buckingham Palace.

'One last task . . .' said Shrimp Simpson, after revealing the award. Two agents had to be landed near Carthage.

'Of course,' said Wilson without hesitation.

He was to travel in the submarine *Upholder*, which had the largest number of kills to her name in the Mediterranean fleet under her by-then famous captain, the tall and bearded Lieutenant-Commander David Wanklyn, VC, DSO and two bars. She had sunk 125,000 tons of enemy shipping in 16 months. Tug was to take the two agents aboard, land them in a rubber dinghy at Carthage and then rendezvous at sea with the submarine *Unbeaten* to get a ride to Gibraltar before going on to the UK.

The landing was completed without a hitch, and Tug went back aboard *Upholder* to sail for the meeting with *Unbeaten* off the island of Lampedusa. *Unbeaten*, it turned out, was limping home, damaged in enemy action. By then the sea had churned up and looked too rough for Tug even to make the transfer. Wanklyn suggested he remain aboard *Upholder*, return to Malta and get a lift to Gibraltar from there. Tug, anxious to get on his way home, decided to risk it in spite of a joking shout from *Unbeaten*: 'Piss off, Tug. We've got two feet of water in the fore-ends and aft. We'll never make it to Gib.' It was a fateful decision. Soon afterwards, *Upholder* was lost with all hands. Tug Wilson was the last person to see the crew alive.

Chapter Three

Tug's last stand

Jumbo Courtney and Tug Wilson were back in Blighty, and Captain Mike Kealy took temporary command of the SBS. The original party, now topped up with additional hands, had remained remarkably intact, considering their hazardous pursuits. In the months ahead and on towards the close of 1942, that was soon to change – decimated by loss of life, loss of liberty and punctuated by some fine stuff for the glory book. There are too many examples to detail, but a few instances will give a flavour of those classic feats of human endeavour, beyond and above the call . . .

There was, for starters, the epic journey of Captain Ken Allott, who was dispatched with Lieutenant Duncan Ritchie, RN, to scout the coastline beyond the British-held position 60 miles west of Tobruk, a mission prompted by GHQ in Cairo. The planners believed they would need to get an idea of the lie of the land in double-quick time. How were they to know that Rommel would soon be rolling the British back to El Alamein, and that Allott and Ritchie were being sent off in the wrong direction?

But it seemed a good idea at the time, and the two officers were ferried 100 miles along German-held coast by motor torpedo-boat (MTB) on 22 May 1942 and dropped off with their folboat and stores (and, for the first time in any SBS operation, a radio) at Cape Ras-el-Tin, deep in enemy territory. They paddled along the coastline, noting the terrain and any troop population and eventually pulled in for a rest at a beach that provided a modicum of cover from low-growing bushes.

No sooner had they landed and shared out some chocolate than the sound of a popular Wagner tune wafted across the dunes as several trucks arrived, disgorging 200 German troops. For several hours Allott and Ritchie, dug into a self-constructed hide behind a few precariously unbushy bushes, watched as the young Nazis performed various physical training exercises, then played some games, one of which appeared to be hide-and-seek. Virtually every bush other than theirs was used in the game, and the troops eventually departed unaware that they had been observed throughout by two British officers who now needed a change of underwear.

The two pushed off to sea again and began to paddle back to base, performing their recce tasks as they went. The journey ahead, often in rough seas, during which the heavy radio was tipped over the side to lighten their load, was completed in five days, often under cover of darkness. From the point they set off to arriving back at Gazala was 150 miles!

Meanwhile David Stirling, the ambitious and empire-building head of the now firmly established Special Air Service, was casting an acquisitive eye over the SBS. Their operations, he conjectured, could easily slot in to a joint command with himself at the helm. He had already established a Special Boat Squadron under Captain (the Earl) George Jellicoe, a 24-year-old, thick-set young man with a mop of curly hair, much remembered at Cambridge, where he had studied before the war, and now an officer of panache, style and wit.

Stirling's little army and the notoriety of its escapades in the desert had grown and grown. He was, said John Lodwick, the Marks & Spencer of the military. His HQ was stacked with the assorted playthings of war which were scarce everywhere else: Jeeps, weapons, stores (variously of German, Italian and British origin), a vast hoard of explosives of every kind and, in an instant, whatever air transport he required as of that moment. For months, while the SBS had been working largely from submarines around the enemy coasts or landing its chaps for highly confidential missions in enemy territory, Stirling's outfit had been rampaging through the countryside, miles inside enemy lines, raiding and pillaging, stealing and killing and causing general mayhem among the outposts of Rommel's Afrika Korps.

Attacks on airfields were a particular speciality, and they had blown up more than anyone else: six air bases in Cyrenaica were put out of action temporarily, forty planes destroyed and an unknown number of German and Italian troops killed. The aura of mystique was also being established, with the standard-issue beret badges with blue wings and a white commando dagger bearing the legend WHO DARES WINS. It was, as a motto of the day and the future, rather better than Jumbo Courtney's invention of EXCRETA TAURI ASTUTOS FRUSTRANTUR, worked out by an Oxford don and which roughly translated meant: BULLSHIT BAFFLES BRAINS.

Stirling himself could see no reason why Courtney's SBS mob should not join his own on selected joint missions, and, indeed, in June they began several back-to-back raids to attack enemy airfields around the eastern Mediterranean. The first of these joint attacks was on Crete. Mike Kealy took three sections of the SBS to the north-west of the island while George Jellicoe led a contingent of SAS canoeists to Heraklion. Kealy's own target, Maleme airfield, was too heavily guarded to attempt their raid. But Captain George Duncan's section made it through the wire at Kastelli field and blew up four bomb dumps in spectacular fashion, killing 70 or so enemy troops in the process.

Jellicoe's attack at Heraklion, with a party that included four French officers and a Greek guide, was also accompanied by a substantial display of fireworks. They were landed from HMS/M *Triton* in captured German inflatables and laid up while a recce was made of the airfield. Sixty-six aircraft were counted, and the raiders moved off on the second day to do their worst. Unfortunately, German guards discovered their wire-cutting entrance to the perimeter defences. Fortunately, before the guards could seek them out, an RAF Blenheim bomber followed three Stukas which were landing at the field and promptly dropped its payload, causing confusion and panic on the ground. This gave Jellicoe and his team the time they needed to set their explosives, timed to go off in 90 minutes.

When the first of their charges began exploding, Jellicoe's party was still inside the perimeter, but with incredible coolness he and his men tagged on behind a German patrol in the darkness and walked boldly out of the main gate, where they promptly split up and vanished into the undergrowth. Jellicoe and the Greek guide managed to reach their rendezvous by walking 120 miles across two mountain ranges before linking up with a rescue contact on the south coast, followed by a safe return to base. The four Frenchmen accepted the kind invitation of a passing Grecian to join him for a meal and were betrayed. In the shootout that followed as they resisted arrest by the Germans, one of their number was shot. The body of the traitor who led them into the trap was later discovered upside-down in a well with a bullet through his head.

To date, the SBS losses in personnel had been remarkably light. That was about to change – and how. Within the next 3 months more than half of the men of Courtney's 42-strong 1SBS would be in enemy hands or dead as, repeatedly, they were asked to undertake the most hazardous and exacting tasks in clandestine attacks. A change in strategy contributed to the losses. The influence of David Stirling became more forceful after Courtney himself left the Middle East in 1942 to return to England for closer liaison with Lord Mountbatten, newly appointed head of Combined Operations. Where originally SBS took light losses on their specialist tasks of hitting railways, running limpet raids on Axis shipping, ferrying agents and making diversion raids ahead of full-scale assaults, they were now being drawn into the work that was previously the domain of the SAS: they were travelling deeper inland, especially to attack enemy airfields.

In July they lost eight key members, all taken prisoner in one hit. With Malta under siege, and the 10th Submarine Flotilla having evacuated its base, SAS and SBS teams were being tasked to attack airfields in the vicinity to protect attempts by Allied convoys to reach the island with supplies and oil. They had been rehearsing with a collection of new devices specifically to be used in rapid attacks on parked aircraft.

On 11 August these eight SBS men, led by George Duncan and Eric Newby, landed on the east coast of Sicily heading for an airfield, where a gleaming collection of Junker 88s was parked.

They reached the field and were dispersing to their targets when they were confronted by Italian guards, who were unconvinced by Duncan's attempts at conversation in the native tongue. As rifles were cocked, one of the SBS men opened fire. Newby's section, meanwhile, took cover but were discovered by guards when one of his NCOs said in plain-as-day English: 'It's time we fucked off.'

They did, firing as they went, and managed to escape the field perimeter. In the darkness one of them fell into the ring of trenches around the airfield and landed on several sleeping Italian soldiers, who managed to keep hold of him and grab his partner. Six made it to the canoes on the beach; one canoe was already damaged and unusable, another sank immediately, and a third, with two men aboard, was picked up the following morning. The last canoe, though upturned, kept the remaining four swimmers afloat through the night, though in the light of day they, too, joined the others in captivity in an Italian POW compound.

In the same month two more members of Courtney's 1SBS, who had been in since its inception, were captured. A section led by newcomer Captain Montgomerie was tasked to attack an ammunitions dump on the North African coast near Daba, one and a half miles behind enemy lines and virtually on top of the El Alamein front line. To reach it they had to pass a tented village of German troops which included a mobile cinema and a canteen full of singing drunks.

The SBS men working in pairs, successfully laid their explosives around the dump and a few more for good measure on tents, wagons, some captured British trucks and even the cookhouse before heading back to the coast for their exit rendezvous. One pair stumbled across a German lookout post, and in the exchange of fire Corporal Gurney was wounded by a burst of machine-gun fire and Lieutenant Mike Alexander stayed behind to help him. Both were captured.

Next, Lieutenant Tommy Langton hit trouble in a raid on Tobruk. It was a two-pronged attack that began on 22 August, when an SAS squadron was joined by detachments of Royal Engineers, Coastal defence and, later, the Long-Range Desert Group. They filled seven three-ton lorries loaded with British soldiers dressed to look like prisoners of war, while the SAS were in German uniform, acting as guards. They were to drive through German lines, intending to reach Tobruk to coincide with the sea landing of the 11th Battalion, Royal Marines, backed up by 150 infantry and machine-gunners. They were to shoot up shore installations and German communications to hinder the advance on Egypt.

Tommy Langton, the sole SBS officer, was riding with the SAS and was tasked to guide the infantry forwards from MTBs while the marines came ashore in Palestine-built landing-craft from two destroyers. The incredible journey of the fake PoWs actually ran without a hitch, apart from one hair-raising moment when Langton and his group, under Lieutenant Roberts, encountered a nest of Germans about to point a machine-gun in their direction. Roberts shot them. On the south side of Tobruk, a building identified as a wireless station was entered; the staff inside were similarly disposed of and the building blown to bits.

On to the beach, and Langton went ahead alone to begin to call in the MTBs. Problems were evident immediately: the landing-craft were generally pretty poor; several simply packed up or were not suited to the rapid landing techniques required. Secondly, as was later discovered, a double agent had forewarned of the attack and, as the chaos of the landing began to unfold, the Germans opened fire from dug-in positions, with tracer bouncing off the MTBs and searchlights scanning the whole area. More than half the force never landed because of the conditions and the inefficient landing-craft. Most of the rest were killed or captured, although mini-battles between groups of British and German troops ran for hours.

The destroyer HMS *Sikh* was sunk by shore batteries; the cruiser HMS *Coventry* and the destroyer HMS *Zulu*, with the unlanded troops aboard, were sunk by dive-bombers on the way back. A young Royal Marines Lieutenant on board *Coventry*, Donald Peyton-Jones, survived and later became Officer Commanding SBS.

Tommy Langton and two army privates tried to make their escape in a beach MTB but couldn't get it started. Then they swam out to an abandoned landing-craft and paddled around picking up survivors, 25 in all from the beach and inshore. Langton led the bedraggled group on what seemed an impossible task of reaching

Allied lines – 700 miles away – through hot Nazi territory, with little food or water and having to dive for cover virtually every few yards.

The trek was to last 78 days, and the last quarter of it in bare feet. Day by day the group became smaller, depleted by illness (mostly dysentery), starvation, German patrols and capture. After three weeks the party was down to six men. Then one more fell ill. Sergeant Evans, dehydrated and ravaged by dysentery, was too ill to go any further and was made comfortable by the roadside to be picked up by the enemy the following morning. Two others, twin brothers named Leslie from the Fusiliers, were next. One of them could not go on and his brother remained with him, to join him in captivity.

Finally, the three made it back to an Allied position – Tommy Langton and two privates. Hillman and Walter, emaciated and bedraggled and with a story of another incredible journey. Langton's only complaint was that he could not get near a radio for world news, otherwise he would have joined Monty at El Alamein. They threw a party for him later. Drink was taken, and Major Mayne accidentally drove a Jeep into the tent. Not many injured. Tommy Langton was awarded the Military Cross and was soon back in action.

While Langton was still marching, four more stalwarts of 1SBS were taken out in an otherwise very successful raid on airfields and fuel depots on Rhodes. The party was led by Captain Ken 'Tramp' Allott – so nicknamed for his total disregard of uniforms and razor blades – and Lieutenant David 'Dinky' Sutherland – the complete opposite, who would rise from a night in the depths of grottiness smartly attired and having used his last mug of water to shave himself.

Their mission to Rhodes was one of the most vital of its time and carried out to perfection. Tramp and Dinky took with them one Greek officer, two Greek guides, Sergeant Moss – a veritable superman – a corporal and three marines. They were landed on the island eight days before the raids were due to begin, bringing ashore a mound of explosives, ammunition and stores on three Carley rafts and one canoe. Each man carried a backpack of

50 pounds (23 kilogrammes) over 40 miles of rough, hostile terrain, deep valleys and steep cliffs to a cave where they would store part of the rations for the return journey. There, they split into two groups, each heading for their respective targets – two airfields from which German and Italian aircraft were harassing Allied shipping.

Each group completed its task with brilliant efficiency, and the two fields were put out of action for several weeks, giving Allied shipping an extremely unusual window of opportunity. Both groups, however, were hampered by deserting guides in their return to the rendezvous, where they would signal to the submarine that they were coming out. German search-parties scoured the countryside. One of the guides was captured and tortured, and they discovered that the rendezvous site was surrounded by 50 Germans. Dinky Sutherland's party split into two, while he himself remained with the Greek officer and Marine Duggan. He never saw the rest of his group again, and from the thud of distant gunfire he knew that they were either dead or captured.

Sutherland and Duggan reached the beach and from a hiding-place in the cliffs could see that the German intercepting force was searching the area meticulously. The Greek officer with them had gone off to try to get information on the others and never came back. Suddenly, amid a lot of commotion and gunfire, it was clear that Tramp Allott's party had been found and captured. Sutherland and Duggan were on their own.

That night Sutherland gave the pre-arranged signal out to sea with his torch in the hope that the rendezvous submarine was hovering somewhere waiting to take them off. Suddenly, Duggan spotted a faint response, flashed through the periscope; it was clearly several miles away.

They had no boats; the only course was to swim for it. They waited for an hour or more until the signal became clearer, but now they were fearful that the Italians had seen it too. They had. An enemy MTB had been launched and was patrolling up and down. Sutherland and Duggan, already weakened by lack of food and the long grind of the operation itself, had a stark choice: to give themselves up or try to swim out to the sub. They chose the latter.

They were in the water for almost an hour and a half, swimming towards the spot where they last saw the signal, with Duggan still signalling with their torch. At one point the sound of motors brought them joy until Duggan shouted 'Dive!' It was the Italian MTB. Minutes later the submarine rose from the depths beside them. Sutherland was dragged aboard, half-dead and seriously ill; Duggan was similarly in a bad way. But they had survived.

One more mishap brought gloom to the SBS and to Jumbo Courtney in particular . . .

Tug Wilson had enjoyed his home leave. He'd been reunited with his wife, had been fêted in Bristol and in his former place of work as the hero returning, and had received the royal congratulations on the presentation of his DSO. The sojourn in England, which he had reached finally in April after the eventful ride home via a limping submarine, was not entirely in the interest of his personal well-being. At one of the several top-secret experimental stations in the South of England, where all kinds of devices, gadgets, aids for agents, and other secret weapons were being tested, Major Malcolm Campbell and his group had invented a mini-torpedo for use by canoeists. (This was the same Malcolm Campbell, later Sir, who took the world land-speed record when his car *Bluebird* exceeded 300 miles an hour on the Bonneville Flats in 1935, and then achieved the world water-speed record in 1939.)

Campbell's device was ideal for the SBS. Instead of having to paddle or swim to enemy shipping and attach limpets – the current practice – they could attack from a safer distance more rapidly with these new hand-held torpedoes, which were powered by a windscreen-wiper motor. Trials had been conducted in experimental pools and home waters, but the torpedoes needed the expertise of a skilled canoeist of the SBS for a practical demonstration.

Tug Wilson was the man selected for the honour. Six of the mini-torpedoes had been produced, and he was to proceed forthwith to Alexandria in the company of a box marked 'Definitely This Side Up'. There he would join the submarine *Unbroken* and travel on to the coast of Italy to attack enemy shipping. This time he would be without his trusted aide Wally Hughes, who was ill. In his place went Bombardier Brittlebank, a solid, unflappable and courageous veteran of the disastrous Rommel raid and who, like Lieutenant-Colonel Laycock, had managed to find his way back to Egypt after enduring 40 days in the desert behind enemy lines.

No account of this adventure can match Tug's own placid description:

> Crotone harbour was chosen by Captain G. W. G. Simpson, commanding officer of the 10th Flotilla, after a close study of aerial photographs, because it afforded maximum chances of success, and of escape after the attack. Periscope reconnaissance of harbour was carried out during afternoon from a distance of about four miles offshore. The target, a merchant vessel, was located in an anticipated position along the northern mole.
>
> It was estimated that the operation, from leaving the submarine to the return, would take about two hours. The commanding officer of the submarine suggested that I should be launched about 2330 hours owing to the phase of the moon, which would rise about 0300 hours. He wanted the operation to be completed and under way from the vicinity of the harbour by that time. It was arranged that on return I was to flash a pre-arranged signal with a blue torch to seaward. If anything delayed my return, an alternative rendezvous was fixed at a point five miles off the harbour.
>
> At 2340 our canoe was launched approximately 2,000 metres off the harbour, with personnel, stores and equipment. There was a slight breeze and a faint swell; otherwise it was flat calm and a clear sky above. At about 250 yards [228 metres] [from the harbour entrance] we split paddles and approached square-on to present minimum silhouette. The boom on closer approach looked rather formidable, but certainly not insurmountable.
>
> However, we decided to investigate the bomb-damaged south mole and see if the breach gave us easier access to the harbour and found a gap that was down to sea-level. Barbed wire and rabbit wire had been erected but not very efficiently.

It was possible without much difficulty to fold this upwards very conveniently over a large piece of masonry, which was luckily just awash with three or four inches of water. Having made the gap sufficiently large, it was then simple to ease the canoe through into the harbour.

Inside the harbour the stillness was intense and the sky clearly reflected on the water. The target was distinctly visible, the funnel, bridge and mast silhouetted against the sky. A large schooner was lying in the middle of the harbour in a line parallel with the target. The breach in the mole was almost directly opposite the target . . . and an ideal position for attack, since the torpedo had a range of only 400 yards.

The chances of being observed at that distance would not be great. Bombardier Brittlebank sat forward using single split paddle, myself aft with torpedoes ready for immediate action. The final approach was made at absolute minimum speed owing to the extreme stillness of the water and phosphorescence stirred up when the paddle was used with other than the smallest effort. The visibility was just too perfect and gave us need for additional caution.

Having just arrived in the attacking position, the stillness was exploded by a challenge from the schooner. This was followed immediately by a shout from the target vessel, then by the noise of people running about and shouting in an unmistakably Italian manner. I decided it would be some moments before they would recover themselves sufficiently and do something reasonable in the way of a countermeasure. I removed the nose cap of one torpedo, placed it in the water and pressed the starter button. It was necessary to make a quarter-turn of the propeller and press the button a second time. The starter functioned and the motor started, sounding extremely healthy.

With the torpedo just submerged, I took careful aim at the target (the canoe being stationary) and with a gentle push released it. Almost simultaneously I ordered Brittlebank to stand by with double-ended paddle in readiness for departure.

Having quickly found my own paddle, I stole a last glance at the torpedo. The white line painted fore and aft along her back was pointing directly at the centre of the target's length. Her depth was about five feet and appeared to be running steadily during the few brief moments I was able to follow her. There was now plenty of commotion, and lights were beginning to appear among the Italian flotilla, but as yet no shots were fired. No definite explosion was heard during retreat, and I could not guarantee a hit. The retreat was made, bearing in mind my instructions and the main point of the operation, and I rather regretted at the time having withdrawn with three torpedoes before making a further attempt in the same or another harbour later in the patrol.

But my instructions were to ensure we were not captured with the torpedoes still in our possession. I still had a formidable salvo of three of them left for use elsewhere, and I was in safe waters outside what had become something of a hornets' nest, with my parent craft in waiting at the rendezvous only some 2,000 yards away.

We made our way to the position and carried out the customary procedure of signalling. This was only used after intensive scanning of the horizon and from a few inches above the water. The swell was increasing very noticeably now, and I continued signalling at specific intervals. Then, after half an hour I located the familiar-looking blob of [what I thought to be] a submarine off my port bow and turned towards it. A moment later I saw a similar object a short distance from the first. It soon became apparent that this was no submarine but two surface craft approaching line-abreast. I turned towards them with the intention of passing between them.

Crouching low in the canoe as the craft bore down on us, I estimated the enemy's speed to be about ten knots, the bow waves now being very marked and about 60 yards apart. On the spur of the moment I quickly launched one of the torpedoes over the port side. A few moments later the knife-edge bows and low waist of the dark-and-light-grey-camouflaged ship, now very close and on my port beam, suggested a light destroyer. Between the two vessels and at such close quarters, I expected some form of challenge, so held the remaining two torpedoes in readiness to be jettisoned. Luckily, the canoe had not been seen by the enemy, and I carried on at a steady speed in a direction opposite to that of the enemy shipping.

A few unhappy moments were experienced in passing through the immediate wake of the two vessels, but the canoe withstood the test without capsizing. I realised that our submarine would most certainly have picked up HE [hydrophonic effects] and would have taken evasive action. With enemy vessels patrolling the harbour area, I gave up any hope of contacting the sub that night. It was by then approximately 0145 hours. The alternative rendezvous was to be at dawn. The weather was gradually worsening. A considerable swell with occasional white horses running diagonally across my rendezvous course created conditions most unfavourable for maintaining an accurate course in an open canoe.

To meet the submarine it would be necessary to square into the weather and patrol up and down for the next five or six hours with concentrated attention. This we managed to do, although the accuracy of my position for the rendezvous at dawn could be no other than a little doubtful. Everything in the canoe was drenched. It was impossible to wipe the compass and binoculars effectively, but Crotone could be seen, however, roughly in the right direction about six or seven miles away.

The sea had quietened considerably at dawn. Having remained in that position for about another two hours without having sighted a surface craft of any description, I decided to try to attract the attention of the submarine by creating underwater explosions. Two four-second hand-grenades were thrown astern after maximum speed had been attained by myself and Brittlebank to avoid possible damage to the canoe by fragmentation. No periscope was observed. I could only conclude that the canoe was not in an accurate position or that the captain had decided not to remain, for very good reasons unknown to myself.

Conditions now demanded that the canoe should be beached

as soon as possible for maintenance, so I abandoned the area rather than run the risk of sinking. I proposed to make a bid for Malta, *some 250 miles away* [author's italics]. The condition of the canoe, however, and the equipment in our possession and the absolute necessity of frequent landings forced us to admit to ourselves that the odds of success of such a venture might be a little in the Italians' favour.

We proceeded south-south-east, towards Capo Calonna. Having rounded the cape, we reconnoitred that part of the coast for a suitable point of landing. A beach was selected, approachable only from the sea, being hemmed in by sheer cliffs. Before landing, the remaining two torpedoes were flooded and sunk some two miles offshore. By then, the canoe was not in a very stable condition. After some twenty minutes' work on her, we pushed off again. It was now about midday.

I set a course to cross the Golfo di Squillace. We passed a number of fishing-craft, and occasionally we were hailed. I replied with a wave of the hand. By six in the evening we were forced to beach again. This time it was not possible to select a suitable beach. We had been observed landing. Some twenty minutes later we found ourselves surrounded by a large number of Italians. Throughout the operation, Bombardier Brittlebank's conduct and reactions to various circumstances left nothing to be desired. Also during subsequent interrogation after capture, he proved to be the model soldier.

Tug Wilson spent the rest of the war in – and escaping from – Italian and German prison camps, a classic PoW story which is a book in itself. In Germany he escaped twice, once from a moving train under heavy gunfire. He managed to get back into Italy in 1943, and became involved in the Rome escape route run by a Roman Catholic priest before finally being betrayed and captured again. He spent the remainder of the war in a German prisoner-of-war camp at Brunswick, along with other British inmates who, as a memorial to their time together, pooled part of their service pay when they returned home in 1945 to fund the formation of the New Brunswick Boys' Club in South London; the club still exists today.

The story of Malcolm Campbell's baby torpedoes was not yet over, however. The result of the trials was unknown. Had the torpedoes worked? Could they inflict serious damage on enemy shipping? They had not been successful, but with Wilson captured they had no way of knowing. Major Vere Holden-White – Harry to his service pals – was the man to find out.

North African invasion for Operation Torch.

CHAPTER FOUR

Harry's game

News item, 7 November 1942:

> The greatest-ever armada of ships assembled for a single operation today landed American troops in Vichy-French North Africa. It brings 140,000 men for the great Allied offensive against Axis forces following last week's decisive rout by the British of Rommel's Afrika Korps at the Battle of El Alamein. As rangers, marines and infantry landed by sea, paratroopers dropped on key airports in Morocco and Algeria. They had taken all their objectives by nightfall. The French had no desire to oppose the Allied forces. The only resistance came from naval and coastal defence guns; two small ships were lost in Oran harbour.

It was the launching of the first major invasion force of the war, famously codenamed Operation Torch. The second string to that assault – the raid on Oran harbour – was codenamed Operation Reservist. No mention was made of SBS involvement because that was a secret. The SBS were among the advance party that carried out a full reconnaissance of the landing-sites for the assault, along with the founder members of new small groups soon to be known as the Combined Operations Pilotage Parties (COPPs), formed by Jumbo Courtney's good friend Nigel Clogstoun Willmott. The SBS had also been earmarked to test a secret weapon, and behind the last dismissive sentence of the news item about the action in Oran harbour and the loss of two ships lay the dramatic sequel to Tug Wilson's trials with baby torpedoes. The man to tell the story was Major H.V. Holden-White, MC, who led the SBS activity in the assault on Oran.

In January 1997 I met him at Huntly, the very pleasant residence for retired officers not far from the sea at Bishopsteignton, Devon. An attendant showed me to his little room, adorned with some of his own fine paintings and other memorabilia from life as an artist, living for a long while in France, after he quit the service at the end of the war. Vere Holden-White is now a frail but thoroughly charming and gentle man who also has an immediate and graphic recall of those days so many years ago.

He goes straight back to that battle off Oran, Algeria, where he was left holding the baby torpedoes that Tug Wilson had tested but had been unable to report back on. 'Bloody things,' said Vere with a mischievous chuckle. 'No bloody good at all. Damn things got ten of us captured, and I told Louis Mountbatten as much!'

Known as Harry in those days, in 1942 Holden-White was a 24-year-old second lieutenant in a battalion of the Royal Sussex Regiment, engaged on home defences since Dunkirk but about to be converted from infantry to a light anti-aircraft regiment of the Royal Artillery. Around that time, Harry's imagination had been fired at the local cinema by some newsreel of Commandos; he volunteered immediately for special duties.

Before he knew what was happening, he was on his way to Scotland, where Jumbo Courtney was hastily assembling a contingent who would form 2SBS, now that 1SBS was under so much pressure at the eastern end of the Mediterranean. The new section would include some returned members of the original section, with new recruits such as Holden-White and the merging of 101 Troop, 8 Commando, the latter hand-picked by its commanding officer, Captain Gerald Montanaro. Montanaro was to be training officer of the new unit, Courtney was commanding officer and the number two was his brother, G. B. 'Gruff' Courtney. Montanaro, in particular, would bring special skills to the training of the new section. Apart from an obsession with canoes which matched Courtney's own, he also possessed remarkable technical qualifications that he could apply to key problems that daily confronted the folboatmen, including the calculation of currents, navigational aids, camouflage and improving the adhesion of limpets to the slimy hulls of barnacled ships.

Their billet was a private hotel in a suburb of Ardrossan, and soon Holden-White was being initiated into the gospel according to Jumbo. After the usual lecture, they were given a tour and shown the folboats they would use: 'a number of canoes stacked higgledy-piggledy against the side of a hut and looking at first sight unprepossessing objects in which to go to war.'

In due course, too, an old gentleman in knickerbockers turned up to face the stolid-looking audience of new recruits. 'This was,' said Harry, 'Mr Branson, the celebrated grass-eater and future great-uncle of the entrepreneur and balloonist'.

> Accompanied by an ancient bicycle to whose crossbar was attached an equally ancient umbrella, this redoubtable man had cycled all the way from London, living on mowings culled from golf courses he passed. He rightly extolled the Japanese method of gathering their food from the countryside through which they walked. Suddenly his eyes lit up as he scanned the ground outside of our hut . . . and with the air of a conjurer producing a rabbit from a hat, plucked a bunch of chickweed and announced that he was going to make lunch with it. With newly awakened interest, we watched in amazement as he doused it with vinegar and bran, which he had brought with him, and solemnly proceeded to eat it.

In the weeks that followed, Harry and his new section passed through the rigours of training as canoeists, swimmers, mountain-climbers, survivalists and the general attributes of advanced boy scouting; the real thing bore no comparison. His tales are filled with the dark humour that goes with capsizing in the rough waters of the Firth of Clyde and being rescued by the harbour-master, and with long treks across Scottish hillsides, jumping in and out of rivers and carrying the canoes on their backs, and with the emerging comradeship among his fellows.

If their training was a trifle hurried and not quite up to scratch, there was a reason: the SBS desperately needed more manpower to match the ambitions and aspirations of Lord Mountbatten and the planners of Combined Operations. And conditions in North Africa, where the Special Forces were in chaos, added some urgency. There, the remnants of 1SBS had temporarily been taken under the wing of the SAS, with George Jellicoe in control but within the sphere of David Stirling, the sole director of the vast and powerful military group he had, by now, built up.

Stirling ran the group largely from his head; he alone knew where everyone was. On the other hand, everyone seldom knew where *he* was – which, most of the time, was racing ahead of the 8th Army, causing mayhem miles behind enemy lines. Then . . . utter confusion. Stirling's luck ran out; he was betrayed, then captured by the Germans while laid up with his column on the night of 23 January. It was days before the enemy realised that it had caught its most wanted man. Two or three months of upheaval and uncertainty among the Special Forces set in, and matters would not settle down again until new commanders were in place. At the time there was much wringing of hands and mutters of 'What do we do now?' Later, the SAS was temporarily wound up, re-forming into two sections. Stirling's original force regrouped under the name of Special Raiding Squadron and were posted as advance troublemakers ahead of the 8th Army in Tunis and later Italy.

Jellicoe, meanwhile, became commanding officer of the SAS-controlled Special Boat Squadron formed principally from Courtney's commandos in the Middle East and from Stirling's own canoeists and raiders; the squadron retained the SAS insignia. It consisted of three detachments of 70 men each, with seven officers. The squadron came officially into being on 1 April 1943 under Jellicoe's command from a base at Athlit.

This combination of SBS personnel caused post-war confusion about the title and an argument over who was entitled to use it (as described in later chapters). 'Special Boat Section' was the title adopted for Courtney's units. 'Special Boat Squadron' was the name of the formation under Jellicoe, who owed his allegiance originally to Stirling. Jellicoe thus began a long and spectacular command with many successful missions. Meanwhile, Roger Courtney was rebuilding his Special Boat Section in Britain. It was a pressing matter with Operation Torch on the horizon. Harry Holden-White was now fired up and ready to go. His first mission in the late summer of 1942 was supposed to be a repeat of the brilliant raid by his training officer Gerald Montanaro earlier in the year.

Montanaro and Trooper F. Preece had been ferried by motor launch across the Channel to Boulogne one moonless Saturday night in spring. Two miles out, they transferred to their canoe and paddled into the harbour to attack their target, earmarked from aerial reconnaissance. It was a German tanker which had taken refuge in the port after receiving a torpedo hit in the Channel. Montanaro and Preece successfully placed delayed-action limpet mines along her side, below the water line, and were about to depart when the front end of the canoe lodged in the hole created by the torpedo and wedged between the inner and outer hulls of the tanker. Although they managed to pull it clear, the canoe was damaged and started to take on water.

In this parlous state they began their difficult two-mile paddle to the launch in heavy seas, Montanaro paddling and Preece bailing furiously. The only resistance they encountered was a German soldier slumped by the wall of the fort at the harbour entrance who did no more than throw a beer mug at them. It missed. They managed to reach the launch just as the charges exploded. An aerial photograph the next day confirmed that they had completed the job the torpedo had failed to do, and sent the tanker to the bottom.

Harry's task was intended to duplicate this exploit. However, the plane that had flown over to take aerial photographs of possible targets was shot down and the job was aborted. Not much later, however, he was thrown into action – with a baptism of fire.

In the second week of October Harry – by then with the rank of captain – was summoned to Lord Mountbatten's Combined Operations headquarters in Whitehall, where Courtney also had an office. There was something big on. Hush-hush. Destination secret for now, but the SBS had an important role to play. Holden-White gleaned enough information to guess that an attack was planned on the Vichy French and that SBS canoeists would be launched at the head of a sea-borne onslaught which, even for one quite new to the service, seemed to nullify what he assessed to be the section's greatest asset, operating clandestinely.

The big one was Operation Reservist, part of Operation Torch described in the news item at the beginning of this chapter, the massive invasion of North Africa coupled with an amphibious attack on Oran, held by the Vichy French, heavily protected by shore batteries and harbouring a number of ships. Opposition inland was judged correctly to be minimal, but the Vichy naval chiefs were still smarting over the sinking of part of the French fleet at Oran by the British in 1940 and would take drastic measures to protect their remaining vessels.

Oh, and one other thing, said Courtney. The SBS had the honour of testing a new weapon, a mini-torpedo designed to be fired from canoes, which would hopefully cut down on the need for limpet mines whose clamping was always a hazardous business. A few days later Harry and Lieutenant E. J. A. 'Sally' Lunn went to an experimental station in Hampshire to see a demonstration of the mini-torpedoes. A stock of them was being prepared which, they were assured, would be dispatched with an officer to Gibraltar, where they would be collected by the SBS *en route* to wherever they were going (then still a secret).

The day of embarkation came. Harry took five pairs of SBS canoeists to Greenock, where they loaded their stores, weapons and canoes aboard two converted American coastguard cutters now under the Royal Navy flag and named HMS *Walney* and HMS *Hartland.* Three pairs led by Holden-White boarded *Walney* while Sally Lunn headed the other two in *Hartland.* Orders were now clear. They were to join a large convoy at Gibraltar, protected by destroyers and submarines. There, the two ships would pick up 400 American troops, who were to mount a sea-borne assault on Oran harbour and hold it until reinforcements arrived from inland.

The SBS role in all of this was to go in first, blowing up shipping in the harbour with the still-experimental mini-torpedoes. Each pair of canoeists was to be given two torpedoes, which they were to release towards suitable targets as soon as feasibly possible. The torpedoes were to be collected in Gibraltar, they were told, where an officer would explain all.

Harry takes up the story:

Well, that was the first thing to go wrong. When we got to Gib, there was no bloody officer to explain it all, no bloody instructions, and the baby torpedoes were in bits. Luckily, I had Sergeant-Major J. Embelin with us, who was a demolition expert, and he was able to assemble them. But we still had only a vague idea about range and so on, and a greater surprise was to come on that score much later.

Another problem for us was launching the canoes from ships. Normally, SBS crews are floated off submarines or lowered from MTBs. These cutters gave us a drop of eight to ten feet and our flimsy folboats could have been damaged. So on the way out we decided to practise and unpacked the canoes we had brought aboard in kitbags to assemble them, staggering about the heaving deck like some mad ballet. Fortunately, the *Walney*'s shipwright designed a sling to lower our boats into the water.

As we sailed into Oran, it was evident that the harbour was a death-trap for a sea-borne assault. Although the overall length of the harbour straddled the coast for about a mile, the opening to it was protected by a boom, which we knew about, of course. Once inside, there was no escape. *Walney* was supposed to ram the boom and, if that failed, Sergeant-Major Embelin, the demolition expert was to break open the boom with explosives. Sadly, he was subsequently killed by French machine-gun fire from the shore.

Anyhow, as soon as we sailed in, the Vichy-French shore batteries started firing. The three SBS pairs on board *Walney* were virtually thrown overboard and started paddling towards the docks. Frankly, I was so bloody glad to be away from it. Soon that feeling turned to guilt as I and my number two, Corporal Ellis, paddled off to find suitable targets for our mini-torpedoes. We had not travelled far when there was a huge explosion. We looked back. *Walney* had been hit by shore batteries and was already sinking. Then *Hartland* was hit; they were being shot to pieces and eventually we learned that around half the men on board were lost. Sally Lunn had been unable to launch his pair of canoes because they were damaged by shells. They joined escaping US troops on Carley liferafts.

Ellis and I paddled on. We had lost sight of our other chaps. We hid behind a barge to get our bearing, and as we did a ship loomed up out of the darkness coming towards us, a bloody great ship, absolutely enormous. Anyway . . . a suitable target, I thought. I fired one of my mini-torpedoes. There was no big bang, although the ship slowed down for a moment. Whether we hit it or not I do not know. She was eventually sunk outside the harbour by one of our subs. Then a submarine came out and I fired my second mini-torpedo at the sub.

Unfortunately, my arm was jolted as I put it in the water, so that one went astray. We watched it go, streaking through the water, but at least it made a bang. It hit the harbour wall just below the lighthouse, which was not, of course, lit. The lighthouse-keeper came out waving his arms; bloody furious, he was. I think he thought he'd been shelled by his own side. After that, there was nothing we could do but go on.

The original plan, in the event of failure, was to paddle back out to sea and get aboard one of the many Allied ships outside the harbour. This was now impossible. *Walney* and *Hartland*, still ablaze and listing, blocked our route. There was no alternative but to go on to the harbour and try to make our escape there and link up with troops coming inland.

Needless to say, the harbours and quays were swarming with Vichy-French troops. Holden-White and his partner Ellis managed to land but were very soon surrounded by a dozen men, who in due course carted them off to a makeshift PoW camp outside the town. The French showed particular interest in the SBS men's clothing – one-piece Tropal suits covering the body from ankle to neck and stuffed with kapok. They bore no insignias to indicate that they were soldiers and thus to be treated as prisoners of war – a fact that

Lieutenant-Colonel H. G. 'Blondie' Halser and Marine W. E. Sparks, the only two survivors of Operation Frankton, at the unveiling of a memorial to the Cockleshell Heroes at Poole. The eight who did not return were drowned or shot by the Germans.

Heroes and legends . . . creator of the wartime SBS Roger 'Jumbo' Courtney with his wife Dorrise in their canoe *Buttercup* in which they paddled the Danube for their honeymoon in 1938. *Left:* Blondie Hasler, inventor of many of the operational strategies on which today's SBS is based, in classic pose.

Nigel Clogstoun Willmott, beach reconnaissance expert and founder of Lord Mountbatten's Combined Operations Pilotage Parties which guided in invasion assault troops and equipment.

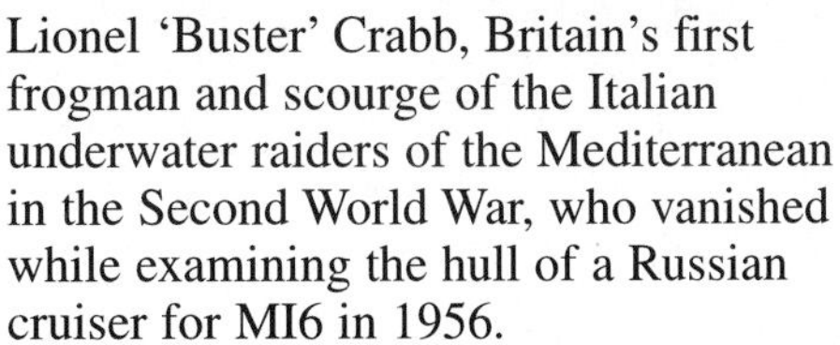

Lionel 'Buster' Crabb, Britain's first frogman and scourge of the Italian underwater raiders of the Mediterranean in the Second World War, who vanished while examining the hull of a Russian cruiser for MI6 in 1956.

Robert 'Tug' Wilson, the Bristol draughtsman who became a courageous canoeist/saboteur.

Canoe-borne raiders
Above: early exercise of Army Commando Folbot troop in 1941. *Centre:* swimmer-canoeists in action in their Klepper during the Indonesian Confrontation in 1963. *Below:* a typical SBS beach landing, though normally under cover of darkness.

Saboteurs, reconnaissance teams and agents were often delivered to their target zone by submarine.

The *Sleeping Beauty*, codename for the wartime motorised submersible canoe developed from an idea by Blondie Hasler for sabotage attacks on enemy shipping. The pilot sat like a racing driver in the cockpit, with a hefty load of explosive charges secured inside the canoe. The *SB*, as it was known, was famously used on Operation Rimau, which originated from Australia for an attack on Japanese ships berthed in Singapore harbour. The raid went disastrously wrong and ten who survived gun battles with the Japanese forces were later beheaded by their captors. *(By permission of the Public Record Office)*

Wartime heroics of Buster Crabb, seen here at work, were subsequently overshadowed by the post-war drama of his disappearance. With primitive equipment, he made hundreds of dives to clear Italian limpets from Allied ships and towards the end of the war helped clear Venice of mines deposited by departing Nazis.

Precarious in the extreme, the *X-Craft* mini-submarine, often leaky and always cramped, in action with top secret COPPs teams guiding the Normandy D-Day troop landings, as they did with all seaborne invasion forces after 1942. On this vessel are Coppists Jim Booth (for'ard) and George Honour in the conning tower.

would cost the lives of other similar adventurers who fell into German hands later in the war.

They were marched to the camp to join the remainder of the US troops who had come ashore from the two sinking cutters and eventually all the other SBS men on the mission. French officers overseeing the remnants of this disaster were friendly enough and referred to them as 'mes amis'. One even said in English: 'Don't worry. You will be liberated soon. The Americans are coming.'

Meanwhile, Sally Lunn, who followed Holden-White to the camp, had been horrified to see one of the mini-torpedoes floating in the water near the quay where he was being marched away. Says Holden-White:

> These bloody torpedoes were supposed to be top-secret. That's why the SBS had been sent to try them out, and I thought I had better get back to England as quickly as possible to report what had happened. We were freed within five days when the troops arrived from inland, but needless to say there was bloody confusion all over the place. We, the SBS, were told we would have to make our own way back to England, so I wandered around to the aerodrome to see if we could find a plane. We eventually got a lift to Gibraltar and linked up with Gruff Courtney. From there we hitched a ride on an American Fortress returning to England. We landed back in Cornwall, where we were immediately arrested. Bloody funny, really. We hadn't got any papers, of course, and wearing these odd clothes, the local police and immigration people surrounded us. We were interrogated for half an hour and eventually, after a few telephone calls, we were taken under close escort to London, where I was finally able to report on the mini-torpedo trials. It was only then, as I explained our efforts to use them, that their range for maximum effect – that is, sinking the target – was [found to be] only 50 yards. We had been firing them from 100 to 150 yards, so they were no bloody use from that standpoint.

In the meantime, Captain Peters, who was in overall command of

Walney and *Hartland*, was killed when the plane carrying him and his report to England crashed on landing at Plymouth. Harry and Sally Lunn were summoned to the office of Lord Mountbatten, a large and sumptuously furnished room on the first floor of the Georgian mansion that housed Combined Operations. Mountbatten was anxious to hear a first-hand account of what had happened. He listened and questioned and was clearly disappointed about the baby torpedoes, for which he had high hopes. Holden-White pushed his personal concerns as far as he dare, hinting that his own bitter thoughts were directed towards 'the shameful waste of life at Oran'.

Mountbatten glared at him but let the comment pass without comment, although there was perhaps a reason for that. In Mountbatten's office at the time was Colonel Robert Henriques, who handled 'public relations'. Mountbatten now wanted Harry and Sally Lunn to agree to be interviewed by the BBC, as it was the first operation of its kind in which British and US troops had cooperated. Though the assault on Oran had ended in disaster, the overall operation had been a huge success. 'I was appalled,' says Holden-White. 'To make capital out of such a catastrophe seemed to me to be an act of betrayal to those who had lost their lives. There were and would be so many disasters. But when you think about it, the odds were very definitely stacked against the SBS and the groups like us, and I suppose when you came down to it it was a case of "If you can't stand the heat . . ." '

Holden-White scuppered Mountbatten's plans for a bit of publicity by standing his ground and refusing to be interviewed; Lunn, seeing the vehemence of his resistance, stood by his decision. Mountbatten had no alternative but to let the matter drop. Harry Holden-White was sure, as he left the office that day, that he had placed his head on the block and it would soon be chopped off.

Not so. Mountbatten grudgingly signed the approval for Harry Holden-White's medal, the Military Cross, for his part in the Oran operation. Then, in late 1943, when Mountbatten became Supreme Commander in South-East Asia, his lordship's long-committed belief in the value of small raiding-units once again came to the fore. Almost straight away, in April 1944, he established the Small Operations Group (SOG) to bring together the skills of the several units involved largely in amphibious raiding, sabotage and recce work behind enemy lines.

Holden-White, now a major, found himself as officer commanding A Group, SBS, running operations against the Japanese on the Arakan coast of Burma. His was one of three SBS groups seconded to the SOG, along with Detachment 385 from the Royal Marines commando assault troops, four Sea Reconnaissance Units (SRUs) and four parties from Combined Operations Pilotage Parties (COPPs).

Mountbatten's commitment to these clandestine raiding-parties was demonstrated by his choice of men to command the SOG: the redoubtable Humphrey Tollemache, a Royal Marines colonel (later Major-General Sir) of vast experience in the Far East and jungle warfare and his number two Lieutenant-Colonel H. G. 'Blondie' Hasler, OBE, DSO.

The mention of that name brings us to the next set of disciplines and traditions, elevated during the war, which would ultimately be incorporated as a model in the do's and don'ts of the post-war SBS.

Chapter Five

Blondie's Cockleshell Heroes

H. G. 'Blondie' Hasler, so nicknamed by his chums in the Royal Marines for his mop of golden-red hair, which he had since all but lost, and a long moustache of the same colour, was a tall and hefty 28-year-old in 1942, an acting major and with a well-known interest in small boats that had been his passion since childhood. He had already been awarded an OBE, Croix de Guerre and Mentioned in Despatches during the Narvik operations. As a career officer, Blondie was projecting his theories about using small craft to attack enemy shipping even before Roger Courtney came on the scene. The previous year he had written a paper on the subject, but his ideas had been rejected. Now Courtney, Gerald Montanaro and others were advocating the same thing and others were following their lead.

There was something particular about Blondie's ideas, though, that distinguished him from the rest. His were perhaps more akin to the Italian way of seawolf activity, filled with ideas involving gadgetry and experimentation. His methodology was not Courtney's way, and they did not see eye to eye.

From the beginning of the war, the Italians had shown themselves to be well ahead of everyone – British, Germans and Japanese – in their perfection of sea-borne guerrilla warfare. They also possessed an impressive array of gadgetry and some deadly missiles – among them breathing apparatus for underwater swimmers, piloted torpedoes, miniature torpedoes and exploding motor boats.

The skill of the Italians began to worry the Allies in 1941, at a time when the British fleet was reduced to two battleships in the Mediterranean, HMS *Valiant* and HMS *Queen Elizabeth*, which lay sheltered behind torpedo nets at Alexandria. At 0330 on 19 December, two Italians were discovered clinging to the anchor buoy of *Valiant*. They surrendered immediately and were taken ashore for interrogation and then, to their dismay, back to *Valiant*, where they confessed that the battleship was about to blow up.

The crew was mustered to deck and the watertight doors were closed, but shortly after 0600 the ship rocked and shuddered as the charge set by the Italians blasted a large hole in her stern. Soon afterwards, *Queen Elizabeth* reared up from two explosions from charges attached below the water-line and both ships were temporarily out of the war. It soon emerged that the explosions had been caused by charges carried by three piloted torpedoes, driven by a team of six men from the 10th Light Flotilla of the Italian Navy, trained to remain under water for miles wearing flexible rubber-suits, breathing gear and fins. Although slow and cumbersome, the piloted torpedoes were to do a great deal of damage to Allied shipping.

In this instance, the torpedoes had been launched from Prince Julio Borghese's submarine *Scire* off Alexandria, two men astride each of the three piloted torpedoes. The men travelled to the target ship, where the time-fused warheads from each one were disconnected and attached to the ships' hulls. They then made their exit on the remaining part of the torpedo and returned whence they came. The operations even drew praise from Churchill as an example of 'extraordinary courage and ingenuity'. Escapes were always planned in advance. But on this occasion the two Italians had to adopt the course of last resort – which was to surrender to the nearest safe haven.

In fact, there was virtually no alternative to capture for the pilots of their next trick – the exploding motor boat. This was a high-powered, one-man boat with a range of up to 100 miles whose bow was packed with 500 pounds (226 kilogrammes) of explosives. The operative would aim the boat with death-defying speed at a suitable target and, at a safe distance for himself, pull a lever that ejected him and a rubber inflatable liferaft into the sea. He would then climb aboard the inflatable and paddle off to surrender to the nearest ship or shore.

The British, intrigued by these devices, captured a number of items – including the exploding motor boat and a human torpedo – which they were able to dissect.

Britain clearly had some lessons to be learned for her own attacking force, especially for use by the small-group raiders. At the time, Lord Mountbatten had just drawn together a number of eminent military and scientific experts to look at new weapons and methods. It was at a meeting of those men at the newly formed Combined Operations Development Centre (CODC) that Blondie Hasler's paper was remembered by one of the committee members – Major Malcolm Campbell, no less.

Hasler was summoned to the CODC's base at Southsea by the head of CODC, Captain Tom Hussey, RN, and was invited to join the study-group. On the first day Hasler was shown the Italian's exploding boat, captured in an attack in Souda Bay, Crete. The following day he was introduced to Mountbatten who made clear that his top priority was to build something similar. Mountbatten seemed convinced that such boats would be ideal for use by British raiders to destroy enemy boom defences, beach obstacles and dock installations. Although the Italians had launched them from surface craft, lowered over the side by derrick, Mountbatten believed that a method could be devised to drop the boats close to the target by air.

After that meeting, Blondie Hasler was given a wide brief to 'study, coordinate and develop all forms of stealthy sea-borne attack by small parties and pay particular attention to attacking ships in harbour'. Hasler went away to draft his proposals for a new specialist detachment. And it was these original theories, dreamed up in a time of dire necessity and expanded later, that were to provide some of the key ingredients in the blueprint for the post-war development of the modern SBS.

His ideas were, of course, linked to the already well-tried and well-tested methods of sea-borne raids by stealth, engineered by the likes of Roger Courtney, Tug Wilson and Gerald Montanaro. For although the exploding boat – codenamed by Mountbatten the

Boom Patrol Boat (BPB) so as not to reveal its true purpose – was his priority, Hasler still based many of his ideas around the use of canoes. Canoeists would be needed, for example, to cut their way through boom defences prior to an exploding boat entering a harbour.

During March and April of that year, Hasler sought out Courtney and Montanaro, the latter bringing his own 101 Troop to Portsmouth to give him a demonstration. Later, after Montanaro's merger with the SBS, Hasler joined them on exercises in Dover, and it was there that one of his key ideas took shape. The canoe, or folboat, used by the SBS was a Cockle Mark I, later replaced by a Cockle Mark I**.

Hasler believed they had limitations for the work he had in mind. He wanted a stronger craft, with a flat strip of timber for a rigid bottom that could take a heavy load and still be lifted over shingle or mud without breaking the canoe's back. Tom Hussey sent him to see Fred Goatley, works manager of the Saro Laminated Woodwork factory, which had recently won a War Office design award for a new river-crossing assault boat.

Blondie described his ideas to Fred, and soon had the Cockle Mark II in production – not knowing that it was to become the carrying craft for one of the most famous small-group operations of the Second World War.

The prototype delivered in July proved to be everything Hasler wanted, a strong but inconspicuous craft, very narrow and low in the water. It measured 16 feet (4.9 metres) in length, and had a 28-inch (71-centimetre) beam and a depth of just 11¼ inches (28.6 centimetres), with a collapsed depth of 6 inches (15 centimetres), and it weighed 90 pounds (41 kilogrammes). It had a flat wooden strip along the bottom made of ⅛-inch (3-millimetre) plywood with shallow bilge keels or runners underneath so that it could be launched from a beach and dragged across mud, sand or shingle. The sides were canvas or rubberised fabric, and the deck was ⅛-inch (3-millimetre) plywood on rigid wooden gunwales. The deck was held by eight hinged struts. When folded, the sides collapsed and the deck lay flat. The cockpit where the men sat was covered with waterproof fabric held by spring clips that disengaged quickly in case of capsize. Normal propulsion would be by double paddles, which could be split to singles at times of quiet operation.

It was designed to carry two men and about 150 pounds (68 kilogrammes) of equipment and stores through rough water. What was also true about the Cockle Mark II was that it would require utmost skill in its handling and in its navigation, especially on a dark night, tossed by rough waters and drawn by a tide flow running diagonally against it. The two-man crews needed utmost practice and training to be able to endure the physical effort of paddling the canoe while reading their charts, establishing their position and setting and maintaining a course by way of a mini-compass and the stars.

The exploding boat, meanwhile, was still on the drawing-board. Not even a prototype had been planned when final details for the establishment of the Royal Marines Harbour Patrol Detachment were submitted in a paper from the CODC to Mountbatten on 12 May 1942. He approved them personally, although he did change the name to the Royal Marines Boom Patrol Detachment, and the RMBPD officially came into being on 6 July.

A memorandum to the Chiefs of Staff noted that the object of the new detachment was to evolve new methods of attacking ships in harbour. The detachment was not intended to specialise in small-scale raids on coastal positions, demolition ashore, reconnaissance of beaches or the landing of agents, which appeared to be adequately covered by the SBS.

The detachment, with headquarters in Southsea, was quite small, initially made up of two sections, each with one lieutenant, one sergeant, two corporals and ten marines, with Hasler himself as officer commanding, and with a captain as second-in-command – a total of thirty men, plus four more in an administrative section. They were all volunteers from the services for 'special duties of a hazardous nature'. (It is interesting to note that one in three of the men in due course won medals for bravery).

Two other sections were added later, and they began training around Portsmouth and the Isle of Wight by day and night, in canoes, assault boats and fast motor boats, the latter acquired from civilian sources.

Hasler had a hand-picked cast. The men had to be young and

fresh – barely out of their teens – and capable of undertaking a training routine that would bring them to the very peak of physical fitness. In the process they went through all-night marches, long swimming routines in the coldest of water, diving exercises, running barefoot across shingle to harden their feet, and paddling canoes for mile after mile. They trained in stealth manoeuvres by sea and in mock escapes from enemy territory.

The RMBPD's daily log reflects a happy, eager bunch of recruits. (On one occasion, as a reward, they were given a private screening of Noël Coward's new film *In Which We Serve*, based on Mountbatten's exploits when he and his crew went down with HMS *Kelly* with all guns blazing.) But none of them yet had the slightest idea what they were training for, and nor did their marine counterparts at Southsea to whom they became a familiar sight, and nicknamed thereabouts as Hasler's Party.

Even as these young men were beginning their training, events unfolding elsewhere were to have a dramatic and immediate effect on their future. On 9 May Lord Selborne, Minister for Economic Warfare, wrote to Winston Churchill about concerns that Axis merchant shipping was running the British blockade. He wrote again on 22 June, and in July Selborne's ministry produced a study that showed that a particularly busy port for the blockade runners was Bordeaux. In the previous 12 months, 25,000 tons of rubber had passed through that port on its way to Germany and Italy. Other cargoes important to the Axis war effort included tin, tungsten and animal and vegetable oils.

With increasing concern in those most depressing days for the British war effort, Selborne wrote again on 5 August offering definite proof that fifteen blockade runners were at that moment in French Atlantic ports and three more were on their way from the Far East. Deputy Prime Minister Clement Attlee passed Selborne's letter to the Chiefs of Staff. Lord Mountbatten, in his capacity of Chief of Combined Operations, sat on the Chiefs of Staff Committee, and it was to him that Selborne's letter was eventually passed for action.

During August and early September the war planners produced a scheme called Operation Frankton. In effect, it boiled down to a

Combined Operations attack on the port of Bordeaux, reached via the Gironde 500 miles south of Plymouth on the Bay of Biscay. The proposals, however, were turned down by the Chiefs of Staff Examinations Committee because of the inaccessibility of the inland harbour, a decision that may not have been unconnected with the Dieppe disaster of 19 August. That raid, also under the auspices of Mountbatten's Combined Operations, was the biggest Allied assault on Hitler's Fortress Europe. At the end of the day, 68 per cent of the Canadian troops and 20 per cent of the Commandos who landed were dead or wounded; 2,000 were taken prisoner, with nearly 1,000 dead and left behind when the battered Allied armada returned home. Though two-thirds of the overall assault force remained intact, this fact merely demonstrated how many did not get ashore. Those who did never got beyond the beach. Nothing in Mountbatten's military career earned him so much criticism as the Dieppe raid.

Even so, Operation Frankton re-emerged in mid-September at planning level, when it was conceded that the port of Bordeaux could be attacked by a small raiding-party, travelling by stealth along the River Gironde to the point where the blockade-running ships would be berthed. Blondie Hasler, by then touting for business for his new detachment, 'now ready for a small testing operation', was called to London. The idea was floated, and Operation Frankton was under way.

On 30 October Mountbatten issued an outline of the operation to the Chiefs of Staff Committee: 'Operation Frankton has been planned to meet Lord Selborne's requirements . . . that steps should be taken to attack Axis ships which are known to be running the blockade . . . [it] is the only one which offers a good chance of success.'

He summarised the intention: officers and men drawn from the RMBPD would be taken to within nine miles of the Gironde Estuary by submarine. They would then paddle the 90 miles in Cockle canoes to the anticipated location of the blockade-running ships. There they would attach limpet mines to as many ships as possible, scuttle their canoes, make contact with patriot French and escape back to England, possibly through Spain.

It all sounded so simple.

Ahead lay four weeks of meticulous planning and final training. All kinds of other hurdles had to be overcome, and scientists were enlisted to help – Professor Solly Zuckermann was asked to provide medical aids for night vision, for instance, and Major Malcolm Campbell to come up with dim-lighted torches by which the men could read charts and compasses. Then came the task of weighing and packing a vast supply of equipment and stores which would have to be stowed on board the canoes while still leaving enough room for the men to complete their journey in relative comfort.

The stores themselves were daunting enough for the anticipated four-day journey along the Gironde by six pairs of RMBPD canoeists to be led by Hasler himself (see Appendix I). The explosives package – 48 limpet mines, 12 grenades, silenced sten-guns, each with 3 magazines containing 36 rounds – weighed 400 pounds (180 kilogrammes).

The men picked for the operation were themselves not told of it – any of it – until the morning of 30 November, when they were safely aboard the submarine HMS *Tuna* and under way to the Gironde Estuary.

They learned of their task only then: to sink the 12 largest ships lying in the Bassens-Bordeaux area. (What followed was immortalised in a not very good film, *Cockleshell Heroes*, starring José Ferrer and Trevor Howard, whose London première Hasler did not attend.)

No written orders were issued. Hasler verbally briefed the men and answered their questions, not least of which was: 'How do we get home?'

The six boats and their crews were split into two divisions: A, led by Hasler himself, and B, led by Lieutenant Mac Mackinnon. Each canoe had a codename; the pairs were: *Catfish*: Major Hasler with Marine Ned Sparks, aged 22, from London; *Crayfish*: Corporal Albert Laver, aged 22, from Birkenhead, with Marine Billy Mills, 20, from Kettering; *Conger*: Corporal G. J. Sheard, from Devon, with Marine David Moffat, 24, from Halifax; *Cuttlefish*: Lieutenant Mackinnon, 21, with Marine Jimmy Conway, 20, from Stockport; *Coalfish*: Sergeant Sam Wallace, 29, from Dublin, with Marine

Bobby Ewart, 21, from Glasgow; *Cachalot*: Marine W. A. Ellery, from London, with Marine Eric Fisher, 22, from West Bromwich.

The submarine *Tuna* reached the disembarkation point on the evening of 6 December and surfaced. A periscope reconnaissance revealed numerous patrolling vessels and they were forced to delay 24 hours. The next night she surfaced again and the Germans' coastal radar station picked up the signal. Searchlights flared along the French coast and all around the entrance to the Gironde Estuary, visible on what was according to the Submarine commander 'a beastly clear night'. But Hasler decided to go ahead.

Up canoes. The forward hatch swung open and seamen crowded on to that narrow stretch of casing, dripping wet, from which the Cockles would be launched. The Cockle crews, faces blackened, stood nervously waiting to go up, saying their goodbyes to the submariners and wishing themselves the best of luck.

Two by two they came out, and then . . . a setback. The sound of ripping canvas. *Cachalot* was damaged, fouled by a sharp corner of the hatch clamp. Ellery called to Hasler. The tear was along the side of the canoe, which he knew immediately could not be launched. Now there were five.

At 2022 they were in the water and heading for the Gironde under a cloudless sky lit by roaming searchlights giving a clear view for the marauding German patrol boats.

That night, with the Germans certain that the submarine, stationary for an hour or more, had unloaded a sabotage party, Berlin issued a piece of disinformation along the news wires: 'Dec 8: A small British sabotage party was engaged at the mouth of the Gironde River and finished off in combat.' Southsea held its breath.

For the remainder of the narrative of this remarkable adventure, there is no better account than the report of Blondie Hasler himself, published here in full, I believe, for the first time:

> The five Cockles Mark II moved off at 0822 . . . led by *Catfish*. Weather oily calm with low ground swell. No cloud. Visibility good, with slight haze over the land. Progress good. At 2350 the boats passed over Bano des Olives [sandbank] whose presence was evident from soundings and the way in which the

ground swell began to build up into steep rollers over the shallows. These rollers would have been dangerous if the boats had been a little further inshore.

The force of the flood tide now began to be felt and course was altered further eastwards to follow the line of the coast, now clearly visible about one and a half miles away. Shortly afterwards, the sound of broken water ahead indicated a tidal race. This came as an unpleasant surprise, not having been apparent from the chart or the sailing directions. Owing to the strength of the stream there was no chance of avoiding the race, which proved quite severe for such small craft. The Cockle Mark II proved quite able to weather it provided it was kept head into the waves and cockpit cover securely fastened.

Immediately after passing the race, *Coalfish* (Sergeant Wallace and Marine Ewart) was found to be missing, and the force turned back to look for it without success. Since both men and the boat had buoyancy equipment, it seems possible that they had not capsized but had turned further inshore on finding themselves separated from the remainder. Nothing further was heard of this boat.

A short time later a second tidal race was heard ahead. This proved to be somewhat heavier than the first, and on emerging on the far side of it we found that *Conger* (Corporal Sheard and Marine Moffat) was capsized, with its crew in the water. As it was impossible to bail out the flooded boat, she was scuttled, and every effort was made to tow the two swimmers somewhat further inshore. During this proceeding, the tide carried the party round the Pointe de Grave, not more than three-quarters of a mile offshore and through a third but less violent tide race. The lighthouse on the point had just been switched on at full strength and lit up the scene quite brilliantly.

The two men in the water were finally left in a position one and a half miles south-east of the Pointe de Grave, since it was considered that to take them any further would prejudice the chances of the other three boats remaining unobserved. From this position the tide should have carried them very close to the mole at Le Verdon, but they were already very cold and unable to swim effectively. Both men were wearing life-jackets fully inflated.

This incident wasted so much time that it was impossible to attempt to reach the east bank of the Gironde that night. Also, the remaining three boats were now closer inshore than had been intended, and the strength of the tide compelled them to pass between the mole at Le Verdon and three or four vessels anchored lying about three-quarters of a mile east of it. These vessels appeared to be of the French Chasseur type. In order to get through unobserved, it was necessary to change to single paddles and proceed with caution, and the three boats separated to a distance of several hundred yards to lessen the chances of being seen.

On getting clear of this danger, it was found that the third boat, *Cuttlefish* (Lieutenant Mackinnon and Marine Conway) had lost the formation. Nothing further was seen of this boat, but there was no reason to suppose it met with any mishap at this stage since it was in perfectly good shape and no alarm could have been raised by enemy without it being audible to the other two boats on such a still night.

The remaining two boats proceeded on course and picked up the west bank of the estuary near the Chenal de Talais, turning south-eastwards in order to continue up as far as possible. At 0630 the first attempt was made to land, but it was found that there was a line of half-submerged stakes on a shingle bank running along the shore, and the ground swell breaking over these obstructions made it impossible to negotiate them in safety.

The boats continued along the coast for some time without finding a possible landing-place, and it was only as daylight was breaking that they were able to get ashore at a small sandy promontory near the Pointe aux Oiseaux. The boats were concealed as well as possible with camouflage nets.

A considerable number of small fishing-boats had begun to issue from the Chenal de St-Vivien and now headed towards our beach. At the same time a number of women appeared walking towards us along the shore. We took cover as well as we could, but it became hopeless when a number of the boats landed on the beach and fishermen began to light a camp-fire and make preparations for breakfast within a few yards of us.

We were soon observed and had to explain that we were British and that our presence must not be revealed to anybody. Some of the party seemed quite unconvinced and declared that we were Germans, but we pointed out that in any case it would be better for them to keep silent on the subject, and shortly afterwards women returned to the village and the men to their boats. At about 1600 some of the women returned for a further chat, but as we were otherwise undisturbed it seemed that they had followed our instructions.

It was not possible to resume the passage until the flood stream began to run at 2330, and as this was low-water springs it was necessary to manhandle boats over nearly three-quarters of a mile of sandy mud before we could launch them. The method was to drag them fully loaded, which was only possible owing to the flat bottom and the strong construction of the Cockle Mark II.

Getting the boats clear of the shore was difficult owing to large areas of outlying sandbanks and breaking rollers which we met head-on. Eventually, we got clear and into the shipping channel. Navigation was easy as the port hand-buoys were all showing a dim flashing blue light. Weather was flat calm, no cloud; visibility good but with haze over both shores. Continuing on the same course, we picked up the east bank just north of Portes de Calonge and followed it about one mile offshore until the approach of daylight made it necessary to lie up.

At this time it became suddenly extremely cold, so much so that the splashes of salt water were freezing on the cockpit covers. We found a suitable field and put the boats in a thick hedge. During the day we discarded certain stores that were no longer any value to us as we got into more inland waters.

The plan for the following night was complicated by the fact that during darkness we would only have three hours of flood tide at the beginning of the night, then six hours of ebb followed by a further three of flood before daybreak. This entailed an intermediate lying up. In order to catch as much of the tide as possible, we started somewhat earlier than was prudent and were seen silhouetted against the western sky as we launched the boats. Frenchmen from a nearby farmhouse came out to investigate and we repeated our story from the day before. They seemed quite convinced and rather upset when we declined their invitation to go to the house for a drink.

At 0630 we began looking for a place for a lying up. It was only after considerable difficulty that we got ashore near a small pier. A quick reconnaissance of the area disclosed what appeared to be a light Ack-Ack position 40 yards away, and in view of that we again embarked and proceeded further south. The situation was getting rather urgent owing to the approach of daylight, and we finally put ashore at 0730 at a point with not very good cover but placed the boats in the middle of a marshy field in long grass with the nets over them. We were not observed at all in this position, although a man and his dog came within a hundred yards of us, and at one time a herd of cattle stood around in a circle looking at us.

It had been intended to carry out the attack on the night of 10–11 December, but we had not got high enough up the river to enable this to be done with any chance of withdrawing into darkness afterwards. It was therefore decided to move to an advanced base close to the target area that night and carry out the attack early on the night of 11–12. The boats were launched at 1845 on the tenth with considerable difficulty owing to vertical and slippery banks. The weather was good from our point of view, being cloudy with occasional rain and a moderate breeze. For the first two miles we proceeded up the centre of the river, then changed to single paddles and followed close along the western passage, which was lined with thick reeds.

After an uneventful passage we passed underneath the pontoon pier opposite Bassens South and found a small gap in the reeds into which we were able to force the boats at around 2300. As soon as the tide began to ebb, the boats dried out and we made ourselves comfortable for the night. Daylight showed us that we had been fortunate in our lying-up place as we were quite inaccessible and well concealed, and at the same time by standing up we were able to observe traffic on the river. Two good-sized ships lying alongside immediately opposite us.

During the day, we rearranged the stowage of the boats so as to have all the escape equipment in two bags, and in the evening we completed the fusing of the limpets. A nine-hour setting was used on time delays. The weather was once again flat calm with clear sky and good visibility. The moon did not set until 2132, and I considered it essential to delay leaving our lying-up place until 2110, which was about 30 minutes later than we would have desired from the tide point of view. At 2100 the time fuses were started.

The plan of attack was as follows:

Catfish: To proceed along the western bank to the docks on the west side of the river at Bordeaux.

Crayfish: To proceed along the east bank of the river to the docks on the east side of Bordeaux, but if no suitable targets were found to return and attack two ships at Bassens South, which we had been studying during the day.

Both boats left the lying-up place at 2115 and separated for their respective attacks. *Catfish* got up past the entrance to the basins without difficulty, except that it was necessary to keep clear of the shore because of a good many lights, particularly around the lock gates.

Eight limpets were subsequently placed by *Catfish* as follows: three on a cargo ship of about 7,000 tons; two on the engine-room of a Sperrbrecher; two on the stern of a cargo ship of about 7,000 tons; one on the stern of a small tanker.

While *Catfish* was a little distance from the side of the Sperrbrecher, and in the process of turning downstream, we were seen by a sentry on deck who shone a torch at us. Fortunately, we were able to get back close to the ship's side and drift along with the tide without making any movement.

The sentry followed us along the deck shining his torch down at us at intervals but was evidently unable to make up his mind as to what we actually were, owing to the efficiency of the camouflage scheme. We were able to get into a position under the bow of the ship where we could no longer be seen, and after waiting there for about five minutes everything seemed quiet, so we resumed our journey downstream.

The attack on the second large merchant ship was rather spoiled by the presence of a tanker alongside her and the fact that the tide was now running so strongly that I considered it unsafe to go between the bows of the two ships; this forced us to attack the stern only.

After all limpets had been placed, *Catfish* withdrew down the river without any further incident. While having a short rest in mid-stream, we were re-joined by *Crayfish*, having successfully completed their attack. This meeting was purely by chance, but it was decided to continue in company until the end of the withdrawal.

Corporal Laver reported that he had proceeded some distance along the east bank of Bordeaux without spotting any targets and, as the tide had turned against him, returned and attacked the two ships previously seen at Bassens South, placing five limpets on a large cargo ship and three on a smaller cargo liner.

In order to reach the Blaye area by low-water slack, it was necessary to abandon our previous caution. At 0600 we separated and proceeded to land independently about a quarter of a mile [0.4 kilometres] apart. Nothing further is known of *Crayfish* and her crew. Having disembarked *Catfish*, the boat was scuttled and sunk.

A full report of the escape route followed by *Catfish*'s crew has been made separately to MI9.

It is desired to draw attention to the part played by the following NCO and men: a) Corporal A. E. Laver, who handled his boat skilfully and displayed initiative and coolness in making his independent attack; b) Marine W. E. Sparks (No 2, *Catfish*) and Marine W. H. Mills (No 2, *Crayfish*), who

> both did their work in cool and efficient manner and showed considerable eagerness to engage the enemy.

Blondie Hasler's report was filed in April 1943 soon after he returned home – following a 1,400-mile journey which was as remarkable as the attack itself, taking him and Ned Sparks through France, over the Pyrenees, on into Spain and finally into British territory at Gibraltar on 1 April, dodging German patrols and the agents sent to look for them all the way.

Mountbatten was moved to send a memo to the Chiefs of Staff: 'This brilliant little operation carried through with great determination and courage is a good example of the successful use of limpeteers.'

The only debatable part of the exercise was its cost. The planners knew from the outset that the chances of the men returning were pretty bleak, but such considerations, at the height of desperation, are not considered in the same light as they are after the passing of years.

It was many months before news of those who vanished from the narrative, two by two, came through. The first, via Red Cross channels, confirmed the discovery of Marine Moffat. His body was washed ashore close to the point where he had been left with Corporal Sheard when their canoe capsized. Corporal Sheard was also believed drowned. As to the remainder, a fuller picture of what happened, though by no means a complete one, was in a report filed to the Office of the German High Command, Foreign Department/Security, by Major Reichel on 12 January 1944 'for possible exploitation for propaganda purposes'.

The report, headed 'Sabotage attacks on German ships off Bordeaux', read as follows:

> On 12.12.42 a number of valuable German ships were badly damaged off Bordeaux by explosives below water-level. Adhesive mines were attached by five British sabotage squads working from canoes. Of the ten who took part in the attack, the following were captured a few days later:
>
> Mackinnon, Naval Lieutenant, born 15.7.21, N. Argyllshire.

Laver, Albert Friedrich (sic), born 29.9.20, Birkenhead.
Mills, William Henri (sic), Marine, born 15.12.21, Kettering.
Wallace, Samuel, Sergeant, born 24.9.13, Dublin.
Conway, James, Marine, born 28.8.22, Stockport.
Ewart, Robert, Marine, born 4.12.21, Glasgow.

Their leader, Major Hasler, and Marine Sparks presumably escaped. Having carried out the explosions, they sank their craft and tried to make their escape to Spain in civilian clothes with the help of French civilians. There were intermediaries in two places on the Gironde, and in a bar. They were brought to the demarcation line by intermediaries with whom arrangements had been made beforehand.

All those captured were shot in accordance with orders on 23.3.43.

CHAPTER SIX

Sleeping Beauty

By now, the intrepid canoeists were performing a broader range of tasks and were diving, with new inventions, activities that would form vital precursors to SBS operations in the post-war years. While Jumbo Courtney's SBS had concentrated largely on surface canoes for the landing of saboteurs, agents, raiding-parties and reconnaissance groups, Blondie Hasler's Boom Patrol Detachment was pioneering a number of new small craft, several for underwater work, which required new skills and a large number of swimmers. In fact, the burgeoning need for swimmers and divers led to the formation of the Sea Reconnaissance Unit, which was attached initially to Hasler's RMBPD.

Experiments were already advanced on a number of craft designs when Hasler had left for Bordeaux. On the assumption that he might not return from that expedition, his second-in-command, Lieutenant (later Captain) J. D. Stewart pressed on with the work. He had served with Hasler in landing-craft operations in Norway in 1940 and enthusiastically supported many of his ideas.

When Hasler got back to the fold after his mammoth journey across Europe four months later, he found that the programme had developed with remarkable speed. Training was in progress for specialist canoeists using a further modified version of his own Cockle design. The group had blueprints for new single-seater canoes and multi-person versions. Meanwhile, would-be pilots were getting the low-down on the exploding boat, while others were being instructed for various tasks, including the latest creation – a motorised submersible canoe which went by the name of *Sleeping Beauty*.

SB was another of Hasler's inventions. In a paper written in late 1940, he had outlined a plan for what he called an underwater glider – a single-seater submersible canoe manned by a shallow-water diver. The Admiralty rejected it as impracticable. Undaunted, he re-submitted the plan a few months later with modifications and explained how the submersible could be used for beach reconnaissance, destruction of underwater obstacles prior to beach landings and for attacking enemy shipping.

By early 1943, with Lord Mountbatten's stamp of approval, a prototype had been manufactured, and it was being trialled along with a number of small surface and submersible craft being produced at experimental stations by the Royal Navy. Mountbatten's Combined Operations headquarters was naturally interested in any craft that eased the route of the all-purpose raiders.

Up to that point, work on the exploding boat had taken priority, and by January 1943 it was undergoing trials. The boat was small – 16 feet (4.9 metres) long with a 2-foot (0.6-metre) draught – and capable of carrying a crew of one with 500 pounds (226 kilogrammes) of explosives with an instantaneous fuse in the bow. It had a maximum speed of 40 knots (74 kilometres per hour) – although it could travel silently at only 5 knots (9 kilometres per hour) – and a range of about 70 miles in calm weather.

Its key purpose was to be taken by air or sea to within range of an enemy harbour, a route through the harbour defences having been ensured by a swimmer-canoeist. The cox'n would then aim it at a suitable target and eject himself at a safe distance, to be picked up by a canoeist or to make his escape in a rubber inflatable to a waiting ship. Trials were already under way for drops by air. Six Dam Buster Lancaster bombers were converted to carry the exploding boats. Lieutenant Cox, RM was awarded the MBE for the first drop – such was its importance.

By August 1943, however, the Chiefs of Staff were still not convinced by either the boat's effectiveness or the procedures to be followed for the safe return of the pilot. Although a number of exploding boats were built, they were never used in any operation.

Sleeping Beauty, on which Hasler had worked with Sir Malcolm Campbell and others, seemed to have more versatile possibilities. The single-seater canoe was 12 feet 8 inches (3.9 metres) long, with a 27-inch (68.6-centimetre) beam, and was powered by an electric motor driven by batteries. The hull was made of mild steel and the deck of aluminium. It could travel on the surface, sailed, trimmed down, or submerged to enable the pilot to attach limpets to enemy ships. The pilot took an unusual position in the craft, lying long and low with his chin almost level with the cockpit coaming. A joystick provided control, and in theory the motor was started by the press of a button (although that did not always happen). The pilot would move the craft slowly forward until the air pressure in buoyancy tanks equalled that of the surrounding water.

Training for *SB*s proved hair-raising for some as they practised submerging in the heavy swell of waters around the Shetland Isles. Two men died in the calm of static training pools during training for the use of breathing sets. The use of such equipment, not common at the time, was very definitely a case of trial and error.

Even so, *SB* was judged ideal for beach reconnaissance ahead of major troop landings and for the more traditional role of fixing limpets to enemy ships, which could be approached submerged and remain so. The submersible had maximum speed of just four knots (7.4 kilometres per hour) on the surface, or around two knots (3.7 kilometres per hour) trimmed down or submerged. It was designed to be carried on a MTB or other vessels, and experiments were also carried out to try dropping it and its pilot by parachute from a Lancaster bomber.

Other small craft, ingenious but of dubious value, were also being built. One of them, from designs by the British Army, was *Welman*, a midget one-man submarine, earmarked for use by the Special Operations Executive in the Far East and by the 2SBS in the Mediterranean. Twenty-nine feet (8.8 metres) long, it could be carried towards the target area in an MTB or on a submarine and was capable of carrying 6 100-pound (45-kilogramme) charges or a single 560-pound (254-kilogramme) charge to attack enemy ships. It was also thought useful for beach marking ahead of invasion.

In trials, however, *Welman* was difficult to navigate, incredibly claustrophobic, and the pilot had to surface to get his bearings. Hasler could see no practical use for it, although Roger Courtney, who was totally sold on the idea, took a team of SBS for practical trials and had supported the notion of setting up a Welman base at Appledore. Further trials raised additional anxieties about the usefulness of *Welman*. One report presented to the Combined Operations Executive complained: 'Eighty-five per cent of trained *Welman* operators conceive a dislike of going down in them. They say there is no way of getting out if anything goes wrong and if the fin drops off under water, no one knows which way up the *Welman* would arrive on the surface . . . the craft roll very badly . . .' Nineteen hulls were built, but *Welman* was used only once, in an aborted operation off Norway.

Then there was *Chariot*, a hefty torpedo-shaped submersible boat, driven by a battery-powered motor with a range of 24 miles. It was a copy of the two-man Maiali (sea pig) used by the Italian 10th Light Flotilla against British ships earlier in the war. Its crew, equipped with breathing sets that would allow six hours of diving, sat in the open astride *Chariot*. The boat could deliver a 1000-pound (454-kilogramme) warhead, which would be detached and hung by magnets to the target. A delayed time fuse would allow the pilots to return to the mother ship aboard the craft without suffering the effects of underwater explosions. *Chariot*'s disadvantage was that it was difficult to manoeuvre, especially in enclosed situations such as crowded harbours. It was not considered a success, and those expected to operate it soon regarded it as jinxed. The charioteers, as they were known, were recruited from SBS and RMBPD. In the first recorded operation, Norwegian blockade runner 'Shetland Larsen' took two *Chariot*s and four charioteers aboard to attack the German battleship *Tirpitz* near Trondheim, Norway.

The submersibles could be slung, hammock-like, beneath the mother boat, and when they got close enough the divers intended to slip over the side and release the two craft for the attack. Unfortunately, about eight miles out they were hit by a major storm. The two *Chariot*s broke free and sank; Larsen had to scuttle his fishing-boat, and all aboard made for shore. The party set off on foot to cross Norway into neutral Sweden. They arrived back in England six weeks later, unharmed but angry.

Next, three *Chariot* teams were taken aboard the submarine HMS/M *P.3111* at Malta and sailed off to sink some Italian ships moored at Corsica. The submarine was hit by enemy action just short of the target area and all aboard were lost. *Chariot*s did however sink ships in an operation at La Specia.

Finally, there was the *X-Craft*, a fully equipped miniature submarine with a range of 1,500 miles, intended again to attack enemy shipping and capable of landing a small raiding-party. Lieutenant-Commander Nigel Clogstoun Willmott was looking for something similar as a recce submarine for his newly formed Combined Operations Pilotage Parties and wanted the *X-Craft*, with modifications. Willmott attended trials of the mini-sub and later described it as 'like living under a billiard-table that leaks'. Living conditions were cramped – no one could stand fully upright – and facilities primitive. Condensation was appalling, causing the labels to fall off food tins so that no one knew what they were about to eat, and body odours became overpowering after a few days. Willmott also spotted other severe flaws: 'It was found desirable for the officer of the watch on the casing to lift his head above water for breathing purposes. He is strapped to the induction pipe and has a bar to which he clings with fervour while floating on his front like a paper streamer on the bottom of the ocean. There is a vacancy for an intelligent merman to fulfil this role.' But Willmott still saw its possibilities, with some modifications, for his own unit, and the *X-Craft* came into service with COPPs during the latter stages of the war and used for the Normandy landings.

Small-party raiders, more often than not, still had to rely on their well-tried and well-tested methods of attack and reconnaissance by canoe. Production of the new craft was slow, and some did not make it into regular service. The Special Operations Executive's Indian Mission, which was based in Ceylon, sent a requisition note for some of all the above for tasks in the Far East. Their order was for 12 *Chariot*s, 9 *Welman*s and 48 *Sleeping Beauty*s, though what exactly they planned for them all was not immediately clear.

They received only 15 *Sleeping Beauty*s, which were to be used on an operation planned and launched from Australia. Though not connected directly with either SBS or RMBPD sections, the story is recorded in the classified history of the SBS, both for its lessons and for the courage of its participants. The operation was also the only one recorded of the intended mass use of submersible canoes (although the RMBPD had trained hard for a plan to drop a party with *SB*s on to the Etang Biscarrosse lake, 50 miles west of Bordeaux, to attack four Luftwaffe Viking 222 flying-boats regularly parked there: the mission was aborted at the last minute because of the weather; the descending parachutes might have drifted off-target in the wind and landed in a nearby pine forest.)

The Far East operation followed an earlier successful raid, codenamed Operation Jaywick, against Japanese ships in the crowded port of Singapore. It was led by Lieutenant-Colonel Ivan Lyon of the Gordon Highlanders, a keen yachtsman and canoeist who was attached to the Special Operations Executive 136 Force, specialising in organising resistance and sabotage. Jaywick was the India Mission's biggest success to date. Lyon's party – himself and three canoeists – approached the port aboard a captured native fishing-junk that had been converted and camouflaged to carry the raiders.

It was moored in a quiet creek among the Riau archipelago of islands, from where Lyon and his comrades took to their two canoes for the final assault on Singapore. They paddled through the filthy waters of this bustling port, unnoticed amid the conflicting smells of diesel and spices and the cacophony of noises and activity all around them. The two canoes moved silently towards their targets on single paddles so as not to kick up any phosphorescence. Unseen, they passed Japanese sentries patrolling the harbour walls.

Once in the port and under cover of darkness, they slipped in and out of the moored ships, attaching limpets to four. They made their escape back to the hidden junk, in which they then proceeded to journey on through almost 1,000 miles of Japanese-patrolled waters to reach the safe haven of the Exmouth Sound, off the north-west coast of Australia. Behind them they left more than 40,000 tons of Japanese shipping damaged or destroyed by their charges.

Buoyed up by the success of that mission, Lyon flew to England

and turned up at the Combined Operations headquarters in Whitehall, where he outlined his plans for a second attack on Singapore, using the new submersible canoes he'd heard about via the India Mission. The plan was welcomed wholeheartedly, especially as Lord Mountbatten, by then leading the South-East Asia Command, had his heart and mind set on – among other things – anything that would weaken the Japanese hold on Singapore and hasten its return to British control. Sub-Lieutenant Riggs of the Royal Naval Volunteer Reserve (RNVR) trained with RMBPD in the use of *Sleeping Beautys* and was then charged with taking them to Australia.

Lyon had gone on ahead to recruit a party of 32 swimmer-canoeists, who were to be known as Group X. After training in *SB*s, the party was taken aboard the mine-laying submarine *Porpoise*, which would deliver them to an island hideaway close to Singapore – and the beginning of what was codenamed Operation Rimau. With them went truckloads of stores: enough food for a month, clothing, weapons, ammunition and, of course, a substantial cache of charges.

Two weeks later, Lyon was taking a periscope recce in *Porpoise*, which was dived off Pulan Merepas, a small island within striking distance of Singapore. This they chose as their advance base for the operation. They unloaded their boats and their stores from the submarine, and Lyon set off with a handful of men aboard *Porpoise* in search of a native junk to capture for use as the carrier for *SB*s on approach to Singapore and in which to escape after the attack.

A long search for a suitable craft proved fruitless, and after five days they had to settle for a conspicuous white junk named *Mustika* that had no engine. The crew of nine Malays was scattered, though in what condition is unclear. Lyon and his own crew set sail for their hideout, where they were soon carting aboard their cargo for the planned assault.

Porpoise left immediately for Freemantle, scheduled to return for a rendezvous in a month to pick up the party. Lyon planned to carry out simultaneous attacks on six separate areas of Singapore harbour, approaching submerged in *SB*s. Ten *SB*s would return to the junk; the other five would travel to hideouts used by Lyon during Operation Jaywick and would be picked up later. All 15 *SB*s would be scuttled after the successful completion of the operation. That, at least, was the plan.

What happened next is, 50 or so years later, still shrouded in the mists of a Japanese cover-up. *Mustika* set sail with her raiding-party, leaving four men at the hideout to guard their stores. At some point during the operation, *Mustika* was challenged by a Malay police patrol. Lyon, certain that they would be discovered with his secret *SB*s on board, refused to heave to and a gun battle followed, killing three men on board the police launch.

Japanese troops, alerted by the incident, began a five-week cat-and-mouse chase for the raiders. Lyon scuttled *Mustika* and the 15 precious *SB*s, and his men paddled ashore in groups in canoes to hide up. They were pursued by Japanese search-parties that relentlessly scoured the islands. Several gun battles followed. In one, lasting a full two days, Lyon and another officer, along with several Japanese, were killed.

Now leaderless, the remainder of Group X continued their desperate retreat from the searchers. More battles followed; another nine men were lost. The submarine *Porpoise*, meanwhile, which should have come to collect Lyon's group, had developed engine trouble, and *Tantalus* came in its place, arriving late because its commander had to engage enemy shipping *en route*.

The remnants of Lyon's party were stranded. The Japanese refused to let go. Survivors were hunted down and eleven were captured, the last one taken 10 weeks after *Mustika* was scuttled. One died from battle wounds; the remaining ten were kept prisoner. On the orders of a Japanese general, they were beheaded on 7 July 1945, a month before the end of the war in the Far East.

Records of a court martial, produced by the Japanese after their surrender, were clearly faked to avoid war crimes accusations. They did, however, note that the men of Operation Rimau died 'in valorous spirit'. The Japanese report claimed that the men were intercepted before they reached Singapore harbour, though evidence suggests that they had, in fact, made it to the harbour and severely damaged some Japanese cruisers.

Thus ended the most ambitious and courageous project to use

Blondie Hasler's submersible canoes. Once again, men were prepared to risk their lives for what were small-volume, high-risk ventures for the sake of damaging or, if they were lucky, destroying a few enemy ships or sabotaging enemy installations, which for the most part were back in operation again within a month or two. The theory was that, cumulatively, the attacks were of great value, tying up or disposing of Axis troops, guns, ammunition, support groups, transport and ships across a wide enemy arena and thus keeping them from front-line positions. And this was certainly true. By the end of 1943 and onwards, swimmer-canoeists and small raiding-parties of the various groups visited briefly in these chapters were working in ever-increasing numbers in every theatre and every department of the war, across the whole panoply of conflict.

There was, however, one more group which forms a key link in the family tree of the SBS of which we have so far only caught a passing glimpse: Combined Operations Pilotage Parties, born initially as a small section to trial a revolutionary concept in beach reconnaissance. COPPs mushroomed into one of the most vital and secret units of the war, and their techniques are still used by the SBS more than half a century later.

Chapter Seven

COPPs

Ronnie Williamson, a softly spoken Shetlander by birth and a Commando in his youth, lives in Edinburgh in quiet retirement, though busy still with matters of military history. He enjoys the reunions with those from the distant days. There are, in 1997, just 18 known operational Coppists left, and today Williamson still looks back with utter astonishment that, as a young man of 19, he was chosen to be part of a group that was given 'Top Priority of the War' – a virtual law unto itself, and to which even senior officers found themselves giving way.

Coppists were members of the élite Combined Operations Pilotage Parties, 50 per cent of whom were officers. Two-thirds of Coppists were naval and the remainder came from the Royal Engineers and Commandos. The group was officially brought into being by Mountbatten at the beginning of 1943 following the disaster of the Dieppe landings.

In a nutshell, COPPs were an SBS-style gathering of swimmer-canoeists, who were to be supremely capable of looking after themselves in any situation but who were also to be trained to perfection in the arts of navigation and hydrography. The men would be delivered by submarine, landing-craft and other carriers – including, later, the X-Craft mini-submarines – paddle inshore in their canoes and then go over the side to prepare a complete reconnaissance of assault beaches, draw their maps and charts to ensure the smooth landing of Allied armies.

The task required many hours of swimming and shore sorties for a complete survey, always in darkness, invariably in enemy territory and often on heavily guarded beaches.

At Mountbatten's insistence, and after putting his proposals direct to Winston Churchill at a private meeting, COPPs were formed on the understanding that they would have to know the secrets of Allied invasion plans ahead of their launch. Given such vital knowledge, the very existence of COPPs was strictly operated within the terms of the Official Secrets Act; their existence was never referred to in any newspaper, or in BBC broadcasts or internal services communications that did not bear the stamp MOST SECRET.

They were given a cover story of being Combined Operations Police Patrols, supposedly checking boom defences, but many senior Allied commanders below the rank of commander-in-chief did not even know of their true role. COPPs commanding officers carried orders signed personally by Mountbatten; their orders were to be produced if challenged by a higher rank, a not uncommon occurrence. COPPs men – even lower ranks – possessed knowledge of future plans in the war often before senior officers of the mainstream services were aware of them, which also put them in a most precarious position if captured. Three COPPs officers were rumoured to have swum out to sea and drowned rather than face torture by captors waiting on the shore. Coppists on missions in the Far East were provided with cyanide pills and anti-shark repellents as standard issue.

The secrecy surrounding COPPs was maintained after the war, even though they were disbanded, because of their hand-me-down connections with modern warfare. Their existence was not publicly acknowledged by the Ministry of Defence until 1959, and only then when the cover was blown by an American researcher. Public Records Office documents relating to COPPs activities did not appear for the full 30 years. Those involved remained remarkably tight-lipped among the wartime memoir-writers.

The reasons for such security dated back to midway through the war. Major troop movements lay ahead and Mountbatten, with foresight inspired by recent experience, began a campaign to ensure that beaches were properly reconnoitred rather than relying simply on aerial photographs or second-hand intelligence – which included prewar picture postcards.

The whole assault area would be examined in detail: gradients of underwater approaches, obstacles, sand-bars, rocks, beach consistency, land surfaces, mined areas, beach defences, beach exits, natural hazards such as cliffs and hills, lookouts, sentry posts, gun emplacements and finally enemy positions . . . all to be mapped and charted ready for invasion troops. At that stage, COPPs would be there again with canoes anchored 100 metres off the centre of the critical beach, shining a shaded torch out to sea over a predetermined arc to guide the assault forces forward. In Sicily, for example, four canoes guided in 3,250 ships.

The task was, as Mountbatten saw it, crucial, and the man he chose to form COPPs – and in effect become the inventor and pioneer of modern beach reconnaissance – was Lieutenant-Commander Nigel Clogstoun Willmott, RN. He was a close friend of and had served with Blondie Hasler in the early Norwegian operations and Willmott, it will be recalled, won a DSO when he saved Roger Courtney's life while they were on the very first reconnaissance operation on the beaches of Rhodes in 1941. Hasler and Courtney were both consulted. Willmott was selected.

They knew he had a particular bee in his bonnet about beach landings. He'd made a study of them, presented reports on Narvik and Rhodes which no one seemed especially interested in and, as a navigator on the Naval Force Commander's staff, he persisted with his theories of converting beach reconnaissance into an exact science. In this he had the intermittent encouragement of Courtney, with whom he had kept in touch. In 1942 Willmott returned from service in North Africa and found himself transferred to the Combined Training Staff in Scotland, where he started a course on beach pilotage for junior officers. In September he was summoned to Mountbatten's office and asked to put together a reconnaissance team to be dispatched immediately to North Africa ahead of the landing in Operation Torch.

Early in 1943, after Mountbatten had visited Churchill and was told to put his proposals before the Combined Chiefs of Staff, COPPs came into being, with barely enough time to train up parties to plot the course for the invasion of Sicily in the early summer.

Ronnie Williamson was little more than a boy when he volunteered for the commandos. After a rigorous selection process, only ten per cent of those who applied were selected for training and about ten per cent of those failed the course itself. Out of a shortlist of six men, a final interview by Captain Basil Eckhard, SBS, produced the three men required for COPPs teams. They then went on a further four months of specialist training.

Ronnie later rose from corporal to captain in 14 months and went on to become a close friend of the founder and his family. (He was best man at Willmott's second wedding in 1982.) Williamson recalled:

> Nigel convinced Mountbatten and Mountbatten convinced the war planners that it would be impossible to win the war unless they could land thousands of men safely on exactly the right beaches which would stand up to the heavyweight back-up of tanks, artillery, shells, transport – the whole mass of an army such as Montgomery's landing in Sicily, brought ashore in good order.
>
> The beaches had to be thoroughly surveyed, the forces guided in and onwards, speedily and perhaps under enemy fire. To have them bogged down in shifting sands, to have vehicles or men drowned, to be unaware of underwater obstacles or mines, to be lacking in detailed intelligence of hazards unseen from aerial reconnaissance photographs . . . those were the nightmare scenarios that gripped Nigel and Mountbatten.
>
> From my own standpoint, it shook one, as a virtual youth, to discover that you were part of something as internationally important as this; it was viewed by all of us, I know, as just a sheer honour to be part of it. You had to pinch yourself to believe it was true. Hitler would have paid millions of pounds to know what we knew. Mountbatten realised quickly that Nigel's job would be utterly impossible unless he was granted Top Priority of the War. I got this from Nigel himself. Mountbatten went directly to Churchill to explain his plans that

would enable Nigel to recruit and properly equip precisely the right people he needed for this vital task. He believed that nothing and no one should stand in their way. Churchill's reply, to my surprise, was that he did not have the authority to grant Mountbatten what he asked. Mountbatten would have to put his proposals directly to the chiefs of the army, navy and RAF – but with Churchill's full approval.

They, in turn, were not at all happy about the top-priority request, in other words giving Nigel the power to overrule senior officers and even civilians to get what he needed. But what choice had they? Either they would have to promote him to an incredible height or else give him the ace of trumps. In the end, entirely due to Mountbatten, Nigel was given the ace of trumps.

That ace came in the form of a personal letter of authority from Mountbatten – golden words from him saying tactfully NOW HEAR THIS. It provided commanders throughout the war theatres with a message writ between the lines. If the officer commanding a COPPs unit experienced any difficulty at all, he was to get on the blower to the Chief of Combined Operations – Mountbatten himself. Under the heading 'Instructions to the Officer in Charge of a COPPs Unit', Mountbatten memoed:

> These instructions should be produced as your authority should such be questioned. On arrival at the station you will be under the orders of the Naval Commander-in-Chief . . . Your normal method of communication should be through the authority under whose orders you are placed. In order, however, that the general organisation, development and training of COPPs units may proceed to the best advantage . . . you should keep the Chief of Combined Operations informed on all matters of detail. This should be done by requesting the authority under whose orders you are to forward a message in the following form:
>
> 'Following for Chief of Combined Operations from COPPs—'

> If requirements are forwarded by letter, it should be addressed to the authority mentioned with a copy to the Chief of Combined Operations. This will enable the Chief of Combined Operations to take preliminary action.

In other words, the authorities mentioned had better watch out, and they did.

Ronnie Williamson again:

> It was quite remarkable. Nigel was given the power to do what he wanted. He was very modest about it, but the reality was that no one could stand in his way. Our COPP units also got pretty well whatever we asked. If we needed a lift on an aircraft-carrier, we got it. If we needed additional equipment, it was there. If we raided the stores of a shore-based unit, there was no comeback . . . quite incredible.

That situation was not easily reached. Some difficult hurdles and resistance had to be overcome. Early COPPs sections, such as the one Willmott took on the recce prior to Operation Torch for the North African assault, were not given the precedence that Mountbatten later ensured. Willmott mustered a force of 18 in haste, virtually all trained navigating lieutenants from the Royal Navy or RNVR and experienced SBS officers. They lacked proper equipment, especially efficient swimming-suits, and Willmott also faced some hostility among the top brass over demarcation: beach marking had always been the preserve of SBS. But these difficulties were overcome and COPPs was founded, initially under the codename of Party Inhuman, which they used for Operation Torch. The reconnaissance was a model of its kind.

It still took a major setback in terms of casualties to prod the powers that be into agreeing to put COPPs on a firm footing in the way that Willmott and Mountbatten had envisaged, with its own headquarters and establishment, training facilities and equipment. At the time, war planners were anguishing over the invasion of Sicily, anticipated for the summer of 1943. Various locations in the south of Italy and Sicily were under consideration. The Allied commanders who would lead the two-pronged assault were more or less agreed that a Sicilian landing could be achieved with the minimum loss of life.

At the beginning of January 1943 COPPs were called into action. Two COPPs sections were dispatched from England and one formed from the Middle East Beach Reconnaissance Unit and supplemented by a couple of men borrowed from the SBS. They met up in Malta and began training procedures. The party badly needed rehearsals but barely had time for them. They were due on the Sicilian recce by the end of February because their reports were required by mid-March. In fact, the assembled company was ill-prepared both in terms of expertise and equipment. That February was wintry cold, their canoes were barely adequate for the weather, and the suits used for lengthy swimming missions were ill-fitting and had a tendency to leak.

The men pressed on. They were taken aboard three carrier submarines from Malta and set off for the Sicilian coast, 75 miles away. There, after dark, they would paddle their canoes to their designated beaches to begin their recce, returning to the submarine on conclusion, the whole operation scheduled for four nights. They were dropped around 2 miles from their recce sites and would paddle inshore to a point around 200 metres from the beach. The paddler would remain in the canoe, suitably camouflaged, and attempt to maintain a stable position, unnoticed, while the reconnaissance officer would slip into the water.

He would be wearing a hefty suit of rubberised fabric, which was supposed to give him buoyancy and protect him from the cold. The suit had a built-in lifejacket that could be inflated by mouth, and pockets laden with equipment, including: a .38 pistol, a fighting knife, an oil-immersed prismatic compass, sounding lead and line, beach gradient reel, an underwater writing-tablet with chinagraph pencil, 24-hour emergency rations in case of separation and two torches to home in on the canoe for the return.

The swimmers were to record every possible detail that would be of use in pinpointing the most suitable assault site, with a profile and description of the geological nature of the beach itself to assist invasion force beachmasters to bring ashore landing-craft and to establish suitable sites for piers and breakwaters.

The Sicilian recce ran into trouble from the word go and stumbled from bad to worse nightly. All the beach sites due for reconnaissance were found to be heavily guarded, with sentries posted at around every 100 metres. The losses began immediately.

First, the leader of the COPPs expedition, Lieutenant-Commander Norman Teacher, RN, failed to return to his canoe and was presumed dead or captured. The former proved to be the case. His paddler, Lieutenant Noel Cooper, an experienced canoeist who had been on Operation Torch as a marker, returned to the submarine rendezvous completely exhausted after a long search.

In spite of that, Cooper went out again with Captain G. W. Burbridge on 2 March. They did not return and were never seen again. On 3 March two of the Middle East group, Lieutenant Bob Smith and Lieutenant D. Brand, failed to meet their submarine, although their navigation was certainly not at fault.

In rough weather, they simply paddled two and a half miles back to the same beach – i.e. seven and a half miles in all. There is no tide in the central Mediterranean, but they had to make allowances for the wind and waves for fine adjustment to their re-set course, which they had carefully memorised. They then paddled 75 miles back to Malta in just over two days and went right up to Grand Harbour in Valletta before arriving exhausted alongside a submarine in Lazaretto Creek. This was a remarkable feat of navigation and endurance without food and water. One week later, the submarine they tried to re-join returned safely from patrol.

On 6 March Lieutenant A. Hart and Sub-Lieutenant E. Folder, also from the Middle East section, did not come back.

On 7 March Lieutenant P. De Kock and Sub-Lieutenant A. Crossley failed to meet their connection, and the following night Lieutenant Davies went to look for them and did not return either. Others also went missing.

Of the sixteen who joined the mission, only four were known to be safe. Five – Teacher, Cooper, Burbridge, De Kock and Crossley – were never seen again, presumed drowned. The remainder had been captured.

The three lost officers of COPPs – Teacher, Cooper and Burbridge – were believed by some to have hit trouble and had taken the ultimate precaution against capture and torture by drowning themselves. Others disagree, and put their loss down to either accident or enemy action. The incident remains a debating point to this day.

In spite of the losses, some of the beach reconnaissances were completed successfully, and for these Lieutenant N. T. McHarg and Lieutenant George S. Sinclair, DSC, RNR, were both awarded the DSO. Smith and Brand were awarded the DSO, while one of those captured, Able Seaman James McGuire, who later escaped from an Italian PoW camp, was awarded a BEM.

In the aftermath it was concluded that the men were ill-equipped and ill-trained. In the haste to get them under way, no homing exercises had been carried out and only three, ironically Teacher, Burbridge and Cooper, had experience of the procedure.

Nigel Willmott, devastated by the losses, vowed that such a catastrophe should never happen again. He insisted that the disastrous results merely confirmed his point – that training procedures for COPPs people were paramount and could not be hurried. The men also had to be properly equipped; without adequate gear, their missions were doomed to failure.

At this point Mountbatten took the operation by the scruff of the neck and demanded full backing from the Chiefs of Staff – which he achieved. They dealt Willmott, as Ronnie Williamson described it, the ace of trumps. Nigel Willmott became the father of COPPs. He based his unit at the requisitioned Hayling Island Sailing Club and went on to train ten COPPs sections between 1943 and the end of the war. Ronnie Williamson recalls:

> Thanks to the Top Priority, we never lost a man in COPP5. Our canoes could and did operate effectively in force eight, while our new equipment was lightweight, tailor-made and state of the art. Hardly a week passed without more high-tech items arriving. It was like the difference between coal-dust and gold-dust. The transformation took only four months and we never looked back.

COPPs took their vital place in the war effort, operating in every theatre and every major invasion of Allied forces. They were there for the Sicilian landings in July 1943, every one of the assault landings into Italy and on into the Adriatic.

Then came the greatest operation of them all, the Normandy landings, where two X-Craft mini-submarines were extensively used by COPPs, with five men aboard at times instead of four. In addition, two regiments of waterproofed tanks were guided 90 miles (145 kilometres) across the English Channel and put into the sea 2 miles offshore from Sword Bay, arriving precisely as arranged at 5.30 a.m. The margin of error allowed was just 40 yards (36 metres). They were right on target. Furthermore, there were no casualties among the COPPs men; instead, deservedly plenty of accolades, honours and medals.

COPPs sterling work continued in major river crossings, such as the Rhine, and in a huge variety of complex assignments with the Small Operations Group in the Far East, especially in preparation for the invasion of Malaya. These were led by Willmott's logical successor, the most experienced Coppist of the war, Lieutenant-Commander Peter Wild, DSC, RNVR. Although all these operations were carried out with remarkable low casualties among the Coppists, the work of such men as Wild was inadequately acknowledged, largely due to the secrecy that surrounded the group long after the hostilities had ceased.

After the war, many of the techniques and unique skills devised and practised by COPPs teams were still totally applicable to modern warfare. From tenuous beginnings, COPPs established the strategy that there should never be large-scale troop landings without prior extensive reconnaissance of the invasion beach, its underwater approaches, its surrounds and enemy positions – techniques that hold good 50 years later and were demonstrated, for example, with the first British task force landings in the Falklands, for which the SBS opened the door.

By the beginning of 1944 the principles of small-group operations which were to provide the foundations of the SBS down the remaining half of the century had been firmly established and were being deployed across the whole spectrum of Allied action. Though many of Courtney's original SBS group had been lost in action or captured, reinforcements were trained and dispersed across the Mediterranean and the Far East.

Three new Courtney-trained SBS groups, A, B and C, were formed to join the Small Operations Group based in Ceylon under the badge of the Royal Marines in South-East Asia Command along with sections from RMBPD, Detachment 385 from the Royal Marines commando assault troops and four Sea Reconnaissance Units, the newly formed unit for the growing emphasis on underwater work. In the coming months the SOG parties mounted no fewer than 174 raiding and recce operations behind Japanese lines before its disbandment at the end of the war. RMBPD also had a section very active in the Mediterranean.

Meanwhile, George Jellicoe's Special Boat Squadron, acquisitive, well equipped and flamboyant, with a force made up of former SBS and SAS sections, bolstered and renewed after losses, had won medals by the bucketful across the whole North African arena and the Italian coastline, prior to and around the time of the Italian armistice. Jellicoe himself led some spectacular missions, by land, sea or floating in by parachute, routing Italians and giving little peace to the Nazis with his island-hopping raids off the Greek and Turkish coasts, around the Mediterranean and on into mainland adventures off the Adriatic and the Aegean.

There was, however, a clear distinction between Jellicoe's Special Boat Squadron and Courtney's Special Boat Section. The Courtney traditionalists considered Jellicoe's group to be an affiliate of the SAS from which it originated, and thus 'not one of us'. Special Forces and private armies all had their own way of doing things. There was undoubtedly dissension between the SBS and the SAS over tactics, and the glowing embers of it remain half a century later.

Gruff Courtney, 30 years after the war had ended, would recall pointedly that when the original SBS was allowed to operate in the specialised roles for which it had been chosen and trained, its casualties in major campaigns were relatively light. Losses mounted after 1942, when Roger Courtney departed the Middle East and 1SBS was employed mainly with Jellicoe on *coup de main* raiding on inland airfields, more properly the province of the SAS.

'The prime function of the SBS,' said Gruff gruffly, 'was to do maximum damage to Axis forces with the minimum of effort . . . weigh the possible loss of two men in a canoe against one or more bomber aircraft in an attack on a railway bridge and you have an example of cost-efficiency.'

He made another valid point that he seemed to equate *his* SBS and sea-borne raiders and recce parties of RMBPD and COPPs. The men whose activities we have followed in this brief sojourn in the Second World War came to the fore on the key principles of the SBS – as volunteers and as men with the physical and mental stamina to sustain them through the most difficult times. They were drawn from all walks of life – from Tug Wilson, the Bristol draughtsman, to Billy Mills, who worked in Kettering Sports and Rubber Store before he became a Cockleshell Hero.

With a few exceptions, such as Roger Courtney himself, they had no exotic past, nor were they undisciplined misfits. They were, however, individualists, loners and survivors whose sometimes latent qualities were spotted by the people who were selecting them for training. 'Their motivation,' said Gruff Courtney, 'was as mixed as one would expect: undemonstrative patriotism, youthful adventure, self-reliance, independence of mind. They were generally quiet fellows but full of spirit. A psychologist might have detected in some a masochistic urge, a hidden death-wish . . . but it never seemed to survive the actual shock of danger. Then, animal instinct for self-preservation could be expected to reassert itself with its usual force.'

It was those men and those characteristics that formed the backbone of the amphibious small-group raiders – another 'few' gathered up and trained in this particular art of warfare. Such men cut a path to the future. They possessed skills that, according to Field Marshal Lord Slim, Commander of the Forgotten Army in Burma, which he led to victory against the Japanese, and later Chief of the Imperial Staff, should not be discarded. 'There is one kind of special unit,' he wrote in 1946, 'which should be retained – that designed to be employed in small parties, usually behind the enemy on tasks beyond the normal scope of warfare in the field.'

Jumbo Courtney, Blondie Hasler and Nigel Willmott, encouraged by Mountbatten, fathered a formation that was born on a beach in

Rhodes in 1941, given a cruel kicking on the banks of the Gironde in 1942, and finally came of age along the coastlines of Normandy and the Arakan in 1945. Traditions and disciplines were formed along the way.

And then, they all came home . . . but to what?

PART TWO

Peace and Wars

1945 to 1970

Hitler gone, the Japanese surrendered after the atom bombs vaporised Hiroshima and Nagasaki . . . and in the context of the war's end the specialist units seemed of little consequence. The stories of the heroes and the legends of the Special Forces were locked away in the filing cabinets marked MOST SECRET and were years away from being told. The spotlight was on the great battles and the great armies, the hundreds of thousands who never came back, the horrors of the German concentration camps and the rush to demobilise. Private armies were disbanded, which pleased many in the military hierarchy who didn't like them, didn't want them and campaigned to have them closed down. Others begged to differ. David Stirling, freed from Colditz and back with the SAS for its last knockings in the Far East, was devastated to discover that his beloved regiment was to be relegated to the Territorial Army, and for a while the amphibious raiders of SBS, RMBPD, COPPs and the swimmers of the SRU who made up SOG seemed to be heading towards the anonymity of a larger command. Barely had they begun unpacking their kit and stacking the stores and equipment being trundled in from around the world than the future reared its ugly head . . .

Chapter Eight

A troublesome rebirth

They were still a pinprick in the order of things . . . 'a speck of flyshit on a map of the world' was one description. Mountbatten was no longer there to jolly them all along. Although he'd had a war to run, there is little doubt that he viewed the canoe raiders of South-East Asia as *his* boys. Now, he and they were no more. He left Singapore on 30 April 1946: the Supreme Commander of South-East Asia was out of a job, along with the rest of them in his Small Operations Group.

The vast territory over which he had administered the British assault on the Japanese invaders was returned to civilian governments. He departed to the sound of a cliché: rumblings of discontent: Malaya, Indonesia, Burma, Borneo, Korea, Vietnam . . . 'I am afraid you are in for a rather sticky time, old chap,' he sardonically and prophetically told one of the administrators as he waved goodbye. United in their resistance to the Japanese, political factions of South-East Asia split wide apart when the Allies withdrew and mayhem took hold. Before long, SOG in the guise of the new SBS would be called back into action. But in 1946 there was little sign that anyone was really interested in what happened to the remnants of that particular party.

Mountbatten's arrival in Portsmouth for a senior officers' course not long after his return gave hope to some – and nausea to others – that he was on the verge of returning to high military office. The new Labour government of Clement Attlee had other ideas and whisked him away to India to oversee the beginning of the end of the British Empire. It would be another decade before the aura of Mountbatten returned, and, as he moved to sort out Partition, the chaps of SOG were struggling for an identity – or at least, those veterans who remained in the service were.

Many returned to civilian life and quite a few others, like Tug Wilson, who stayed on and rose to the rank of lieutenant-colonel, did not remain with the amphibians. He later returned to front-line action in Korea. Roger Courtney, ill since 1942, retired and died in 1947. Nigel Willmott returned to the navy and then went home. Things could never be the same. The impetus of war which allowed the creation of private armies and small-group raiders had gone; in its place was an anticlimactic void.

A million service personnel had been demobilised by the end of 1945. Bankrupt Britain had to tighten its belt yet again. Deep cuts in service personnel and economies across the board were being demanded by politicians. Special Forces, and their surrounding collection of experimental stations and support staff, were a small but obvious target. Who would need them in an age of A-bombs?

The War Office Tactical Investigation Committee took soundings from commanders on the future use of Special Forces. There was formidable opposition to them from commanders in all sections of the armed forces, but, equally, many remained convinced of their role in modern warfare, particularly in some of the looming troublespots, where the terrain was rough and the natives restless. Expert testimony on where those troublespots were likely to occur led the committee to conclude that 'short-term, shallow-penetration' sections should be raised and trained under the auspices of the Royal Marines.

The SAS, on the other hand, was given no quarter. Two months after the war ended, 1SAS, 2SAS and HQSAS were disbanded, while the Belgian 5SAS was handed over to the Belgian Army. As a compromise to some loud howls of protest, a new volunteer SAS regiment was to be raised as part of the Territorial Army. The mantle was passed to a distinguished old volunteer unit, the Artists' Rifles, and on 1 January 1947, the unit became the 21st Special Air Service Regiment (Artists) TA.

The sections of SOG that remained intact were placed in the charge of the Royal Marines. It would take another five years or more before any cohesive policy for their future emerged, largely because of the vacuum in terms of direction that came with post-war blues – plus the dire shortage of cash and calls for economy.

The nucleus of men who would take the organisation forwards came principally from SOG – the remains of Courtney's SBS, RM Detachment 385, Sea Reconnaissance Unit, Combined Operations Pilotage Parties and Boom Patrol Detachment. The men had returned home from Ceylon in MV *Athlone Castle*, arriving in November 1945. In fact, only a small number from each group opted to stay on, and after their leave they reported to the Westward Ho! Hotel, which was the wartime headquarters of Combined Operations Experimental Establishment.

They amounted to fewer than 60 men, who formed up under the command of Blondie (now Lieutenant-Colonel) Hasler. He, determined to keep those wartime disciplines alive, set about producing a draft plan for their future. What remained of Hasler's former creation, the RM Boom Patrol Detachment, moved from its wartime base, HMS *Mount Stewart*, to the rather less salubrious surroundings of Harris's Boat Yard, Appledore, under the command of Lieutenant P. G. 'Pug' Davis DSC, a future commanding officer of the SBS.

By then, his detachment consisted of just three officers, eight other ranks and two maintenance ratings – along with their stock of *Sleeping Beautys* (now to be known as Motor Submersible Canoes), their exploding motor boats and a very useful depot ship, MFV MV *Celtic*. But Davis, too, had aspirations.

With the likes of Field Marshal Slim supporting a continued life for small-party raiders, Hasler was heavily promoting the idea of a school that would serve all sections of the armed forces to keep alive and develop their skills. Early in 1946 the Admiralty gave approval to the opening of the School of Combined Operations Beach and Boat Section (SCOBBS) at Fremington, Devon. Hasler produced a paper, his vision of the future, which turned out to be a significant blueprint, defining the role of modern amphibious Special Forces, combining all those small-party skills from the war for a single unit of saboteurs, sea-borne raiders and intelligence-gatherers.

In future warfare, Hasler wrote, there would still be a need for infiltration by small parties of troops for the key elements that had proved so successful in the war: reconnaissance of enemy-held areas, beach survey, small-scale raids, with independent objectives or in support of larger operations, ferrying agents and supplies for them. He correctly forecast that an increasing number of special operations would be entirely air-borne, but where stealth and surprise were important the approach by water would still often be the only practicable method – hence the SBS motto created 10 years later: NOT BY STRENGTH, BY GUILE.

His proposal was for SCOBBS to train a substantial pool of men who would carry out water-borne operations in small boats (such as dories, canoes, inflatables and so on) and by swimming and wading. 'Such men,' Hasler wrote, 'must from the nature of their work be courageous, intelligent and resourceful. Normally the required standard can only be reached by training specially selected volunteers with a high proportion of officers and NCOs. This unit would also contain a number of specially trained RN officers with navigating or hydrographic qualifications to lead teams on beach survey operations (former COPPs role). All SCOBBS-trained ranks of the armed forces would operate in uniform . . . They may, of course, be required to work in conjunction with plain-clothes agents for certain operations.'

Hasler's vision – though perhaps not fully appreciated then – would stand the test of time. The following passages, edited here for the sake of brevity and quoted directly from his previously unpublished document, could easily have been used as the starting-point, for example, for the recapture of the Falkland Islands 35 years later:

> Requirement: When the balance of power in a particular theatre of war is in favour of the enemy, so preventing large-scale operations, small-scale raiding is of the highest importance, both in keeping up morale and in forcing the enemy to deploy large forces in static defence tasks . . . [and] while the enemy is deployed in strength ensures that there are plenty of good targets.
>
> Transport: Long-range operations must be put in by large aircraft, submarine or large surface vessel. Short-range

operations can be transported by small aircraft, coastal forces, landing-craft or sometimes overland. Where there are no off-lying obstacles or risk of enemy detection, parent vessels can launch parties close to their objectives. This enables a simple means of approach, such as swimming or a manually propelled small boat.

Approach: Where parent vessels must launch parties further off, or for an operation lasting several nights, with the force remaining concealed during daylight, the approach will call for small powered craft (which may themselves carry canoes, swimmers, etc.).

Lying up: In daylight, lying up will be necessary either afloat, in a boat of low silhouette lying some way offshore and suitably camouflaged, or ashore, in thick scrub or mangrove or on some inaccessible feature. If the boats cannot be concealed ashore, they may sometimes be deliberately submerged under water. Alternatively, the use of a local type of craft may enable the force to move by day even in fairly congested areas.

Advance base: The object is to establish inside an enemy-held area a static advanced base, from which sorties are made against local objectives. The base may well operate for some time without detection.

Withdrawal: Parties usually withdraw by retracing their approach route [to rendezvous with parent vessel or transport], but should this fail there would be a delayed rendezvous at a different place, and/or an escape plan to be used after all rendezvous have failed. Alternatively, the main plan for the withdrawal may be for the party to link up with pro-allied guerrillas, or an existing escape organisation; or in the case of certain tactical operations, to stay put until overtaken by the advance of the main force.

Suicide jobs and capture: It has not been the British policy to send a member of the armed forces to do work which is certain to end in death, or even in capture. In 1943–5 both the Germans and Japanese executed many British ranks who had been captured in uniform, on infiltration operations; but these men were captured through failure of the plan, not as part of it.

Some enemies have an unenvied reputation for extracting information from prisoners by torture, and men captured on infiltration work are particularly liable to suffer in this way. These facts cannot be allowed to interfere with the intention to press forward with such operations, but the following precautions should be taken:

1) Men sent out on an operation, including the OC, must never be briefed with more than the minimum information to enable them to carry it out, and 2) the whole party must be well briefed with a convincing cover story, which they can bring forward if forced to say something. 3) If a man who is otherwise sound has a dread of capture and its consequences, he should be allowed to take 'sudden death pills' with him if he wants to do so.

Difficult landing: A valuable characteristic of well-trained infiltration parties is that they can land at places which would be impracticable for a larger force; for example, through surf, or over cliffs, rocks or soft mud. This factor should be exploited to the full on a defended coast. Even on an undefended coast, most of the easy landings are usually in use by the natives and are better avoided.

Weather and climate: On an open water, wind of over force three may make it impossible for canoes and other small craft to carry out an operation. Water and air temperatures have a marked effect on the methods which can be employed. In the tropics both small-boat work and swimming becomes far simpler in that there is no need to keep the body dry; on the other hand, coral, sharks and sting-sores must be reckoned with ashore. In the Arctic swimming is only practicable in a limited way with the aid of a watertight suit, and for boat work the main problem is to keep the body dry and warm. Snow-covered country offers considerable difficulties to infiltration parties, but this is partly offset by the long hours of darkness in the winter season, and by the large proportion of uninhabited country.

Much of what Hasler identified as ideal working practices for the sea-borne raiders holds good as we approach the millennium, and his strategy will become apparent over and over again as these pages progress in our story to the present day.

Hasler's proposals were adopted more or less as written, except in the area of control. In his vision, the school of small-party raiders should train élite squads who would be attached permanently to larger commands. The school itself would be run by Combined Operations, without specific allegiance to any one of the main service groups. In the end, SCOBBS was placed under the command of the Royal Marines. Within a year it was merged with RMBPD and renamed COBBS – Combined Operations Beach and Boats Section. At the end of August 1947 both units, consisting of 6 officers, 25 other ranks and 8 ratings, plus 17,500 cubic feet (495 cubic metres) of boxes of stores, 5 motor boats, 12 dinghies, 26 canoes and a small mobile crane, were packed ready for their move to the Royal Marines base at Eastney, Portsmouth. Their task was set out in a memo from the Commandant General, Royal Marines, to the Chief of Staff, Combined Operations: to select and train officers and other ranks in the skills inherited from SOG and to test and trial new and experimental equipment.

An air of secrecy still surrounded this tiny group of water-borne nomads, especially concerning its inheritance of beach reconnaissance and pilotage skills. It was noted in an article by a COBBS officer in the Royal Marines magazine *The Globe and Laurel* that November. 'The days of WWII private armies are finished,' he wrote. 'In their place in the corps a unit which will retain all the flexibility and originality of its predecessors has been formed. For two years . . . it has carried out much research into small craft, frogmen, parachuting, long-range penetration, cliff-climbing and concealment . . . What we need now is a little less secrecy so that the remainder of the corps realises what we are doing and why we are doing it.'

The secrecy was not entirely across the board. In fact, in the early days the new formation was used as something of a showcase for both recruitment and public relations. From the beginning, SCOBBS and its successor, COBBS, carried out large numbers of demonstrations around the country. Frogmen were, to the British public, a completely new and exciting force, and swimming-baths all over Britain were clamouring to get a visit from these strange creatures in their black suits, masks and flippers. Several war veterans, too, were used in demonstration teams to show off other aspects of amphibious raids. Many in the service regarded these demonstrations as a rather humiliating activity. 'Frankly, we didn't like it,' one of their later additions, Captain Len Holmes BEM, told me. 'It was seen by most of us as play acting, a gimmick. No, we didn't like it at all.'

Lieutenant Pug Davis, a tough, small man so nicknamed for his pugilistic appearance and earlier life as a services boxer, won a Distinguished Service Cross for landing with six men to search for a patrol of 2 Commando on a heavily defended Dalmatian island in 1944. Now he was traipsing around supervising frogmen demos. He sent a detailed account of a visit to Sweden, and his report was found buried away in the Public Records Office at Kew. Davis reported: 'The naval attaché of the British Embassy . . . told me the purpose of our visit was threefold – to further Anglo-Swedish relations, to interest the Swedish Navy in frogmen to buy equipment from Great Britain (export drive!), and make the Swedes more reliant on the Royal Navy for training and information.'

The frogmen were fêted, photographed and cheered, and Davis gave a 15-minute interview on Swedish national radio . . . and at the conclusion . . . the defence minister presented them with a little bronze plaque which was suitably engraved.

All very nice, said some, but this ain't what we're here for. A top-level report to the Chiefs of Staff, in a later review of Special Forces, agreed, and made the point quite bluntly: 'Too much time is being taken up acting as clockwork mice for harbour defence exercises and doing parlour tricks at demonstrations.' But if there was ever a danger of the amphibious raiders slip-sliding away into the ignominy of such ventures, international tensions came to their rescue.

A few headlines: Berlin under siege from the Russians; Fierce fighting in Palestine between Arabs and Jews; Flare-up ahead of the creation of the state of Israel; Communist 'rebels' battle with British troops in Malaya; North Korea proclaims itself a republic under

Kim Il Sung; Shanghai falls to Mao's army; The IRA vows to fight for a united Ireland . . .

The troubles that were to rebound down the century were stirring by the summer of 1948. By then, the designation of the COBBS team had been changed yet again, this time to become the Small-Raids Wing (SRW) of the Royal Marines Amphibious School of Eastney. Apart from training and exercises – and prompted by the international tensions – new operational tasks were approved by Combined Operations headquarters. The SRW's new brief included offensive raids and harbour attacks, deception raids, intelligence sorties, rescuing air crews and PoWs in enemy territory, and ferrying 'clandestine operatives' and stores into enemy territory.

In the summer three frogmen were dispatched to Palestine, where British forces were in action to quell continued fighting between Arab and Jewish troops and assorted guerrilla groups. They were tasked with finding and removing limpets attached to ships in Haifa harbour. They included Sergeant 'Sticks' Dodds, so called because he began his military life as a drummer universally called Sticks, who later commanded the SBS. He was awarded the Military Medal for the operation.

The success of this mission reminded the military of the usefulness of small-group raiders, and other tasks soon began to emerge. The first major European exercise since the war, Exercise Kiel/Elbe, took the whole force through the Kiel Canal and on into the Elbe, in which live limpets were used in mock attacks. In the escape and evasion phase of the exercise, more than half the SRW team evaded capture. Another major exercise took them to Northern Ireland, where they carried out mock offensive raids and escape and evasion tactics against the Royal Ulster Constabulary in the mountains of Mourne.

Even so, the SRW remained principally an instruction and demonstration unit. Demands on its limited personnel left little scope for deployment, and this was recognised. As the new decade turned, the commanding officer of the Amphibious School, Lieutenant-Colonel Houghton, was ordered to form an operational section which would henceforth be known as 1SBS, and more or less kept apart from the training routines of the SRW.

Marine Jim Earle was a new boy at the SRW at the time and recalled the activity. He had joined the service as a tearaway youth in 1947, with starry-eyed visions of becoming one of the blacked-up commandos who figured so often in the newsreels at the local cinema. He was posted to 40 Commando in the Middle East, saw action in Palestine as a sniper, and was among the last British troops to leave Haifa. He did a stint in Hong Kong, had a short stay in Cyprus, and back in Britain his sergeant-major volunteered him, as a punishment for some misdemeanour, for the notoriously tough SRW course at Eastney. 'I knew very little about the SRW,' said Earle, when I interviewed him at his home in Wiltshire. 'I knew even less about the SBS. I don't think I'd even heard of them. But I was a good swimmer and a good shot . . . got through the selection week and was accepted for the Swimmer Canoeist 3 course; they ran through grades SC3, SC2 and SC1. The course lasted about five months in three phases, intermittently progressing through the disciplines of swimming and diving, canoeing and small craft handling plus navigation and recce, then finally the tactical phase, which was escape and evasion, mapreading, survival and a parachute course.'

There were a dozen potential recruits on the course, of whom five were eventually accepted. He is the last survivor of that intake. The remaining four had been aboard HMS/M *Affray* in April 1951 to get experience of leaving and re-entering a submarine prior to an exercise. With 75 men aboard, the 1,600-ton vessel vanished mysteriously several hours after leaving port and was reported missing when contact ceased off the South Coast of England.

The submarine's disappearance baffled naval experts for many days. There were numerous theories, and it was believed she had battery failure. To aid them in their search for *Affray*, the Admiralty took the unusual step of consulting a spiritualist, who apparently told them where to look. It still took weeks to locate the craft, and, with air long expired, all hands were posted as lost.

At the time the SRW was under the command of Major Donald Peyton-Jones DSC, 'a vague but lovely fellow' who stayed until 1951, later, after leaving the service, becoming a vicar. (It was long-held ambition. He took the trouble to discover the name of the

German who had bombed him during the war and wrote and told him that on that day he had decided he would take the cloth.) Under Peyton-Jones, Jim Earle moved quickly into a tactical team of the SRW which was responsible for training courses. With demands on personnel increasing, three instructors were posted elsewhere, and he was presented with immediate scope for advancement, progressing from marine to sergeant within 12 months and becoming the youngest NCO in the section.

As a member of the Tactical Training Team, he discovered for the first time some of the history of the SBS, COPPs and RMBPD; their wartime stores were at Eastney. Some of the material was still packed away in boxes at Fremington and was eventually brought to the Eastney base. Said Earle:

> It was like an Aladdin's cave; the most interesting equipment we'd ever seen. Apart from the weapons, fighting knives and communications gear, there were all kinds of oddball things. There were some false rubber feet, for instance, so that the wearer could track around the beach and leave native Asian footprints instead of European ones. There were boots with thick felt soles for silent marches. There were lots of trip-switches, various booby traps, a mass of cameras and special photographic equipment, lots of literature on special operations – and all kinds of good equipment. It was a whole new world to me and, of course, a lot of the gear was used for our courses. In fact, a lot of the courses were built around the equipment we found in the stores, and during the whole time I was there, throughout the 1950s, we were developing courses and resurrecting a lot of the old skills.

Earle recalls the re-formation of 1SBS, which would include several of the originals from Courtney's SBS.

> There were still a few names from the past among them. They were sectioned off into a Nissen hut on their own. We called them the old and the bold. Those who had been in SBS during the war kept themselves pretty much to themselves. Probably

> thought we were all a bunch of fairies. But 1SBS came into being, for a specific reason that we didn't know about at the time. Everything in SRW and SBS was done on a need-to-know basis. If you didn't need to know, you weren't told. That was the nature of the place, and everyone respected that.

The reactivation of an SBS unit was probably inevitable in view of international tensions. Several discussion papers were drawn up on the future role of the section, allied to its possible deployment in some of the envisaged troublespots. This renewed interest in Special Forces coincided, not unexpectedly perhaps, with the troubles in Palestine and the Far East. In Malaya the CTs (Communist Terrorists) had taken a hefty toll in their guerrilla warfare against the British-installed Federation of Malay States.

By the spring of 1950 almost 2,000 civilians, police and soldiers had been killed by the CTs, who had moved back to their jungle hideouts that existed during the war. They also had an ample cache of weaponry, courtesy of the British military, which had armed their underground army to fight the Japanese. Guerrilla leader Chin Peng had been given an honorary OBE in the Victory Honours list.

Now, in what became known as the Malayan Emergency, the same arms were being turned against the British, a salutary lesson that was never heeded (as Saddam Hussein proved years later). The probability of Britain becoming involved in jungle warfare focused minds on Special Forces. The War Office also issued a new directive for the use and training of 21SAS (Artists) TA, by then a strong volunteer force of reservists and Territorials.

The directive, issued on 2 January 1950, arose partly because 21SAS was sending personnel to the Amphibious School for instruction in sea-borne techniques. Combined Operations headquarters judged this to be 'using up valuable time of instructors' and that they would merely be encroaching on the role of the SBS. Areas of operation for SAS personnel were clearly defined – deep penetration into enemy-occupied territory – and their training should therefore take account of specific tasks, which would include: harassing the enemy, impeding enemy movement, destroying stores, equipment, bridges and railways, reporting on suitable targets and operating as reconnaissance for air-borne divisions. Training would be required to a 'very high standard'.

An SBS training directive, on the other hand, showed a clear distinction. It was very much on the lines outlined originally by Hasler. It stated: 'They must reach a standard of self-reliance which will enable them to land from a submarine or carrier with necessary equipment and weapons, establish themselves ashore, live and evade capture . . .' The planners added the proviso that since detection could have serious consequences in compromising the security of future operations, SBS men must be sufficiently skilful 'to be relied upon in suitable circumstances'.

In the middle of this flurry of fresh activity, an internal row broke out when it became known on the service grapevine that the name assigned to the new operational party was Special Boat Section. The commanding officer of 21SAS (Artists) TA wrote to the Commandant General Royal Marines, to complain. They had no right to use the title SBS, he declared, because the wartime SBS was part of the SAS and wore the same badge. Using the letters SBS would therefore be wrong! This totally inaccurate generalisation of the situation brought a firm rebuke from the Commandant General, Royal Marines. He pointed out that the Special Boat Squadron (Jellicoe's army) operated under the auspices of the SAS and was part of it. The claim for the title was not valid because it was never recognised by the War Office as a regimental title. RM, conversely, could use the title through its inheritance of its own SBS antecedents. The dispute reached the Chief of Combined Operations Staff, who promptly ordered them to settle it over a gin and tonic. The upshot was that RM continued to use SBS as a functional title. Dispute solved, and SAS (TA) retired still smarting!

Later, the SAS once again attempted to call their boat parties SBS. Combined Operations headquarters stopped them and again put down a formal distinction between the two:

SAS . . . recce at division level, deep penetration raids, harassing the enemy well behind the lines, and training partisans.

SBS . . . operations against ships and coastal installations, shallow penetration raids by water, beach reconnaissance, smoothing the path for difficult landings, and ferrying agents.

Tasks that could be done by either were harassing raids against coastal targets, landward reconnaissance, capture of prisoners and 'eliminating undesirable people'. One important difference still remained, however. SAS was a unit of the Territorial Army, while the SBS were regulars.

Chapter Nine

Pug takes on the Reds

Pug Davis was being sent to stop the Reds. It might have brought a few guffaws in the bar at Eastney as the 1950s dawned, but it was no joke to him or the military planners. The red shading on the map on their wall swung into a huge arc across Eastern Europe, the Soviet Union, China and down across Indo-China into Vietnam and North Korea. The Cold War was at freezing-point. There were Reds under every bed, rumours of spies in the British Secret Service, and Senator Joe McCarthy shot to fame with his Un-American Activities Committee alleging Communist infiltration of the Federal government of the United States.

Joseph Stalin, meanwhile, had made friendship pacts with the victorious Mao Zedong, given his support to Ho Chi Minh as leader of North Vietnam and likewise to Kim Il Sung, whose generals were at that moment planning the invasion of the southern half of Korea. But at the beginning of 1950, Germany once again was the focus of Europe's attention. The Soviets were pillaging their occupied eastern section and running it with an iron fist through their puppet government. Berlin became the centre of everything after the year-long blockade by the Russians ended in the summer of 1949, broken by the extraordinary airlift of Allied supplies to the city. Besieged by hundreds of thousands of East Germans fleeing to the West, the city was full of intrigue, swarming with black marketeers and flooded with agents and spies from all sides. It was the beginning of that era of Checkpoint Charlie, the Third Man and all that.

The creation of the Democratic Republic of Germany in October 1949 was worrying Britain and her NATO allies. After securing its domination of the Eastern Bloc, the Soviet Union had effectively moved to the front door of the Western alliance. Would Stalin now push on into the rest of Germany? Alarm bells were ringing loudly through the corridors of Western military power. Speculation of an imminent Russian advance was sufficient for NATO commanders, with British and American agreement, to increase the number of their troops in West Germany and to form a strategic defence that included specific tasks for an SBS-style force.

In February 1950 Lieutenant Peter Davis, today 'the legendary Pug' to all his former colleagues, was ordered to form a detachment from the Small-Raids Wing in haste to join a Royal Navy Squadron on the Rhine. Davis recalled the moment for me, chatting at his home to which he had retired from the service with the rank of lieutenant-colonel. He joined the Royal Marines in 1942, was decorated, as mentioned earlier, for leading a landing-party to search for a British patrol from 2 Commando, and was one of the few 'hostilities-only' officers to become a regular after the war. 'The "w" word was being mentioned again,' he said. 'There was a real panic on.'

Having spent too much of his time in arranging frogmen demonstrations in the preceding few years, Pug was glad to be back in operational mode. He explained: 'NATO had by then drawn up an operational plan to meet a possible move forward by the Russians. The British Army of the Rhine (BAOR) would fall back to a position on the west bank of the river, which itself would then form a natural defended barrier to a Russian advance. And that's where we came in.'

With 1SBS committed elsewhere, Davis collected his new SRW detachment of 12 men to join the Royal Navy Rhine Flotilla, which became the RN Rhine Squadron, with about 250 men of all ranks, based at HMS *Royal Prince* at Krefeld on the Dutch border. The SRW detachment was known initially as the Royal Marines Demolition Unit, but Davis lost no time in preparing a paper on the possible tactical missions for his unit, from organisation to equipment. This he presented to the Staff Officer, Operations, of

Techniques learned in the Second World War were soon being called upon.
Above: a team of divers won medals for their work clearing limpet mines from troopships in Haifa during the Israeli crisis of 1948, Sergeant 'Sticks' Dodds and Lieutenant Henry Musto (*left and centre*) were both future Officers Commanding, SBS.
Below: SBS teams joined 41 Independent Commando RM and US troops in the early stages of the Korean War to lead sabotage teams blowing up railways and vital installations, landing on a hostile coastline in their canoes and inflatables from submarines and ships stationed up to five miles offshore. *(Royal Marines Museum)*

Beach reconnaissance remained a crucial task after the Second World War and canoes remained a principal craft: here Len Holmes, a long-serving SBS member instructs new recruits.

The scene looked casual enough and their equipment in austere post-war days was described by one commanding officer as consisting of curios and museum artefacts. It fell to the SBS to make detailed charts and reports on dozens of beaches and landing areas throughout the 1960s in such sensitive zones as the Middle East, North Africa and the Federation of Malaysia (see Appendix II).

One for the album: in the Second World War, they were sabotaging each other's ships and coastal installations. In Malta, in 1959, 6SBS carried out numerous exercises with their Italian counterparts of Reparto Sabotatori Paracadutisti.

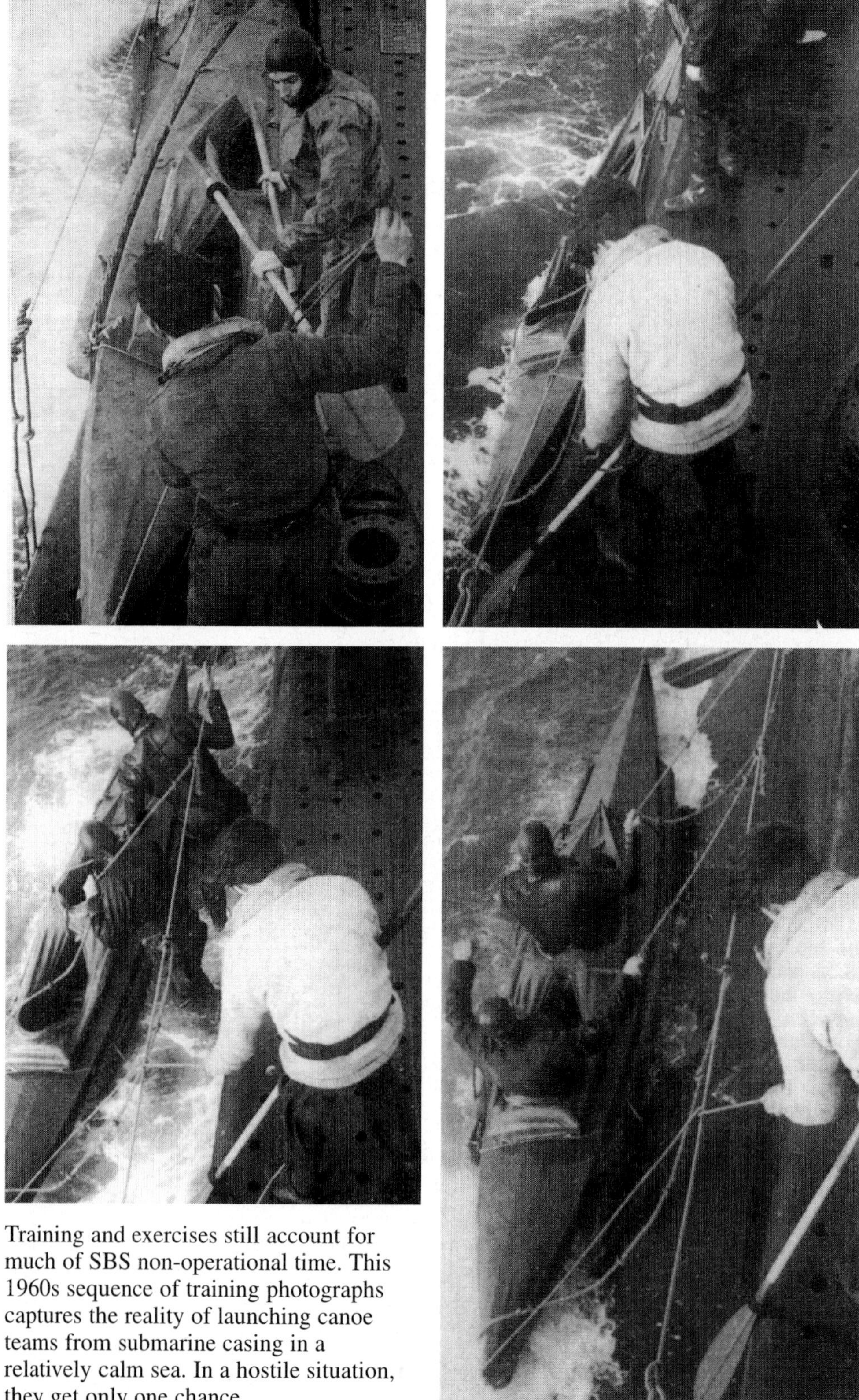

Training and exercises still account for much of SBS non-operational time. This 1960s sequence of training photographs captures the reality of launching canoe teams from submarine casing in a relatively calm sea. In a hostile situation, they get only one chance . . .

Small inflatable craft, like the one above, were developed for use in the Second World War, mainly for downed pilots, and eventually adopted by the SBS as an alternative (though not a replacement) to canoes. An outboard motor was later added – in this case an Atco lawn-mower engine.

Early multi-personnel carriers were a precarious mode of transport through choppy seas.

Faster, more powerful inflatables developed through the 1960s and 1970s brought added dimensions to SBS ability to insert both small and large raiding parties.

A four-man SBS patrol with stores and equipment required to put just two swimmer-canoeists into the water en route to a target in the Arctic during a 1972 exercise. The men had exited from a dived submarine with their gear, then skied across country and spent some time lying up, before finally swimming to the target and returning by the same route.

the Rhine Squadron, Major N. Tailyour, DSO RM, a supporter of the SBS, who submitted it to the Admiralty and won approval for the formation of 2SBS. The creation of the unit was completed in the summer of 1950, and manpower was increased later in the year and again in 1951 to create 3SBS. The SRW section based at Eastney was renamed Special Boat Wing to accommodate the revival of its operational activity.

The principal SBS role was to utilise the Rhine as the major defended obstacle to troop movements from the east. The men were tasked specifically to rehearse stay-behind parties on the eastern side as the British Army fell back. These parties would provide reconnaissance and intelligence reports on troop concentrations and carry out sabotage raids. The remainder of the SBS would, in the event of war, blow up barges that populated the river to prevent their use by the Russians and create hazards to crossings, attack bridges and generally make a nuisance of themselves. Their tasks required men with a high competence in swimming, diving and craft handling in fast-flowing waters, as well as an expert knowledge of demolitions.

The extent of the preparations, the potential involvement of the SBS and, to some degree, the seriousness with which this operation was being treated are seen in previously classified exchanges between the Rhine Squadron and the War Office in London in the latter half of 1950, viewed for this work. The squadron requested as a matter of urgency the supplies for SBS use of 10,000 limpets, hawser cutting charges to destroy enemy pontoon bridges, 31,000 pounds (14,000 kilogrammes) of plastic explosives, 11,000 detonators and 62,000 magnets to attach the charges. Unfortunately, the War Office could locate only 4,000 limpets in the British Army of the Rhine, although another 6,000 were said to be in British Army stores somewhere in England. It would attempt to retrieve them and supply them as soon as possible. Combined Operations Experimental Establishment was also alerted to begin trials on fixing limpets to wooden hulls, which were found in many of the Rhine craft.

Meanwhile, all around the SBS was the activity of the BAOR and the Rhine Flotilla itself. Preparations included full-scale exercises and training.

Captain Len Holmes BEM was an SBS corporal at the time of the West German crisis. He had been drafted to the Rhine to join the new 3SBS and found the place buzzing when he arrived. 'There was massive troop movement around the Rhine. The whole atmosphere was very tense,' Len recalled for me at his home.

> Every day there seemed to be some sort of political reprisal or tit-for-tat exchanges going on, and everyone was very conscious of it. Certainly, the army manoeuvres or exercises were of sufficient strength to show the Russians we weren't there for our health. They were posturing too. We had major rehearsals in which all nations with soldiers on the Rhine took part: British, Americans, Canadians and French. Vast areas of Germany were turned into an exercise arena with literally thousands of men taking part. There were always a few casualties, quite a few people killed being run over by tanks or other accidents. It was pretty well unavoidable with the amount of weaponry and machinery about the place.
>
> The SBS practised being left on the east bank of the Rhine and hiding up. These invariably started up travelling in a Jeep with a radio operator and two swimmer-canoeists. We would keep with the Jeep for as long as possible, until we got into an area where we would be able to see 'enemy' troops building up. It was only an exercise, but even so a very close simulation of the real thing. The Red troops were positioned and moving forward very much as the Russian Army would have done. So we moved around on country lanes until we reached an area where the Red troops were discovered and began reporting it. When the build-up of troops became so great that we could no longer use a vehicle without being discovered, we would ditch the Jeep and go off on foot into the countryside, all the time reporting the Red troop movements.
>
> By that time most of us could speak some German, and we would hide up in local farms and villages. Some of them wondered what the hell we were doing, because we would be wearing pseudo-civilian clothes, blue trousers and old sweaters. Communications were difficult. We were still using

> wartime radio equipment, a massive, heavy thing in a suitcase, which hardly lent itself to clandestine work. The exercises were extremely realistic, and you knew full well that if you were captured by the Red troops you would spend a long time being interrogated and, believe me, that's a very uncomfortable experience. You got as good a grilling as you might expect from the enemy. All of us took them very seriously.

The Rhine Squadron which included 2 and 3SBS, was based at Krefeld, with a training area 25 miles away at Four Lakes Camp, near Venlo on the Dutch border, where they set up a hutted camp in the woods and practised shooting and demolition training. Training in diving was performed in Moehne Dam. The camp was also to be the assembly site if war started.

Plenty of other tasks filled their time, such as diving in German rivers to locate equipment – even tanks! – lost during exercises. It was not uncommon for the tanks to be driven accidentally into the Rhine in darkness. Searching for them was a hazardous task in the fast-flowing waters because the exercise called for SBS divers to 'walk' the river to find the lost hardware. Len explained the procedure: a heavy-duty wire was strung across the river, which was around 200 metres wide, and seven or eight soldiers gripped each end. Eight SBS divers then went hand over hand and positioned themselves at intervals along the submerged line, which was walked downstream by the sappers on either bank until the tank was found. 'You could never see it,' said Holmes, 'because the water was pitch black. You made contact by running into it. Then the diver would pop up to the surface and shout: "Found One." The fast-flowing current at times reaching 7 knots (13 kilometres per hour) meant we were unable to leave marker floats. The positions were noted, and the tank would be dragged out by the army, once again using divers to attach wires. Of course, we couldn't stop the Rhine traffic while we were searching. If a barge came along, the sappers just let go of one end of the line and the divers were swept into the bank in a tangle of arms and legs.'

Still, as Len Holmes recalled, there were compensations, such as winter training, with skiing at Winterburg, Bavaria, where all SBS sections took part in the BAOR military ski patrol races. SBS sections also took part in the major BAOR exercises each year, such as Broadsword in 1950 and Counterthrust and Jupiter in 1951, with their numbers now swelled by the temporary inclusion of 4 and 5SBS formed from RM Force Volunteer Reserve. As the tension eased between the Soviet Union and the West, the German-based units found less taxing tasks in their itinerary, including two annual cruises down the Rhine to Holland to take part in sea-defence exercises and in the autumn up the Rhine to St Goar in time for the wine festival. Someone, at least, had a good nose for organisation!

Trouble was brewing on several other fronts – and running in tandem with the German expedition. First, Korea, south of Manchuria, with the Russians not far away through their port of Vladivostok, Japan to the east and the Yellow Sea to the west. An SBS recce team would report on the mountainous peaks that ranged the full length of the Korean peninsula and on the icy winds that swept down from the Manchurian plateau.

The recce would show that the peninsula's east coast had virtually no tidal range, yet on the west it was as much as 36 feet (11 metres). A very tempting railway line wound through tunnels along the full length of the east coast between Hamhung and Ch'ongjin. This would be the first target of an SBS unit attached to a newly formed British contingent, 41 Independent Commando RM. The unit was mustered specifically for Korea and coastal raiding. It would stand for one year, perform the tasks that were needed of it, return home and disband.

History drew the battle-lines. In 1943 Western allies pledged to make Korea an independent state. When the Soviet Union joined the war against Japan, they insisted a demarcation line along the thirty-eighth parallel, and as the Iron Curtain slammed shut Korea was split in two. On 25 June Kim Il Sung sent his troops south across the thirty-eighth parallel to pick up the other half of the country. It was an uneven match.

His armies were Soviet-trained and heavily equipped. Eight divisions led by mighty T34 tanks simply ran over the southern force, which was barely stronger than a gendarmerie. The South

Koreans were backed into a corner with only light support from the United States.

The British Pacific Fleet was patrolling those waters west of Korea and was committed to the United Nations. The American 7th Fleet patrolled the east coast, which was more suited to amphibious operations. The US Marine Corps Historical Records Officer provides the following summary of the British involvement:

> In August 1950, Admiral C. T. Joy, USN, Commander of the United Nations Naval Forces, suggested a small-scale raiding-force should be formed with the object of operating against the Communist lines of communication. The original intention was that this force should be composed of volunteers from the British Far Eastern Fleet [for rapid deployment]. However, it was decided to enlarge the original conception and send out a Royal Marines commando unit . . . to be placed under United States Naval Command and equipped and maintained by them.

Having accepted the invitation to provide such a force, the British found themselves in a quandary. The most suitable unit, 3 Commando Brigade RM, was already committed, fighting the terrorist campaign in Malaya. Plans to form a special unit were advanced quickly, and at the same time a small party of volunteers was sought from SBS units to run sabotage operations.

The commanding officer was given three weeks in which to recruit, train and prepare his force. Half of the men were drawn from Royal Marine establishments in the UK and the rest from a draft which was at that moment on its way to reinforce 3 Commando Brigade RM. The former were given a vast series of jabs and flown in haste to Japan in a chartered BOAC aircraft. Though hush-hush, a British newspaper got hold of the story and ran headlines: 'British Volunteer Unit for Korea.' In fact, the only volunteers were SBS and, according to archive reports, 'the reaction was swift . . . the CO received a host of letters from angry wives. They were concerned that it looked as if their husbands preferred service in faraway Korea to domestic bliss'. Several husbands also received some poignant letters of reprimand from anxious wives as the Korean situation flared up in newspaper coverage.

And so . . . 41 Independent Commando RM, joined by SBS volunteers and commanded by Lieutenant-Colonel D. B. Drysdale RM, were dispatched at once to a US naval base at Yokosuka. From there they were to be sailed to the east coast of Korea for Operation Double Eagle – operating as part of a US Army raiding-unit from the submarine USS *Perch* and assault personnel destroyers USS *Bass* and *Wontuck*.

Five SBS men were among the first in action, carried aboard *Perch* which has some historical significance, as the craft was the first troop-carrying submarine to be used in any raiding-operation of this kind. She was converted so she could carry a large number of men and a massive array of equipment that was capable of launching one motor boat, ten ten-man rubber boats and around seventy raiders with their stores.

For their first outing, the force embarked in late September 1950 and had a week to get used to life on board and carry out rehearsals. On 1 October they arrived off the target area on the east coast of Korea, where the railways and tunnels were visible. Periscope reconnaissance was carried out from the submarine submerged about seven miles offshore for a landing on the first night. However, a number of North Korean patrol boats were spotted, and they did not go away: mission aborted. The following night they were more successful and began their first operation, which set the pattern for months to come. The fear of mines and coastal radar forced *Perch* to stand off at around eight miles from the coast. There, she launched her light motor boat and ten inflatables with raiders aboard and then submerged. Using a telephone link to the surface craft, *Perch* towed the line of small inflatables to within five miles of the target area and then cast them off. The motor boat then towed the inflatables to within half a mile or so, and from there they were on their own, paddling. At 300 metres, the swimmers went in for a final recce, signalled the all-clear, and the raiding-party came ashore.

The men headed straight for their target, carrying anti-tank mines, which they laid beneath long stretches of the railway. They returned to the beach and prepared for the rendezvous with their motor boat and mother ship and had the satisfaction of hearing several huge explosions as a train came along.

Other SBS men had joined marines on *Bass* and *Wontuck*, both of which were able to sail closer to the shore during a misty, dark night. They launched their first assault party from three miles off, with landing-craft towing ten inflatables. Between them, they carried a cache of 4,410 pounds (2,000 kilogrammes) of explosives. The charges were placed in a tunnel, culverts and bridges. When they had exploded, the men went back and set anti-personnel mines in the craters of their explosions and hastily departed under enemy fire. It was during this retreat that the SBS lost one of theirs: Corporal Babbs, ironically one of the more experienced among them, and one of the few with operational parachute wings. Babbs accidentally shot himself while paddling his inflatable towards safety and did not recover from his injury.

After these initial sorties, 41 returned to Japan to be re-assigned to the US Marines at the very time the Chinese threw in its lot with North Vietnam. SBS reinforcements were waiting, including Sergeant Sticks Dodds, along with equipment and canoes. They began going ashore in two-man parties for recce and sabotage missions, which were carried out with considerable success – provided they had been given the correct intelligence, and that was not always the case.

In February Dodds and his number two, Corporal Edmonds, were sent to ambush an enemy convoy as it passed a certain point in the coast road; they were to set charges and blow up the road as the convoy passed. They were briefed on the mission on board USS *Wontuck* by a CIA man, who claimed to know the beach well and told them to look for a large building at one end.

They paddled for miles, up and down the coast, trying to find the building but saw no sign of it. Finally, they went ashore and discovered that the building was in fact a large rock. The CIA had misread aerial reconnaissance photographs. The delay allowed the enemy convoy to pass through unhindered, but Dodds and Edmonds blew up the road anyhow.

Apart from one daylight raid in April, all the unit's tasks were clandestine missions performed at night. As the RM Corps Historical Records Officer noted: 'Most of the personnel were permanently based in islands off Wonsan on the east coast of Korea some 60 miles behind enemy lines. From here they carried out raids that varied from two-man canoes to forty men in rubber inflatables. Tasks included beach reconnaissance, capture of prisoners, blowing up railways, ambushing roads, and generally keeping the enemy occupied on his lines of communication.'

Both SBS and marines had become skilled in close approach work in rubber boats and canoes. Unlike British tactics of canoe pairs, the Americans preferred mob-handed missions, with charges carried by humping-parties, laid by assault engineers, while a covering force would form a defensive circle around them. It would take around four hours to lay the charges in 10-pound (4.5-kilogramme) packs connected in a ring with cordtex for simultaneous detonation.

Once the fuses had been pulled, and the order to withdraw given, the force would fan out again, return in a line to the beach and re-embark under the direction of a beach-master until all were clear. They would paddle out to the waiting landing-craft, which would begin the long tow back to the waiting ships. Although the US Navy was officially dry, officers would invariably break out the medicinal brandy after a successful operation.

As their stay progressed, one troop established an advance base on Yo Do Island, with motors, tents, landing-craft and canoes, and were joined later by other marines to launch clandestine missions. Another troop did the same on Modo Island, establishing a more permanent outpost – only to have it temporarily flattened by a typhoon – from which to carry out mainland recces. Other, smaller groups established observation posts among the outer islands, where they would remain for up to two weeks at a time.

Towards the end of the year, their activity was toned down while the United Nations tried to get peace talks under way. Although it would take another two years, and a good deal more fighting, before armistice was finally achieved, 41 Independent Commando RM formally stood down in December 1951 and disbanded on its return to England on 22 February 1952. SBS men returned to Eastney, minus two: Corporal Babbs and Sergeant C. E. Barnes, the latter killed in engaging the enemy during a raid; he had been Mentioned in Dispatches. Sergeant Dodds collected another medal, the DSM, to add to his MM from Haifa.

'So ended an eventful year,' wrote an RM historian who was there, 'involving most types of operations . . . Many lessons were learned and many friendships cemented . . . A great experience and one which no one who served in 41 Independent Commando is likely to forget.'

Chapter Ten

To save a king

The SBS men returning from Korea brought with them stories of an experience remembered. They rabbited on about the gear, the abundance of stores, good weapons and good food. No hunting around for equipment, as they had to do in 1950s Britain, which was still in the grip of severe austerity. The armed forces were no less focused on their spending habits than the rest of the population. Politicians demanded cuts. Prudence was a regular visitor.

Major Hugh Bruce, RM, was used to making do and mending in Colditz and had to do something similar when he took over command of the SBS. As he told me:

> On the one hand we were charged with encouraging new recruits during a period of moderate expansion through demands of military activity in the Far East. On the other, our range of equipment was pretty old stuff, largely from wartime stock and quite inadequate to meet current needs. Homing devices were primitive, navigation aids almost non-existent, beach survey equipment was made up of curios and museum artefacts, and clothing and suits were poor and of the wrong material. It was all very well to say that we were keeping in touch with wartime techniques, and indeed teaching them to trainees and trainers, but it really was a burden to have to use wartime equipment too.

To top it all, the Joint Intelligence Bureau produced a study criticising the lack of beach intelligence both in the UK and areas abroad in which Britain had a specific interest, and Operation Sandstone was launched in early 1950 as a joint task between the hydrographic section of the Royal Navy and the SBS. The navy were to survey British beaches and the SBS were to do the same abroad over coming months and years. Most were done clandestinely without the knowledge of the country's government. COPPs equipment extracted from the remains of their wartime stores was largely used. More modern equipment came along eventually, but the style and report format were virtually the same as those created by Nigel Clogstoun Willmott.

Hugh Bruce, then a captain, came to the SRW/SBS in the early 1950s and brought a new impetus in terms of leading from the front. Bruce, a strong, forceful man, scared of nothing and no one, was liked by all. His own background lacked the cut and thrust of SBS field action, but he made up for it in other ways. He was taken prisoner during the defence of Calais in 1940 and took no further part in the war, at least not on any military front. Like all the British in German prison camps, he felt it his duty to escape and get back home. He worked on numerous escape schemes and got out himself three times, spending many weeks on the loose before being recaptured on each occasion, usually through betrayal.

Finally, the Germans took him to Colditz, along with other famous escapers and personalities such as David Stirling and Douglas Bader, where he spent two and a half years on the escape committee, planning the breakouts later famously re-enacted in books, film and a television series. 'In the process,' Bruce recalled, 'I learned much about disguise, deception, impersonation and some of the skills of moving through enemy countryside at night and lying up during the day. I learned about travelling incognito and how to forge papers.'

Like many in the SBS, he was a canoeing and yachting fanatic, navigated for yachts of several nations and took part in several transatlantic races. He also formed the RM Canoe Club and broke the record for a two-man canoe crossing of the English Channel and came second in the 124-mile Devizes to Westminster canoe race in 35 hours and 7 minutes. So, the SBS had a generally good egg at the helm at a particularly crucial time.

When he arrived, first to head up training and later to take over as officer commanding, Bruce discovered that the SBS – though reactivated on the back of a training school – had no current instruction manuals. He created, typed and bound three volumes as aids for instructors. Later he wrote the handbook, too, entitled *SBS: Capabilities and Techniques*. It was an uphill struggle without finance and resources. Bruce recalled:

> Training and safety were paramount. Every operation, every exercise, needs a full recce, complete information; otherwise you are courting disaster – as happened so often in the past, when men went barging in without full knowledge of what might confront them. It's no good training up men who are going to get put out of action on their first operation through lack of knowledge, fitness or not being sufficiently skilled in the use of equipment, or indeed of not having the right equipment at all. SBS operators for all grades faced a pretty stiff selection procedure, and the pass-rate was incredibly low because of the standards demanded.

At the beginning of 1952 Bruce suddenly found he could use the cheque-book again. This brief and welcome respite from cash starvation had less to do with the current well-being of the SBS than an operation for which he had just received his top-secret orders. He had been instructed to prepare for a clandestine recce in advance of a possible evacuation of British nationals from Egypt. At least, that was the cover story. It was almost certainly untrue, and he was never told exactly what the operation was intended for because he never actually got to the point of 'need to know'. The jigsaw can now be pieced together.

Bruce was allowed to purchase new equipment previously requested and refused, including new drysuits for beach reconnaissance, swimmers and reels to develop distance and sounding lines, bought from Ogden's Fishing Shop in St James's Street, London. Why? The countdown to what history now terms the Suez Fiasco had begun.

King Farouk was in trouble. The dissolute and bulbous playboy monarch, last surviving member of the Mohammed Ali dynasty, which had ruled Egypt since the early 1800s, was on the verge of being ousted. Rumours of his imminent demise through assassination or some other non-accidental misfortune were rife, and he was holed up with resident harem in his magnificent Ras-el-Tin Palace in Alexandria. Gamal Abdel Nasser, head of the Society of Free Officers and courted by the Soviets, was dedicated to liberating Egypt from what he considered its three main evils: the monarchy, imperialism and feudalism.

Although the British government had withdrawn its troops from Alexandria and Cairo in the late 1940s, it could barely contemplate the risk of losing control of the Suez Canal. Two world wars had demonstrated the importance of the waterway to British security and trade. Britain retained a heavily manned base that had grown, Topsy-like, along the west bank and had become the last great monument to the country's military and economic strength in the Middle East and North Africa. Nasser wanted them out. Britain, in company with France and other foreigners, had run his country for too long.

Nasser was talking loudly about cancelling the Suez Canal Treaty, and King Farouk was shuddering in his palace. Back in Britain, Hugh Bruce was studying his secret orders. The plan, that March, was to send destroyers into King Farouk's private harbour, 10 miles east of Alexandria, ostensibly to rescue British nationals but more likely, in the first instance, to bring out Farouk himself. No one was saying. Bruce was to take a recce party to get the lie of the land; he gathered five of his best operators and flew to Malta.

More details emerged. The staff of the Commander-in-Chief, Malta, had drawn up a plan to send the SBS party into Alexandria by merchant ship. They would wear civilian clothes and, on reaching the harbour, transfer to a dory to conduct their clandestine recce. Bruce was not at all happy with the plan and put forward an alternative: they would be taken by submarine as close as possible to the harbour and travel the remaining distance by canoe. Their swimmers would then go over the side, complete their recce and return to their canoes and to the submarine. This was accepted, and

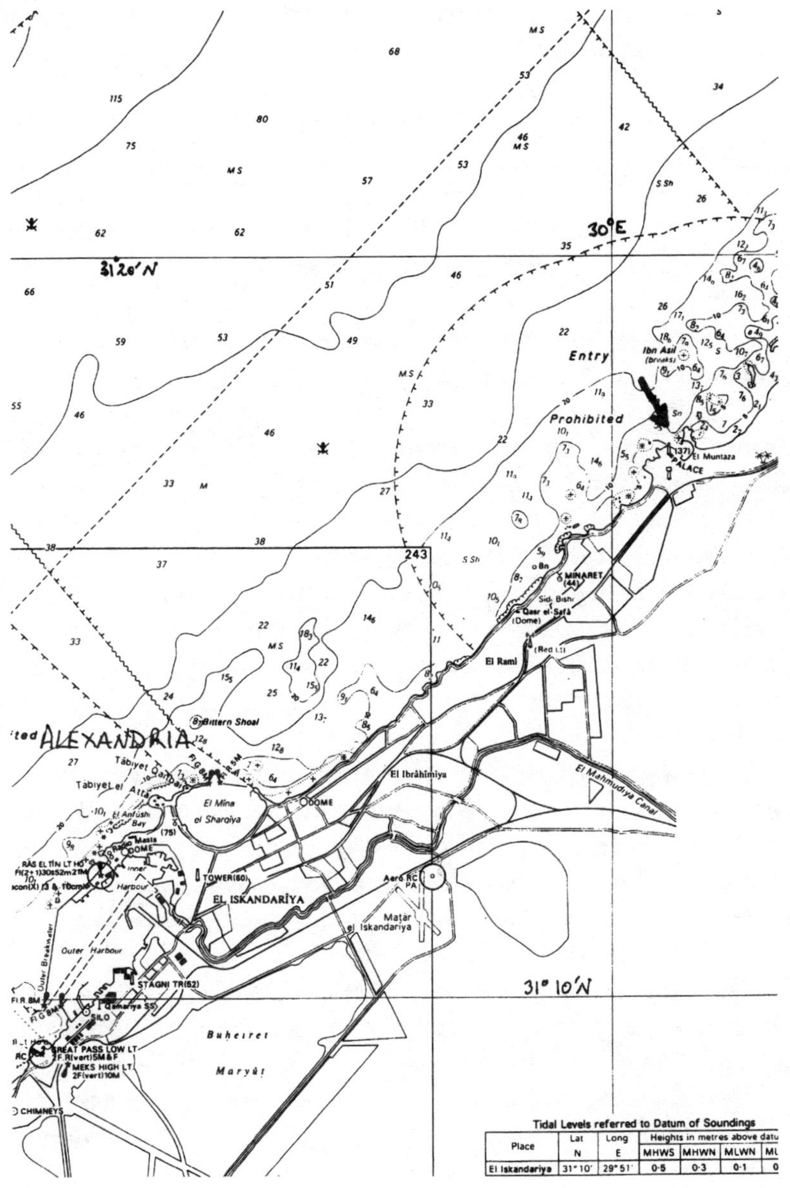

Beach recce for King Farouk's palace.

the team spent the next couple of weeks rehearsing and training. But Bruce began to get a distinct feeling that the operation was becalmed. Sure enough, after six weeks in Malta it was aborted and the SBS unit returned to base in early April.

By the end of May the operation was on again. Lord Mountbatten was now in charge, having just arrived in Malta as Commander-in-Chief of the British Fleet in the Mediterranean. Captain Bruce was otherwise engaged, and so he sent Lieutenant H. B. Emslie, MC, RM, to lead the party. The men were flown to North Africa and then travelled on to Tobruk to join the submarine HMS *Teredo* under the command of Lieutenant-Commander L. D. Hamlyn.

Hamlyn was also kept short of detail. Mountbatten told him to leave Malta and proceed westwards and await further instructions – and, by the way, 'Keep your mouth shut afterwards!' About what, Hamlyn had yet to discover. While at sea he received a signal to proceed to Tobruk. There, he learned he was to take the SBS party aboard, with the intention of floating the men off in canoes at Alexandria. They carried out a few hurried rehearsals by day on a deserted beach, and then the submarine headed off to Alexandria, intending to drop the SBS team about three miles from Farouk's harbour.

Under starlight, four of the team left the submarine in two canoes and paddled in closer. The swimmers, Lieutenant Emslie and Sergeant Moorehouse, made a final check of their suits and equipment, put their writing-tablets over their wrists, slipped into the water and swam into the harbour, splitting up when they were close enough to begin their individual tasks.

The submarine remained at a discreet distance until dawn, when Emslie and his partner returned, their recce completed. SBS Marine Geordie Vardy, keeping watch on the bridge with night binoculars, spotted the second canoe heading back but with only one man, Marine Langton, aboard. Langton reported that his swimmer, Sergeant Moorehouse, had not made the rendezvous.

Hamlyn ordered the submarine to dive and set a course for the pre-arranged alternative rendezvous, ten miles away to the south-west. As they approached it, they found an Egyptian sonar-operating frigate with an aircraft circling above, seemingly on a joint search.

Hamlyn thought this was too much of a coincidence and headed back out to sea and signalled to the C-in-C, Malta, for instruction. He was told to make for Port Said, though was given no explanation.

The mystery of Sergeant Moorehouse's whereabouts began to unravel. After completing the recce of his designated zone, two sentries sitting smoking on the harbour wall delayed his exit and he missed the rendezvous with his canoeist, Marine Langton. So he had to swim for it, out of the harbour and down the coast towards his next rendezvous. After travelling about five miles, he ditched his one-piece swimming-suit so that he would not be too heavily questioned if caught, and then, wearing only his underpants, stopped for a rest. Moorehouse was discovered – according to his own account – resting on a buoy by a coastguard patrol boat to whom he told his cover story that he had fallen overboard on a fishing trip.

He was taken ashore and asked to be put in touch with the Royal Navy or the embassy. Eventually he was taken under escort dressed in Arab clothes to Fayid, half-way along the Suez Canal, where he was handed over to Major Gordon Sillars, RM, of naval intelligence. He was given more appropriate clothes and sent to Port Said. When Lieutenant-Commander Hamlyn arrived in *Teredo*, he found him waiting on the jetty.

The navy had apparently asked the Egyptians for help in locating a man lost during an exercise, which accounted for the fact that there was an aircraft and frigate searching the second rendezvous spot. Moorehouse had not revealed the true reason why he was out alone, almost naked in the water, and the Egyptians seemed satisfied with the explanation.

To Lieutenant-Commander Hamlyn, the episode remained annoyingly unexplained. He was never told of the purpose of the mission, was not involved in its planning, nor debriefed at the end of it. Moorehouse was not entirely frank with him, either, when he was questioned aboard as to what exactly happened. Moorehouse died some years ago, and Emslie was killed on active service. Today, Major Bruce believes that the operation achieved its aim in making a full recce of Farouk's harbour.

The lack of information supplied to the operatives at the centre of this intrigue was and, to a degree, still is fairly typical. MI6 and the CIA hovered in the background of this particular mission. The CIA were clandestinely funding Nasser because it was against the British policy of attempting to make the corrupt monarchy work. The British hoped to keep Farouk alive and well, and hopefully return him to power if Nasser staged a coup. Farouk was to be rescued by a raiding-party if a coup seemed imminent.

In the end, the good work of the SBS team wasn't necessary. On 23 July 1952 Nasser seized power, and the same evening he peacefully ejected his unwanted king, who was allowed to sail comfortably away to the fleshpots of Europe, his possessions stowed in 200 trunks. But, of course, that wasn't the end of the matter . . . not by a long chalk.

Hugh Bruce was already planning another series of events that eventually became tiresome because, again, they were not what the SBS was about. 'That didn't stop us throwing everything into them,' said Len Holmes, who took part, 'and especially Hugh Bruce. He was hard physically and mentally, and his big claim to fame from the SBS point of view was his meticulous planning. And what came next was not going to be any different.' The Admiralty had commissioned the SBS to test the security of all Royal Navy bases and air stations throughout Britain with saboteur or terrorist-type penetration that the SBS was itself famous for, intermittently over a period of several months. This was to be followed up with an extensive infiltration exercise against submarine defences on the Clyde, with raiding-parties using both surface and submersible canoes. Len Holmes recalls:

> On the face of it they were exercises that sounded pretty innocuous. Boring, we all thought. But Bruce had souped them up so that they were as close to the real thing as you could possibly get – even to the point of cutting wire fences, charging in with a lorry packed with SBS raiders, clearing buildings filled with 300 to 400 matelots with tear-gas, and making one helluva racket. When it became known on the grapevine that

> the SBS was attacking bases, it became extremely hazardous, with our small group being confronted by a large crowd of sailors carrying pickaxe handles.

Bruce's mock base attacks unknowingly laid ground rules for the future, when the SBS was charged with creating a maritime protection force for the security of Britain's coastal oil-rigs, offshore installations, and for counter-measures when the IRA began targeting mainland military bases. Bruce's time in command was also marked by the development of many new SBS training techniques. He initiated experimental work on the underwater release of SBS operatives from submarines, making it unnecessary for the vessel to surface.

He also began extensive trials dropping SBS raiders, their boats and stores by air, landing them by parachute into the sea close to the target area, saving the problem of the need for a submarine to hang around in hostile waters. It was the first time ever that the SBS dropped swimmers already dressed in full underwater kit, oxygen diving apparatus and fins. One other important development was the introduction of the first custom-designed underwater breathing sets for use by SBS teams. Colour-Sergeant Jock Swan received the Herbert Lott prize for work on this project. Piece by piece the SBS was building its stock-in-trade for the developing needs.

Curiously enough, it was also underwater work that led the SBS into a period of temporary decline, a time when, through no fault of its own, few called on its services to the point where it was almost being shunned. The troubles arose merely by association with the generic term of frogman following an MI6-sponsored mission that ended in disaster and brought unexpected implications for the SBS.

To the underwater fraternity at large, Commander Lionel 'Buster' Crabb was something of a legend. He made his name in Gibraltar in the early stages of the Second World War when, with hopelessly inadequate equipment, he led Britain's first team of frogmen to combat the attacks by Italian underwater teams on Allied shipping at Gibraltar. As we have seen in earlier chapters, the Italian 10th

Flotilla, with piloted torpedoes, well-trained divers kitted out with flexible rubber suits, breathing gear and swimfins, and exploding motor boats, was causing havoc in Mediterranean harbours under Allied control, and especially at Gibraltar. The Italians' most spectacular successes came in 1941 and 1942, attaching warheads and mines to the hulls of British ships.

Buster Crabb was 32 years old and could barely swim the length of a swimming-pool on the surface when he joined the battle against the Italians in November 1942. Nor did his background recommend him for such work. After an apprenticeship in the Merchant Navy, he had lately been drifting aimlessly, with a variety of jobs ranging from petrol-pump attendant to selling advertising space.

His only pre-war contact with the water was through a friend who was trying to market the invention of a Frenchman who had designed a pair of rubber swimfins for flippers which Crabb personally had little faith in. At the outbreak of war, he volunteered for the Royal Naval Volunteer Reserve but was rejected on account of his age, and he returned to merchant shipping as a gunner on a tanker. A year later he managed to transfer to the Royal Naval Patrol Service and then volunteered for special duties, which led him eventually to join a Royal Naval Mine and Bomb Disposal Unit. He took a two-week course in explosives, and that was sufficient for him to be given a commission to lieutenant and, soon, to lead the Royal Navy's hastily prepared Underwater Working Party in Gibraltar.

There, two Royal Navy divers, equipped with the most primitive breathing gear, swam around and under Allied ships looking for mines and warheads. The original plan was to bring the charges to land, where Crabb, was bomb-disposal officer, would disarm them. That was often impracticable, and Crabb was soon dealing with the charges himself below the surface, never knowing when they might explode and take him with them. From then on, his contribution to the Allied war effort was remarkable, filled with acts of tremendous courage and endurance. Fear was not a word in his vocabulary, and he and his colleagues in the naval team pushed themselves and the boundaries of safe diving to the very limit.

After the war Crabb found himself once again in limbo. He devised many money-making schemes to utilise his skills, from discovering the size of fish shoals for herring trawlers sailing out of Great Yarmouth to underwater photography. He turned up at the SBS headquarters when Pug Davis was running the frogman demonstrations – 'and he still couldn't swim far on the surface,' Davis told me. Crabb was re-called periodically by the Royal Navy as a member of the RNVR and helped in the search for the lost submarine, *Affray.* He was employed on occasional and secret missions for British intelligence, including one still-classified 'underwater job' in the Suez Canal zone in 1953 and the examination of the Russian cruiser *Sverdlov* when she visited Portsmouth in 1955.

In April 1956 Crabb, then 46 years old, was overweight, unfit and in debt when he was approached for another intelligence mission. An agent of MI6 contacted him and outlined a proposal for a particularly sensitive task – to examine the bottom of an important Russian cruiser, the *Ordzhonikidze*, when she arrived in Portsmouth with an escort of two battleships, carrying the two Soviet leaders, Khrushchev and Bulganin, on a goodwill visit.

While MI5 were bugging the hotel rooms of the two leaders in London, MI6 hired Crabb to investigate the hull of the cruiser. Although never publicly revealed, it can now be confirmed that MI6 wanted Crabb to measure the cruiser's propeller and to discover how the ship could travel at twice the speed originally estimated by British naval intelligence. The Royal Navy urgently wanted this information. MI6 itself was also anxious to listen into the ship's cipher machine transmissions to try to break the cipher.

An attempt had been made to inspect the cruiser when she came into British waters a year earlier, using the one remaining serviceable X-Craft mini-submarine which MI6 kept at Stokes Bay, three miles from Portsmouth. On that occasion the mission had been aborted because of tight security around the ship.

On 17 April Crabb checked in at the nondescript Sallyport Hotel, Portsmouth, using his own name, accompanied by a tall, blond-haired man aged about 40, who signed himself in as 'Smith'. The following day Crabb had a reunion meeting in Portsmouth with some old friends from the Gibraltar era. That was the last anyone outside MI6 saw of him. He was not seen leaving the hotel on the nineteenth, but as dawn broke on that day he was taken by a small launch from Portsmouth harbour to a suitable distance offshore, donning his diving gear as they went.

He took an oxygen breathing set so that no bubbles could be seen on the surface. At safe range, he slipped over the side and swam towards the target ship well aware that he might have to dive below the 33-feet (10-metre) safety margin for oxygen breathing gear. What happened next remains a mystery; all that can be said is that Crabb got into some kind of difficulty – either through a heart attack, oxygen poisoning, getting caught in the propeller blades or being captured by the Russians.

When he did not return, panic hit the MI6 operatives managing the operation – and it rose all the way to Cabinet level. Feverish attempts to keep the developing fiasco from public view merely enhanced the mystery. Three days later 'Mr Smith' arrived and paid the bill for the hotel rooms for both of them, in cash, and took away Crabb's belongings. The newspapers had already got wind of Crabb's disappearance but had been put off from publishing the story by an Admiralty spokesman, who claimed that Crabb's next of kin had yet to be informed. On 29 April the Admiralty finally put out a statement claiming that Crabb had disappeared and was presumed dead after 'failing to return from a test dive in connection with trials of certain underwater apparatus'. On the same day a detective superintendent from the Portsmouth force arrived at the Sallyport Hotel and removed four pages from the hotel register, warning the hotel owner to say nothing to anyone since the matter was covered by the Official Secrets Act.

On 4 May Prime Minister Anthony Eden, faced with mounting pressure for an explanation of what exactly had occurred, ducked behind the barrier of national security:

> It would not be in the public interest to disclose the circumstances in which Commander Crabb is presumed to have met his death . . . It is necessary in the special circumstances of this case to make it clear that what was done was done without the

> authority or knowledge of Her Majesty's Ministers. Appropriate disciplinary steps are being taken.

Hugh Gaitskell, leader of the Opposition, retorted: 'The suspicion must inevitably arise that your refusal to make a statement on this subject is not so much in the interests of public security but to hide a very grave blunder.'

The Soviets promptly added their own contribution with letters of indignant protest. The Soviets' note stated that a frogman had been spotted at around 7.30 a.m. on 19 April, swimming between the Soviet ships. The British reply conceded that was a possibility, but that Commander Crabb's presence within the vicinity of the Soviet ships was totally without authorisation and was regretted.

The absence of a body and the scent of espionage brought days of newspaper speculation, discussing the possibility that Crabb had been captured, perhaps tortured, even taken to Moscow by the KGB. Finally, a Commons debate on his disappearance was granted on 14 May and lasted for more than an hour and a half. Gaitskell once again laid into the government and to the secret service, which was 'patently mixed up in this affair', although he added that he recognised that the nation would be poorer without men like Buster Crabb. Anthony Eden deplored the debate and insisted that national interests were of first importance. 'I confess,' he said, 'that all I care about is that our discussions with the Soviet leaders should in truth prove to be the beginning of a beginning . . .'

The mystery only deepened when a headless body of a frogman was washed up on the shore and was tentatively identified as Crabb's. Much later, further intrigue was added by the claim by Soviet defector Anatoli Golitsin that the Soviets had been forewarned of the impending visit to their ship by Crabb through a security leak from within MI6.

In the bloodletting that followed the débâcle in the higher regions of MI6, there was a throwback to all associated agencies, and to frogmen in particular – which in turn meant the SBS. For months afterwards the very mention of underwater activity brought a minor knee-jerk reaction among the naval and military hierarchy.

Lord Mountbatten had no such qualms. He had recently doubled his area of responsibility with his additional appointment as Allied Commander-in-Chief, Mediterranean, in which role he reported direct to the Supreme Allied Command, Europe. Now, in addition to his role as Commander-in-Chief of the British Fleet, he had the authority of NATO over the French, Italian, Greek and Turkish admirals, each commanding their national navies in the Mediterranean, and consultative powers with the American 6th Fleet.

Among his immediate NATO tasks was to prepare an immediate plan to prevent Russian submarines from leaving the Black Sea in the event of war. This, he proposed, should be achieved by the laying of a complex system of mines. These plans, and the focus on other regions around the Mediterranean where sabres were being rattled, such as Cyprus, Egypt, Libya, other parts of North Africa and the Arab oil states, brought a renewed urgency for beach reconnaissance for the Joint Intelligence Bureau. This was to be given priority treatment, overseen by AI9, a sub-section of JIB, and a major reconnaissance programme was set in motion which would go on from the mid-1950s well into the 1960s.

The JIB would require hugely detailed reports, charts and photographs which, in the main, could be obtained only by clandestine methods, inserting SBS men in civilian clothes disguised as tourists or locals. This brought fresh demands on the SBS. Mountbatten's own liking for small raiding-parties and recce teams, along with general intelligence-gathering, was the background to the hurried formation of 6SBS in Malta.

Recruiting the group fell to Pug Davis, who was about to join 42 Commando when 3 Commando Brigade, Royal Marines, returned from the Far East and took up residence in Malta. Initially, Davis recruited from the ranks of 42 Commando, which was a far from satisfactory arrangement, given the training and expertise required for beach recce and other SBS specialist tasks. A few months later the RM Commandant General formalised the establishment of the Malta party, and a new section, with one officer and ten other ranks, was formed in the UK and posted immediately to Malta, where it would for many months hence concentrate on the beach recce work required by the JIB, along with a busy schedule of other tasks.

Training and development exercises were carried out around the waters of Malta, and it was an easy launch-place for other rapid missions of both recce and insertion. The exercises came as a prelude to the Suez crisis of 1956.

On 13 June the last British troops had been withdrawn from the Suez Canal garrison, where they had been for so long. The canal was to remain in the hands of the Anglo-French Suez Canal Company, which had originally constructed it. Before the month was out, President Nasser nationalised the company, beginning a series of events that some would compare to a Greek tragedy.

Eden dithered for months, and by September the Chiefs of Staff were being ordered to prepare a full-scale invasion of Egypt, codenamed Operation Musketeer, supported by the French with some side action by the Israelis. Mountbatten was among vociferous opponents to the very last. As a serving officer, he could do no more than comply or resign, which he contemplated doing.

At Poole, 1SBS had been placed on alert, and within days half the section was given orders to proceed at once in support of Operation Musketeer to conduct a clandestine operation in Alexandria. They were given a specific task: to cut cables drawn across the harbour entrance which were being used as a boom to prevent ships from entering. Before leaving the UK, 1SBS carried out deep-dive experiments using charges. The noise was so loud, however, that a thermic cutting lance activated by oxygen was specially developed by the Admiralty Materials Laboratory at Holton Heath.

The SBS team, led by David Leigh, left by Sutherland flying boat as civilian passengers. They flew to Malta, where they were kept apart from 6SBS for security reasons. They had a further rehearsal in Malta which included practising departure and return with cutting gear from the submarine HMS *Totem*. Four canoes loaded with their equipment would be floated off. They would paddle as close as they could under darkness to Alexandria harbour, where four swimmers would go over the side and complete their task. Political uncertainty intervened. Operation Musketeer was stalled, revised and then given a new direction, and 1SBS was re-called to the UK.

Next, there was curious talk of a plan to assassinate Nasser using SAS/SBS-type raiders. The hare-brained scheme was supposedly invented by MI6 and was said to have been 'favourably viewed' by Eden, though it was never activated. One of the reasons was that in the intervening period most of MI6 'assets' in Cairo had been uncovered and neutralised by Nasser, with a little help from the Soviets acting on information supplied by the British traitor Kim Philby.

The SBS was mobilised once more. Lieutenant Henry Musto, Officer Commanding, 6SBS, in Malta, was ordered to prepare his section for a submarine-borne mission off the north coast of Egypt, ahead of British landings. The men were to prepare a detailed recce of the beach landing-sites. Musto found the plan full of inherent dangers. Nasser's army was well equipped in surveillance, radar and coastal monitoring. The closest the submarine could get to deliver the SBS was 12 nautical miles (22 kilometres) offshore. The men would have to paddle to the coast in manual canoes and come ashore on a bland coastline that offered virtually no protection or cover; more than likely they would be shot to pieces.

Just before they were due to sail, the task was cancelled. Instead, 6SBS boarded HMS *Ocean* with 3 Commando Brigade bound for Port Said. The British paras dropped in to coincide with a landing of commandos on 6 November, five days after the British jet bombers taking off from Cyprus bombarded military installations around Cairo and the Suez Canal zone. The French landed in Port Fuad and the Israelis invaded from the east. Tough fighting ensued, though British casualties were light.

The attack was, as history would show, ill-timed and ill-judged. The commandos went in on the day of the US presidential elections and quickly gained control of the docks, the airports and the outskirts of the city. The American government of General Eisenhower was openly hostile to Prime Minister Eden when it learned of the attack. Thirty-six hours later, the United Nations imposed a ceasefire. Britain retreated with humiliation. Eden and his Suez masterplan were finished, and King Farouk spent the remaining nine years of his life gambling and womanising in Monaco.

Farouk wasn't the only monarch that the SBS got involved with. In 1959, a drama developed in Libya, where Britain's good friend,

King Idris, seemed destined for a fate similar to King Farouk's. Intelligence sources had uncovered an assassination plot by left-wing opponents supported by factions in the military. Idris immediately fled to his fortified palace in the desert and appealed to the British for assistance. The Foreign Office in London alerted Malta, who put 6SBS *en route* to Tripoli. A contingency plan would be worked out on the way. Somehow, they were going to reach the palace and, if necessary, get the king out. By the time they reached their point of assault, however, some gunboat diplomacy had achieved its desired effect and the SBS men were stood down. King Idris negotiated a token 'invasion' by 3 Commando Brigade, RM, as a demonstration that the British were on his side. When the forthcoming arrival of the commandos was made known, the threat to the king's well-being evaporated. He continued to live on a knife-edge and survived for another ten years before a group of revolutionary army officers, led by a young subaltern named Muammar Gaddafi, seized power while the king was visiting Turkey.

The SBS did not waste the journey to Libya. The men conducted beach recces along the whole stretch of coastline between Tobruk and Tripoli, where some of the waters were still mined from the Second World War. In fact, the SBS was still continuing with its task of beach reconnaissance on all coastlines designated by the Joint Intelligence Bureau. They landed on Cyprus, for example, at the height of the EOKA terrorist campaign and, under the guise of civilians having a beach party, surveyed numerous beaches that would be suitable for troop landings should they become necessary. By the turn of the decade, few coastlines of strategic interest around the Mediterranean had not been charted. Elsewhere more pressing matters were occurring . . .

South-East Asia.

Chapter Eleven

Undrinkable claret

Now the SBS is in the jungle, answering the call of a Company Commander in 42 Commando RM. Out of the torrid, monsoon-drenched undergrowth, with perspiration patches under his arms and down his back, strolls Pug Davis, a little more rotund now but as pugnacious as ever. He's running Pugforce in the Borneo 'confrontation'. There standing before him is tall and lanky Sergeant Len Holmes, reporting for duty.

First it was Germany and drowning tanks. Then Malta and all that, and now the sergeant and his section are in some godforsaken sweatland of the Far East, where headhunters abound, to paddle their canoes down mosquito-infested waterways, taking care not to hit the booby traps, holed up in unprotected lookout posts in the middle of mangrove swamps, surrounded by guerrillas ready to cut them to ribbons at first chance and mingling with Gurkhas, supposedly their friends, ready to do the same if Len doesn't give the right bird-call when entering camp!

Pug's call to the wild was welcomed. The life-blood of the SBS was being 'tasked', as it still is. One of those latter-day stalwarts, Captain Neil Johnstone, an SBS officer for almost 30 years, made the same point as many of those interviewed for this book: 'Special Forces can only thrive if they are being tasked. Without tasks, we're not working . . . If we're not working, people start to question our *raison d'être*.'

The core of SBS operations moved to the Far East as Britain

attempted to oversee the orderly transfer of independence to its far-flung colonial outposts. The Malayan campaign had kept British forces busy virtually since the end of the Second World War as they battled guerrilla opponents to the creation of the Federation of Malayan States, later to become Malaysia. The SAS was reactivated into regular service with the formation of 22SAS with four squadrons. At the end of the campaign it was reduced to two again as Whitehall once more cut the defence budget.

The SBS had only a brief involvement in Malaya, when a section was formed from the ranks of 3 Commando Brigade specifically to find and capture a guerrilla leader. In 1961 a decade of political and military manoeuvres in Malaya seemed on the brink of collapsing. Military analysts were predicting a Communist 'domino' effect throughout South-East Asia. Americans would soon be pouring into Vietnam, the French having retired hurt.

Britain was committed to a heavy slice of action through its three dependencies on the island of Borneo. There, it was responsible for the defence of the Sultanate of Brunei and the colonies of North Borneo (later Sabah) and Sarawak.

Those states, it was hoped, would join the Federation of Malayan States to form a powerful and stable alliance. The 'Mad Doctor' Sukarno, president of Indonesia, was doing his damnedest to prevent it. The three British protectorates shared borders with Kalimantan, the Indonesian region of Borneo which accounted for three-quarters of its land surface. Sukarno wanted control of the remainder, to add seven and a half million inhabitants to the hundred million he already ruled. His further ambitions, inspired apparently by the Japanese plan in the Second World War, was to take over the whole of the Malayan states, with it the plum target of Singapore.

In 1961 he was poised to continue. For a year or more, Britain had been engaged in quelling riots in Brunei, largely locally inspired but fuelled by Sukarno. Guerrilla forces, backed by Indonesia, were also playing havoc in the other two dependencies by attacking strategic installations. In the same year the British government approved a hurried, if limited, military response from an initial force drawn from the Gurkhas, 42 Commando Royal Marines and the Queen's Own Highlanders.

The force resolved the Brunei crisis, freed hostages and restored order, but it was already clear that a new campaign was looming in the territory that the British hated most, jungle and swamp in a climate that ran the gamut of extremes.

Orders called for 2SBS to join 42 Commando from Malta to Singapore, and were later joined by 1SBS to create the largest single gathering of SBS personnel outside Britain since the Second World War. The men were to remain there until 1971, along with SAS squadrons, one of which was led by Major Peter de la Billière, future commander of British forces in the Gulf.

The Borneo clash was never classed as a war, just 'a confrontation'. It was confined mainly to the borders and coastal areas of the four regions of the island. The British military was tied to strict terms of engagements, codenamed Claret, which became otherwise known as 'the golden rules'. The Claret Reports of operations during this period were regarded top secret. As such, public knowledge and perception of the Borneo confrontation was unlike Korea, for example. It did not rate among the more celebrated victories of the British armed forces, even though it was precisely that. When set alongside the record of the French and the Americans fighting guerrilla warfare, the British and her allies repelled the Sukarno-backed invaders in one of the worst regions on earth for conventionally trained soldiers – the island where in 1995 a team of British soldiers on a training expedition became hopelessly lost.

The SBS succeeded, as one Special Forces commander was heard to say, with one hand tied behind its back – because of the strict rules of confrontation in a bitter struggle fought in wild, dense, watery and mountainous terrain, terrain far more hostile than the Americans faced in Vietnam. The 'golden rules' for the Claret operations were quite specific and limiting.

The rules were drawn up with two key thoughts in mind: first, the British government did not want to become drawn in to a long-running jungle war in which heavy casualties might be inflicted on British and allied forces; secondly, the terrain was so hostile that troops should not be risked on deep penetration. The overall penetration across the border into Indonesia allowed was just 5,000 metres although this could be increased to 20,000 metres for specific operations authorised by the director of operations. He in turn had to get permission from London; there could be no diversion from that chain of command, regardless of how urgent the situation on the ground and in the jungle might appear at the time.

Only experienced troops were to be sent across borders, no attacks were to be made with the sole aim of retribution or inflicting casualties on the foe, and there would be no close air support except in an extreme emergency.

The army's overall commander in Borneo was General Sir Walter Walker, who was also brigade major-general of the Gurkhas and a man of somewhat enigmatic behaviour. He was also a supporter of Special Forces. He had used the SAS and, briefly, SBS in the Malayan campaign, and he planned to use it at the forefront of intelligence-gathering over what was effectively an 800-mile front. The SBS, in particular, would be sent covertly into the toughest terrain for reconnaissance where guerrillas were most active.

Walker also knew that small parties were likely to be better received by local populations whose loyalties, in those wild regions, were never certain. The 'hearts and minds' of the locals were as important as hitting the rebels. Both SBS and SAS parties, moving into the countryside, won the support of villagers with gifts and favours such as medical attention or supplies.

They needed all the help they could get. Teams of three or four SBS men were sent into the jungle or the swamps to scout for the army patrols. There, they would build their hides and stay for three to five days at a time, radioing back to base ('when the damned radio worked!') with hourly reports. Quite often, they set up shop only to find they had pitched their hide in a position almost face to face with the enemy. They had to avoid fire fights. They were there to observe and track the movements of the guerrillas, establish their coming-from and going-to directions, their base camps and their numbers.

From this information, the assault force could take them on. It is beyond the scope of this book to record more than a summary of the events in what became a five-year campaign, but after a shaky start SBS operations came thick and fast. They reached a peak under its commanding officer, Captain David Mitchell, who had teams working throughout the theatre, often leading recce tasks himself, being landed into the most difficult regions and conditions. Mitchell himself was awarded an MBE for gallantry in 1965.

A flavour of the activity, however, can be gleaned from a ground's-eye view by Len Holmes, then an SBS sergeant who was involved in much of the campaign. His jottings, told in a matter-of-fact way that almost plays down the dramas, make it clear that the key to the SBS presence was their total invisibility:

> We arrived in Singapore at a time when the furore of the Brunei revolt was beginning to fade, and the prospects for peace in the region seemed quite good. The SBS had settled into a normal training routine, and sport was the order of the day. The section was based in HMS *Terror*.
>
> The first indication of trouble came when we received a signal ordering us to Tawau, a major timber port on the eastern tip of North Borneo at the point where the border converges with Kalimantan [Indonesian Borneo]. Guerrillas backed by the Indonesian military had infiltrated the border area, killed pro-British headmen and terrorised the local population.
>
> The terrorist action was centred on the island of Sebatik opposite Tawau Port. The island was divided, one half being under British control, the other Indonesian. The terrorists had attacked a kampong [village] on our side of the border, and it was anticipated that further attacks were likely to follow. The region was a mass of mangrove swamp intersected by rivers, and the army in Tawau requested small-boat patrols to police the waterways.
>
> We installed ourselves with an infantry platoon of the Leicestershire Regiment, based in a saw-mill on Sebatik Island. An observation post was established by building a hide in a large tree on the border headland. We used our own inflatable craft and purchased longboats to patrol the rivers.
>
> Small military craft of any sort were not available. The patrol channels were very shallow and unmarked; there was always the possibility that any of our craft would run aground and become an easy target. Channels had to be

marked with poles, and this enabled us to keep a close watch for terrorist incursions. It also seemed to keep them at bay. Terrorist activity in the area had virtually ceased after two months.

We were summoned back to Singapore and had barely had time to unpack our stores and equipment when we received a signal from 42 Commando, located near the Sarawak area of Borneo. Intelligence reports predicted a large sea-borne incursion by IBT [Indonesian Border Terrorists] at the west end of Borneo. We loaded all our equipment back on to a Beverley aircraft and flew this time to Kuching via the RAF staging-airport on Labuan Island. From there it was a short hop by twin-rotor helicopter to Sematan, the nearest kampong to the incursion area, where a company of 42 Commando were based.

We were met by Pug Davis, the company commander, who had been my CO in Germany. As a former SBS officer, Pug had realised that this could be a worthwhile task for the section. Within 24 hours of the signal arriving in Singapore, we had two craft patrolling the headland where the border came down to the coast. This entailed carrying boats, engines and stores over a very shallow gradient beach, and with a 30-mile approach to the operating area it meant that this system of surveillance could not be maintained for long. Two three-man observation teams were inserted onto two headlands near the border.

Len's account of the first teams describes a pattern which was to be repeated many times by all members of the SBS section during the coming months:

Two teams were landed by inflatable craft, both within a few hundred yards of the border and we were effectively operating in no man's land. You never knew when you might come face to face with the IBT.

The OP [observation post] teams were put ashore on a rocky, wave-swept headland where no person in his right mind would have expected us to land at night. Having shut off the engine and paddled in the last hundred yards we searched for a large flat rock on to which to hold the craft while we unloaded our equipment. The first man ashore moved into a position where he could watch the approaches to the area and give covering fire if we were attacked. Within seconds of the touchdown, the craft was pushed off and withdrew seawards.

Two men were left in the craft to return to base when the team was landed. Two were considered necessary; in the event of engine failure – a frequent event – there was still enough manpower in the craft to enable it to be paddled to shore. But soon, the return journey was left to one man because of shortage of personnel and loss of speed in the craft through carrying one extra person on the outward voyage. The boat-handler was left to return to base alone. If the engine failed, he either fixed it, waited on a sea anchor while another craft came to his aid or got swept ashore and picked up later.

The OP team moved to the jungle's edge and established a position where they could have the maximum view to seawards and then waited undercover for daybreak. At first light a quick reconnaissance was made for evidence of terrorist tracks. If we were satisfied we had a safe hide, one man was on watch to seawards while the other remained in a defensive position to protect the team. The third would brew the tea, make hourly radio contact, passing on our intelligence reports, attend to the waterproofing to keep the equipment dry and take his turn to sleep – in that order. It was monsoon season at the time; nothing stayed dry for long. We were to maintain this routine for three days, and then we would be taken off and replaced with another team.

On the third day of our first watch, sea conditions were so bad that there was no hope of us being picked up, and behind us the countryside was swarming. Communications were also a constant problem. The A41 VHF radio we were using to link OPs, boats and base had a range of 20 miles. We were 30 miles out and, even with a 40-foot aerial at our base, radio contact was a hit-and-miss affair. As always, we had an alternative RV [rendezvous point]. It was located on the other side of our headland, where there was a small island close inshore, sheltered from the storm.

We set off, carrying our gear, to reach the RV but hit jungle territory so dense and wild it was impossible to cut through and reach the other side by the RV time. The only option was to go into inhabited areas, where the IBT could be in residence. That worry had so concerned 42 Commando that they had earlier withdrawn a ten-man section from a bunker position they set up nearby to keep local residents loyal and ward off terrorists. Intelligence reports indicated an imminent large-scale incursion, and we were walking right into it.

We set off towards the village just before dark so that if we got involved in a fire fight we could track off into the gloom. We moved cautiously through the native huts and came upon a Chinese store, the only place which had any lights showing. The Chinese family, after the first shock of seeing three armed and rather trigger-twitchy men burst into their home, made us welcome and seemed quite hurt when we left one man outside in the dark to keep watch.

We stayed in the store for a couple of hours, drinking tea, and then suddenly a yapping dog brought us to our feet, weapons at the ready. It turned out to be a false alarm. The dog, foraging in empty food cans under the hut, had got its tongue stuck between the lid. The Chinese thought it was hilarious. After the adrenalin surge had subsided, we laughed too.

We headed off to the RV and reached it ten minutes before pick-up time. No sign of the craft. We were in a very exposed position, sitting ducks for the IBT, and we decided to wade out to an island 100 metres offshore. We had just set off when, to our intense relief, the RV craft came into view. It was always a great feeling to see your mates in the pick-up craft.

For the next two months we maintained both OPs and offshore boat patrols in the Tanjong Datu border area, sending intelligence back. Eventually, the wear and tear on craft and operators caused by the long sea approach to the border meant we had to operate from coastal minesweepers which patrolled further out to sea. It was while I was on board one of these ships that we received a signal instructing my team to make a daylight landing in Milano Bay to establish if the IBT had moved into 42 Commando's old strongpoint.

My first reaction was that someone must be joking, but who was I to question the wisdom of such an exercise. I briefed the ship's captain on our task. He thought we were mad. The ship sailed into Milano Bay and dropped anchor 1,500 yards off-shore, and we lowered our own craft. The ship's coxswain came along so that he could take it back to the ship and wait events. We were landed well to the flank of the strongpoint. One man with a light machine-gun would wait at the water's edge to give us covering fire if we hit trouble. We ran up the beach and into the cover of the coconut grove 150 yards away. Once there, we would give him cover while he joined us, and then we spread out, moving cautiously towards the strongpoint. Fortunately for us, IBT had vanished.

The journey did have its compensation because next we moved to Turtle Island, half-way between Sematan and Tanjong Datu, the classic example of a tropical island, 400 to 500 yards long and, with the exception of the rocky shoreline, covered with dense rain forest. This cut our approach passage to the operating area by half, and we were able to keep our craft closer to the water's edge and avoided the effort of carrying our equipment over several hundred yards of beach every time we launched.

The beach, which was the only all-weather landing-place, also catered as the nesting habitat for the turtles, and it was not unusual to see dozens of them at night laboriously digging their egg-laying holes. Where the tongue of the beach joined the solid mass of the island, a beautiful wooden villa had been constructed in the edge of the trees, and it was here that we made our base for some weeks. The villa was only normally inhabited during the turtle egg-hatching period and was overseen by the curator of the Sarawak Museum, a former member of the Special Operations Executive who had stayed behind in Malaya after the Second World War.

This idyllic tropical island, which was ideal for the SBS team's clandestine mission, was also secluded enough to leave only one man guarding the stores. Now, with SBS operations groups dotted around the theatre, manpower was under pressure. It was while they were on Turtle Island that a couple of well-known SBS stalwart characters, GH and PW, arrived to throw some experienced weight before them. Both were SBS long-term tough guys and had been out tracking for 42 Commando. When they arrived on Turtle Island they had just survived a dramatic fire fight with a 40-strong party of IBT.

GH, a sergeant, was leading a DPT (Dog Patrol Team) with PW acting as signaller, and a Dyak tracker and a dog. They had been dropped into the jungle by helicopter after reports that a large band of IBT was making its way back across the border. The dog picked up the scent, and the trackers pursued at great speed. By nightfall they could still not report a confirmed sighting. GH knew that the IBT were still too far from the border to cross it before dark, so decided to take a chance and keep going, even though this meant that his team would not have time to find a lying-up area before dark.

They had moved on only a few hundred metres further when the tracker put his hand up, signalling movement ahead. GH moved off the track, peered through the undergrowth and found himself face to face with IBT sentry. The troop was in the process of preparing camp for the night. GH fired first, shot the sentry and then raked the area with his sub-machine-gun; several IBT dropped to the ground. The IBT reacted quickly. The tracker was wounded in the arm from return fire. GH was shouting orders to non-existent troops. He and PW, using rapid fire and movement, managed to dodge the IBT and escape.

As soon as they'd lost them, GH stopped to radio the position of the IBT, but the commando reaction was not fast enough to stop them crossing the border safely that night. For his leadership and bravery under enemy fire, GH received a Military Medal to add to the Distinguished Conduct Medal he had earned as a young corporal for a similar incident against the terrorists in Malaya ten years earlier. Later, he was also awarded the British Empire Medal and the Meritorious Service Medal and became the most decorated post-war NCO in the Royal Marines. Len Holmes continued his account:

> By then, it was time to move on from Turtle Island. Once sea conditions improved, the IBT began to use the route again. The risk of the base being overrun was too great, and soon afterwards, the section was withdrawn again to Singapore after two more months of sheer, continuous effort. We once more had to go through the major task of moving all our equipment.
>
> The phrase most often used about us was the 'lightly equipped fighting troops' – typical marine sarcasm. Each time we moved, we had to move house. We never knew what our role or method of operation would be when we arrived in Borneo, and had to take our whole range of boats, diving equipment, radios, weapons, ammunition and explosives with us. The total aircraft payload for it was in the region of 30 tons for a 15-man section. This meant that every one of us had to move two tons of stores from base to truck, truck to aircraft, aircraft to helicopter, helicopter to truck or ship and then finally into a new base.
>
> So in spite of periods of high drama, the overwhelming memory of these initial operations is inevitably one of acting like coolies. Fortunately, the hierarchy had now realised that small-boat presence was needed at both Tawau and Sematan for the foreseeable future. Another 1SBS section had been flown out to Singapore from the UK and had acclimatised themselves while we were in Borneo.
>
> Half of this section was to be based in Tawau, where they had supervised the installation of a motley squadron of small boats manned by the local army unit and Malay troops. This unit became known as the Tawau Assault Group and took over all the tasks we had performed during our first period in Borneo. A purpose-built boat-shed, office and store had been built on the waterfront for the SBS which was within the

security of the local army compound. One section, complete with all its stores, could now operate on specific SBS tasks without being side-tracked on to defensive patrolling.

For the next two years both sections were based in Singapore but supplied an officer, sergeant-major and two subsections (sergeant, corporal and two marines) on a three-monthly rotation to carry out operations in Tawau. The whole of Malaysia was now on a war footing. Indonesian agents had been stirring up the local population, creating general unrest. There were strikes and riots, and a constant bombardment of militant Indonesian propaganda created rumours of amphibious landings and air raids.

Singapore itself was threatened with invasion by Sukarno, and from an early stage it had been realised that if the British were ever to be able to leave the area, the resistance to Indonesian aggression must begin with locally based forces. The SBS had been instructing the Malaysian Special Forces in raiding techniques, but there was insufficient time for intelligence-gathering before action was required. The periods spent by the sections in Singapore alternated between training the Malaysian and South Vietnamese forces in raiding, and carrying out the operations which would provide the Malaysians with the information on which they could act.

No British personnel, alive or dead, or their equipment, could be allowed to fall into enemy hands and become a source of embarrassment to the UK government. Permission for SBS raids had to come from the Cabinet Office in London, and these were approved only if it could be seen that the planning was so precise as to limit failure to the absolute minimum.

By this time Indonesian forces were preparing camps on several islands within a few thousand yards of Singapore from which they could carry out military raids or launch terrorists against Malaysia. Some could easily be approached from territorial waters by launching our craft from a surface ship; others, set further back, would have to be approached by submarine. That was a complication because of the shallow approaches in some areas, and could work only if the sub

> surfaced several miles offshore then submerged, towing the canoes into the area by using the periscope. The new OPs were to be mounted on islands just off Singapore.

One night the SBS target was a small island, little more than a coral reef and with virtually no cover, where an IBT encampment was located. The recce OP was assigned to another of the SBS stalwarts, Sergeant CC, who had a marine as his number two. They paddled from their submarine to an offshore position, where the two operators would swim ashore and recce the defensive positions around the camp which the Indonesians had built on the island. To make sure they could locate the canoe again, one swimmer carried a thin fishing-line paid out from a reel in the canoe. The line was staked into the beach at the water-line and left while the reconnaissance was carried out.

When the work was done, enemy positions noted and landfall charted, the two returned to discover that an unexpectedly strong tide had washed away the stake, string and canoe. After a vain search swimming around the bay using compass bearings, they were approaching the time for their RV for pick-up by the parent craft. They would never make it back in time. The sergeant faced a choice: to return to the island and risk being captured, tortured and probably executed or to simply swim out to sea. Mindful of the 'golden rule' about being captured, he chose the latter. They began swimming seawards in the hope of making the rendezvous. Fighting strong currents and a hefty swell, they swam on, but found no trace of the parent.

Five hours later they were all but done in, at least 12 miles from land, with a vast open sea ahead of them. By sheer chance they were spotted by a Royal Navy Coastal Minesweeper patrolling in international waters and picked up and returned to base. Sergeant CC, the man who faced one of the most awkward decisions of his life, was awarded the British Empire Medal for his courage.

Back to Len Holmes's diary of events:

> Tawau, in the north, beckoned again, but this time the emphasis was no longer on the defensive. Tasks allocated to the section were definitely offensive.

Over the preceding months, the Indonesians had established a considerable amphibious force at Nunukan. Two large landing-craft were permanently at anchor offshore, and a regiment of Alligators [Armoured Amphibious Personnel Carriers] were positioned in a large waterfront compound next to Nunukan jetty. Both landing-craft and Alligators indicated the arrival of what was probably Indonesia's élite fighting force, the KKO [Korps Kommando Operatives], Indonesia's marines. We were asked by DOBOP (Director of Borneo Operations) to carry out a sabotage raid on the Alligators and put as many as we could out of action. At first glance the operation looked feasible; the distance from the nearest border point was only 1,000 to 1,500 yards. Theoretically, it was well within the range of swimmers towing explosive charges. However, the lack of knowledge of tidal currents created the need for caution. The experience we had gained when working in the area some months previously had shown there could be strong currents during spring tides and moonless periods which we would need to operate in. For these operations, two canoes and two assault craft were used. The canoes paddled to within 200 yards of Nunukan jetty, anchored and measured the stream every 30 minutes over a period of 3 hours. Meanwhile, the two assault craft maintained a position on the border; one was fitted with outriggers so that if necessary the canoes could be picked up quickly.

The other assault boat was fitted with a crossbar so that a bren-gunner could wrap his legs around it, leaving his hands free to operate the machine-gun. The task of this craft if the canoes came under fire was to head towards the enemy, spraying them with bullets, while the other craft picked up the canoes and withdrew them. The only way to get accurate fire from a bouncing and moving craft was for the bren-gun to be fired from the hip. By using a mix of one ball to one tracer ammunition, the gunner could see the direction of his shots and spray on to the target. Even then, the results were hardly pinpoint, and we had bullets from one of our craft go through the sides of the other.

> The system of measuring the tide's strength was typical SBS stick and string. While they were at anchor, the rear-seat canoeist let a partially filled plastic bottle attached to 50 feet of buoyant line into the water. The time taken for the line to go taut and the compass bearing of the direction it took was then recorded to measure the strength of currents.
>
> We established there was a 2-knot current setting towards Nunukan along the route the swimmers would have to take. With a surface swimmer's speed of at best 1 to 1.5 knots we could reach the target but could not guarantee that they would be able to return. As a result of this information the plan to attack the Alligators was cancelled. It also became known that the KKO had a forward base on their side of the border. Two operations were mounted, involving two canoes paddling along the main Nunukan Channel and setting up a hide in the mangrove, providing confirmation that the KKO were based there and could be dealt with in due course.
>
> Two recces of an Indonesian listening-post were also carried out, and from the info provided the post was attacked and wiped out by a troop from 42 Commando [led by an SBS officer who was awarded the Military Cross].

Next, Holmes's section was sent back to Sematan.

> Our original small camp with 42 Commando had mushroomed into a large defensive compound manned by a company from 2/7th Gurkhas, and it was from there that they once again began inserting three-man teams into OPs near the border, where they could report any incursions.

They were out on jungle patrols, up to 17 days at a time. Apart from their OPs, SBS were used to resupply them with ammunition and food. The two groups had much in common in their operational tactics. As the Gurkha history records, its operations in the jungle were governed by stealth and silence: no rifleman was allowed to eat, smoke or unscrew his water-bottle without his platoon commander's permission. At night, sentries checked any man who snored. Whenever the company was on the move, a recce section led the way, their packs carried by men from behind. Because of the long approach marches, each man could carry six days' rations . . .

Although on the face of it the sideline task of resupplying the Gurkha patrols provided the men with the security of being based within the safety of a Gurkha compound, it turned out to be one of the most hazardous they'd face, and the dangers did not always come from the enemy, as Len Holmes explained:

> A few of them spoke English, and they insisted that we identify ourselves by giving a special bird-call. I can assure you it is extremely difficult to whistle anything when you're standing alone in the pitch dark trying to locate a bunch of trigger-happy Gurkhas. Life in the Gurkha compound was far from happy. They themselves are delightful, child-like warriors, but living among them produced many problems. Our food was produced separately because theirs was too highly spiced for our consumption, and we had a navy cook using two Primus stoves producing meals from food bought locally. Washing had to be done at different times as our nudity offended their modesty.
>
> Most of us were only getting a few hours' sleep each night and were only in the camp for a rest one day in four, yet we still had to man the compound defences at stand-to each night and morning. The British officer in charge of them was also senior to our officer and clearly did not believe that the Special Boat Section were as special as his Gurkhas. That, coupled with his overbearing attitude, produced a rebellious response from our chaps which at one stage looked as though it might erupt into a mutiny. Only a great deal of common sense on the part of our team, and a visit from our brigade major, who managed to curb some of the Gurkha officer's inflexibility, prevented a most unpleasant incident.

It was a curious confrontation, particularly as the Gurkhas and the SBS, in many respects, shared a common philosophy. Their raids were by stealth, to the last moment, then all hell would break loose.

Towards the end of the SBS's unhappy attachment to the Gurkhas, they received information that an IBT camp was located on the Indonesian coast just across the border from Milano.

The SBS was tasked with determining if it were still in use. If it were, the Gurkhas would mount an attack on the camp. A long-range patrol from the Gurkhas was sent to establish the jungle track the IBT used to get to and from the camp. To get SBS recce canoes within easy paddling distance of the camp, an assault boat towed them to within a mile or so of the landing-spot. The canoeists could have paddled the distance easily, but they needed a fast craft close by if they had to make a sharp exit. A coastal minesweeper was positioned a mile or so offshore, where she could sweep the area with her radar for enemy craft. The canoeists arrived at a point 200 to 300 metres away from the suspected IBT camp, and then made a landing near the camp's position. They hid their canoes at the back of the beach and waited until daylight before scouring the area to find the camp. The thick jungle and the threat of booby traps called for a daylight recce and even then only with extreme caution. If they were discovered, they were to make their way back over the border on foot, leaving the canoes behind.

After a slow search they found the camp set in a jungle clearing slightly inland from the coast. The area was deserted, but there were clear signs that the IBT had been training for a water-borne incursion. Not long afterwards, the Gurkhas stumbled on another guerrilla camp. As recorded in their historians' description of the action, the recce party discovered a riverside Indonesian army camp against whom the Gurkhas were vastly outnumbered. It was day-break, and the Indonesians were taking a breakfast of spit-roasted pig.

The patrol edged close and prepared to launch its attack: 'A 3.5-inch (8.8-centimetre) rocket flared across the river and exploded among the breakfast party. Their hut disintegrated in a ball of flame, the men hurled in all directions. As the two assault platoons moved in . . . they were confronted by a number of totally naked, panic-stricken enemy rushing from it. These were quickly dealt with and, covered by fierce fire from the support group, we assaulted the base. Resistance had ceased but a number of dead lay scattered about the camp and blood was everywhere.'

Len Holmes looks back at his time in Borneo as a contributor to an effort which reflected great credit on the SBS as a whole. He points to the words of Colonel J. P. Cross in his book *Jungle Warfare* who in comparing the Confrontation to Vietnam said '. . . in both Malaya and Borneo their enemy were at least as formidable as the Viet Cong in the early 1960s and Indonesia just as strong militarily as North Vietnam.'

Britain could have had Vietnam on its hands if the campaign had been mismanaged, and there is little doubt as to the value of SBS intelligence-gathering tasks in avoiding an escalation of the Confrontation into a full scale war.

Chapter Twelve

Paddy and the goldfish

Major Pat Troy, a 1950s old boy of the SBS, arrived in Singapore as a young career-minded captain in 1965. The Borneo Confrontation was still on, and he had been expecting to take command of L Company in 42 Commando, having just spent a chilly year or so with the RM Falklands protection force, NP 8901. He went straight into a Jungle Warfare Course in Malaya in anticipation of his new post. Many old friends and acquaintances were around, including David Mitchell, officer commanding of SBS in Singapore, who was also moving on. A new man had been earmarked to take his place but suddenly backed out.

Pat Troy was dragged reluctantly to succeed Mitchell, and the chap who turned down the job went to 42 Commando, where in due course he became a company commander and adjutant. So, he is not one of Troy's favourite officers. 'Having said that,' Troy told me from his home, 'I thoroughly enjoyed my time back with SBS. Although operations in the Borneo Confrontation were scaling down when I arrived, there was still plenty to do and we did carry out a lot of worthwhile work, particularly in experimenting with exit and re-entry of SBS teams from dived submarines on which Paddy Ashdown, who joined us in 1966, took an active part.'

Troy had been through the SBS mill at the time when its instructors included a number of old stalwarts of the section and some of them were still around. 'In those days, few officers saw the

SBS as a good career move,' said Pat Troy, and continued:

> We had no one at the top fighting for us in the RM. There is no doubt that there was a strong body of opinion in both political and military circles that Special Forces were an expensive luxury . . . that they denuded lots of units of their best men, their leaders, and they'd have far more effect if they remained with their unit. I must admit I had that feeling, too, when I was a company commander in 42 Commando. I had an excellent company and, given the time and the tasks, I reckon I could have picked guys out of my company to train up to the job. I used to feel quite strongly about SBS demands for special equipment. They'd have a bee in their bonnet about some particular thing, and finally they'd win and it would be bought, and when that particular person left it would remain on the shelf in the stores. Demand, demand, demand, all the time.

It was also true that some RM officers still regarded SBS men as overbearing eccentrics, diffident to authority and always asking for expensive new toys. They also had a tendency to shy away from other formalities, like uniforms and hair length. It was a standing joke that when they were going on parade, it took them a month to prepare! And wasn't it one of Troy's young trainee officers, Neil Johnstone, who turned up in battledress wearing brown shoes? 'Go away and do not return until you find some suitable footwear!' And, yes, the same Neil Johnstone who became one of the longest-serving officers in the SBS is right when he says: 'For years we were never really flavour of the month, if for no other reason than the fact that we seemed to collect a bunch of guys who had a reputation for being – shall we say? – difficult. Some of them *were*, and equally a lot of those guys went on to become real stars of SBS operations and a good many of them made their name through it.'

Major Troy admits, however, to learning an early lesson or two among them:

> Once, the Dutch asked us to attempt to break into their naval base to test their security. They'd been doing it for a number of

> years using the Dutch marines. They wanted us to take it on and bring a fresh approach, see how far we'd get. There were about a dozen of us, going in night after night. Jim 'Horse' Earle, my colour-sergeant, noticed I was trying to get a piece of the action myself. He bluntly pointed out that it wasn't my job. He took me to one side and said, 'Look, we know you can jump as high as we can and run as fast and as far and can swim and dive. But you're our OC. Your job is to tell us where to go and what to do, how to do it. And if things go wrong, get us out. If you're with us, you can't do that.' Point taken.

Now, in 1965 he somewhat reluctantly found himself OC in Singapore and incidentally confronted by the need to acquire equipment, about which he had been critical in the past. Within a few months he was joined by Paddy Ashdown, who came to the SBS after a lively spell of operational action with 42 Commando. They had both served together earlier, in the Far East. Singapore was a married posting, and Paddy had his wife with him. He spoke fluent Malay and thus had a strong rapport with the locals.

By now, apart from its operational duties, the SBS was heavily engaged in training Malay troops in the defence of their land. Selected forces from the South Vietnamese Army and, later, US Marines were also given the benefit of SBS experience in jungle and swampland warfare for their battles with the Viet Cong and the North Vietnamese Army. Initially, specially selected small groups from the South Vietnamese Army were given jungle warfare training and underwater instruction. Later, the US Marines were grateful for advice on operations in bad terrain, but their years of ineffectual confrontation with the Communists and their eventual withdrawal proved how right the British planners had been to restrict Borneo to border confrontations and not even attempt to get involved in a jungle war.

Meanwhile, Pat Troy still had some important operations, and was working well with submarine commanders. Several islands within a few thousand yards of Singapore provided good cover for Indonesian guerrillas as a base for their raids. The SBS recce teams could reach some by launching canoes or inflatables from a surface ship. Others, further afield, had to be approached by submarine, which not only put the men at risk but the submarine too. Nothing had changed in that regard: a diving submarine makes a very loud noise and draws attention not only to itself but to the men it has just floated off. It was an age-old problem, wherever the SBS men were carried by submarine.

Trials started earlier in Singapore by David Mitchell, with Len Holmes and Corporal Bob Beers during the intermission from operations, were aimed at establishing safe techniques for the exit and re-entry of SBS swimmers, their gear and boats while the submarine was still dived. They were being run under the codename of Goldfish. Similar work was being run in the UK, but Singapore had the weather and the water that made it ideal. The trials and experiments which began in these years and pursued back in Britain would provide the basis for vital improvements to the way SBS teams were delivered to an operation.

Pat Troy and Paddy Ashdown, who served together in 42 Commando, were deeply interested in the theory of underwater exit and re-entry, and they had the support of Commander John E. Moore RN, Commander of the 7th Submarine Squadron, who was not only willing to have his boats mucked about with for experiments but also acquired much of the gear. By then all British submarines were equipped with BIBS and TABS (Built-In Breathing System and Tower Air-Breathing System).

Installed for the escape of the crew, these systems involved pipelines running throughout the boat. In an emergency, the crew could plug in a tube with a demand valve and mouthpiece. The escape tower through which the crew would have to pass to exit was in effect a small dry and wet compartment. A system of vents and floodpipes allowed escapees to enter, close the lower hatch and then flood the compartment until the water pressure was equalised with that outside, then open the upper hatch to make a free ascent to the surface.

There was a single escape tower in both Fore and Aft of the submarine in compartments which needed flooding. The built-in breathing system meant that while this was going on the men could plug in a mouthpiece and stand, rather like tube-train commuters, waiting to go. For the Goldfish experiments, the escape tower was the only access in and out of the boat. The tower, like a large tube about 4 feet (1.2 metres) in diameter and 5 feet (1.5 metres) in height, was just forward of the conning tower in the A-class submarines then in use (they were phased out in the 1970s). Other submarines had two single escape towers.

For the Goldfish trials, high-pressure air cylinders were tied inside the conning tower, with air lines and mouthpieces. Also secured inside the conning tower was a rope with a small float attached to it so that on reaching the surface the swimmers could clip the air lines and mouthpieces on to it ready for their return and re-entry into the submarine.

Paddy Ashdown was one of the key members of the team when the Goldfish trials were reaching a successful conclusion, and it was Commander Moore (a future editor of Jane's *Fighting Ships*) who provided the boats, the air tanks, and the kit to make the trials all come together. As Pat Troy recalled:

> We were on an exercise when we first decided to put Goldfish to the test and do some serious exit and re-entry trials in the submerged submarine in a mock-attack situation, as near as possible to the real thing. John Moore didn't tell anyone we were going to do it. Two pairs – Paddy Ashdown and Ted Lonnegan, each with a marine – were suited up and prepared for exit while Moore weaved the submarine in and out of the ships in a deep-water bay. The two pairs swam to the ships and placed charges on the hulls successfully without being spotted. Unfortunately, as we were leaving some sharp-eyed lookout spotted our tac periscope. He didn't know what it was, so he went to the radar. He vectored a boat on to it and we hit it and holed it. We had to do an emergency surface to check for damage. At that time, Paddy and his partner were still in the tower, draining down. The boat surfaced beside Ted Lonnegan and his marine, who were just about to start re-entry procedure. It was a very good test, however, and Paddy wrote up the paper, and much more work was done both in Singapore and in the UK to perfect the procedures.

Ashdown was also working on parachuting men into submarines at sea. The problem with carrying SBS personnel in submarines was the overcrowding, as well as the men getting unfit during long journeys and, crucially, not having up-to-date intelligence. The canoes or inflatables, their engines, and their mass of gear and stores took up a large amount of space in already cramped conditions, conditions submariners had moaned about since they began carting Tug Wilson around the Mediterranean. Unlike the US, Britain had no personnel-carrying submarines, so Troy began exploring the possibility of getting the SBS to operations by air.

SBS parties in Malta, including Jim Earle and Len Holmes, had already done a good deal of work in this area, especially at the time when 'Sticks' Dodds was OC of 6SBS, although dropping men by parachute was usually for direct raids by air without involving a submarine.

Pat Troy's variation on that theme was to load up a submarine with some of the gear and then rendezvous with an aircraft somewhere close to the target zone, where the SBS men and their additional kit would be dropped into the sea, picked up and taken in by the sub for the last hop of their journey for the clandestine raid. They practised the techniques by day and by night. The RAF were very keen on the routine, too, and Troy secured great cooperation from them. The SBS also practised parachuting to the submarine while it was still submerged, with the men entering without surfacing using the techniques developed for Goldfish.

The trials were all completed very successfully, with rubber inflatable craft being brought out through the torpedo tubes and outboard motors through the conning tower. The SBS trialists managed to get motoring without the submarine surfacing. The experiments continued – and would do so for the next decade or more – and next Troy and Moore began working on a motorised underwater towing vehicle that could pull an SBS diver and his load of explosives. John Moore got hold of a Mark XXIII torpedo. Royal Navy engineers at the submarine depot-ship HMS *Medway* adapted it to Moore's specifications and added extra batteries to convert it to an underwater tug.

Paddy Ashdown was one of the test drivers, and it worked successfully enough for designs of a similar underwater towing vehicle to go into production under the codename of Archimedes, or Archie as it was affectionately known. That particular design was not ultimately successful, but the same principles were used for underwater tugs and Swimmer Delivery Vehicles that remain in service today.

Troy recalled one more rather ironic event before Ashdown left Singapore to go off to China to continue his studies of oriental languages. The Singapore contingent of the British armed forces was putting on a show for Harold Wilson's visiting Secretary of State for Defence, Denis Healey. At the time, Healey was planning to axe various prize possessions of the navy, including cherished aircraft-carriers.

He'd had a good look around, been into a carrier, talked to the troops and so on. By the time he reached the SBS and submarines, he'd got a big gash over his eye, having hit his head somewhere along the way. He complained that they kept putting him in smaller and smaller boats. He joked about it and said thank goodness it had happened in a small ship: 'You can imagine the headlines. "Healey Leaves Carrier with a Black Eye." '

His hosts then invited him to inspect the submarines. The SBS was to pick him up in a motor launch and deliver him to the submarine where Captain John Moore was waiting. There were chaps jumping out of aeroplanes and swimmers coming up all around the submarine and so on. It was Paddy Ashdown who went to pick him up in a Gemini, brought him back to Moore's boat and eventually returned him. 'Anyway,' said Pat Troy, 'we eventually got a signal from Healey saying how much he'd enjoyed his day with the navy and especially the stage-managed finale. Some time later I was up in the House of Commons, by which time Paddy was leader of the Liberal Democrats. I bumped into Healey and I asked him if he remembered the day with the navy. He did . . . remembered it very well. And no, he didn't know it was Paddy Ashdown who had driven across in the Gemini to the submarine.'

Paddy Ashdown left Singapore and the SBS after a two-and-a-half-year stint. He had been studying oriental languages at a college in Singapore and moved on to China to continue his studies. He went to an SBS reunion in 1996 – just like the old days, except that he was famous now. He was invited to do the draw, but the hubbub and noise were such that he couldn't be heard. Ashdown got on to a chair and bellowed: 'Shaaaddup!' Of course, they all jeered and yelled back: 'Shut up, Paddy, you're not in Parliament now.'

CHAPTER THIRTEEN

White arses in the moonlight

Beach recces! Dozens of them throughout the 1960s. A whole decade of scouring, plotting and charting the coastlines of the Middle East, along with a good deal of other intelligence-gathering, a fair few fire fights and a remarkable shoot-to-kill engagement fell to the lot of the SBS in a series of operations in the Middle East that ran parallel to their presence in Borneo. They were to be followed in by the SAS and other contingents of British troops, called to action once more in the deserts and desolate mountainous territory of southern Arabia.

A brief summary of events: in the aftermath of the Suez fiasco, President Nasser vowed to kick the British out of the Arab world. The southern coastal lands, from Yemen on the Red Sea around to Qatar in the Persian Gulf, were on a knife-edge. Across the Gulf, Iran and Iraq were staring at each other menacingly. Nasser stirred the pot, the Soviets threw their might behind the Marxist rebels of Yemen and anyone else willing to take their handouts, aided by the knowledge and contacts of the British traitor Kim Philby, who vanished from Beirut in 1963 and turned up later in Moscow.

British influence, political and economic, over this string of sheikhdoms, sultanates and monarchies had become the focus of bitter reaction among Arab republicans. The one remaining vestige of colonial power in the region hung tenuously in the balance in the protectorate of Aden, which Britain had ruled for 128 years. This last strategic base had been its fortress guarding the southern access to the Suez Canal at the mouth of the Red Sea and at the tip of what would soon become the People's Democratic Republic of Yemen. By 1960, it was surrounded by hostility.

British troops had faced increasingly bloody skirmishes with the Yemeni rebels since 1955, and by the early 1960s Aden was virtually under siege. The British-friendly ruler of the Yemen, the Imam Mohammed al Badr, was deposed in September 1962, and within the month Egyptian troops rolled in to support the Marxist regime. The Imam fled to the mountains and came to rest close to the border with Saudi Arabia, whose king remained a supporter. From there, and with the aid of privately contracted British mercenaries, including former serving members of the SAS, he directed a guerrilla war against the Communists for the rest of the decade.

The Conservative government of Harold Macmillan had vowed 'no surrender' to the Marxists and Nasserite factions. The Labour Party of Harold Wilson's was not so sure, and within 18 months of coming to power in 1964 it confirmed Britain's withdrawal from Aden, leaving its base to fall into the hands of the Soviet satellite.

Between the departure and arrival of new political colours at Westminster, British troops became ensnared in a sustained campaign of terrorism and guerrilla warfare around their Aden base which threatened to spread into the Trucial States (now the United Arab Emirates) fronting the Persian Gulf. If that wasn't enough, Iraq's Nasser-friendly military rulers announced they would reclaim Kuwait following Britain's ending of its protectorate of the oil-rich little state.

Britain promised to continue its military support of Kuwait and also reaffirmed its friendship with Iran, which would receive some long-term assistance in the way of training of its Special Forces from the SBS. The Israelis, meanwhile, were standing by, secretly backing the anti-Communist factions of Yemen and preparing to act when the moment was right.

Out of this turmoil, as history now records, the dominoes fell one after the other. The worst-case scenarios of the military analysts who had called for the supreme intelligence effort at the back end of the 1950s were ticked off, year by year, and onwards down the century: British withdrawal from Aden, the Six-Day War, the

Palestinian crisis, Gaddafi seizing power from King Idris in Libya, Middle East terrorist outrages, plane hijackings, hostage-taking, the 1970s oil crisis, Lebanon, Iraq v. Iran . . . and so on.

The SBS was again in at the beginning and would remain well into the crucial stages of most of the above events, carrying out top-secret recces and raiding-missions under the auspices of the Amphibious Warfare Centre and the Joint Intelligence Bureau's AI9 and MI6. SBS involvement was, as ever, a prelude to all that was to follow as the British military planners and intelligence analysts continually updated assessments of the region, identifying the troublespots, forecasting dangers to Britain, her economy or her allies, and determining best sites if and when invasion or withdrawal of troops and British nationals became necessary. All eventualities needed to be covered.

At the turn of the decade, as things were hotting up in Aden and elsewhere, 6SBS based in Malta sent a detachment to Bahrain, from where they would be deployed throughout the Arab southern regions. The SBS teams who came to Bahrain over the next ten years or so were given a fairly long leash, often working on their own initiative, usually dressed as civilians or disguised as Arabs, but all the time reconnoitring the scenery of the coast. Jim Earle gave me this account:

> JIB wanted reports on beaches throughout the Middle East, assault and withdrawal sites, very detailed recces – bearing capacities, underwater obstacles, beach profiles, exits, cover . . . everything. We were doing that from Qatar in the east to beyond Aden in the west. I spent two weeks learning how to speak a bit of Arabic, and how to conduct myself with Arabs. We were being sent away on our own, as a sub-section, and we knew it might be necessary on occasions to wear Arab clothes. We were administered, supplied and looked after by JIB, which was tremendous because wherever we went they always had a secret squirrel who could fit us up with the most amazing stuff. I'd meet the squirrel, who would give me directions of where to go, what to do, and keep in contact throughout. He'd have the up-to-date aerial photographs, which he'd marked, and hand

over to me for guidance. Around those areas we had to make a full beach recce. I would work under him while I remained in his area.

As an example, we were sent into Kuwait at the time of a dispute over borders with Iraq. The oil states were all in a tense mood, with Nasser and Israel, Iran and Iraq all embroiled in their historical differences. The possibility of an Iraqi invasion of Kuwait had blown up again in July 1961, and intelligence reports from Baghdad reckoned the Iraqis were about to send troops towards the Kuwaiti border. 45 Commando were mobilised to make a show of strength by turning up in Kuwait. If a full-scale shootout developed, more troops would be needed. JIB wanted precise beach recces of Kuwait, their existing ones being out of date. At the time I was down in Oman – also facing trouble with left-wing rebels – with my section when I received a signal ordering me to report to Bahrain forthwith. There, in the naval base HMS *Jufair*, we met the JIB rep. We saw him on a Thursday, and he explained the task. There were clear-cut rules about any intelligence work in Kuwait, and they were scared shitless about disturbing them. He asked me what kit I wanted, and I gave them a list. It was ready to be collected on the Monday.

They flew us up to Kuwait City and there we were met by another JIB squirrel. He directed us to recce the oil company base outside of Kuwait. We commandeered some transport – two Dodge powerpack vehicles – and drove down to Mina' al-Ahmadi, where I saw a second squirrel, a retired naval commander. He gave me precise directions as to what we were to do. There was one road straight out, two lanes, 50 miles long leading to the beach. We travelled along it until we reached a villa, which they had acquired for our use. We arrived there and just took it over for the period we were there, using it as the base while we conducted a full beach recce along the whole stretch of Kuwait coastline.

It took us about a month for that particular recce. But there were many others . . . Aden, Yemen, Muscat, Oman, a large section of the Arabian coastline and across into East Africa.

> Nine times out of ten we were in these places just prior to trouble, or withdrawal. In the two and a half years I was on the Bahrain posting, it was almost entirely spent on beach recces. Some of the time we were in places we shouldn't have been, and there were occasionally some tense moments with the local militia or rebels. There was a lot of anti-British activity. We were well armed and well equipped, but we were instructed to avoid trouble. We had to be invisible. We'd run rather than engage in a fire fight because that would destroy the object of the task. Once you engaged in a fire fight you'd lost. You might win the fight, but you've destroyed the object. We were forced into returning fire once or twice in the Gulf of the Yemen areas, but that was because we were being shot at – we just did enough to clear our escape.

With the continuing threat of Iraq invading Kuwait, the SBS was ordered to send a permanently based detachment to Bahrain. Lieutenant Neil Johnstone – he of brown shoes with battledress fame – was attached to 2SBS in Singapore, where during his tour with them he became a familiar figure thereabouts, driving his little MGTC. It was around this time that 2SBS was extended to cover the Middle East; the detachment later became known as 3SBD. Johnstone was tasked with taking, initially, a five-man team to HMS *Jufair*, the shore base in Bahrain, to work with the Amphibious Warfare Squadron. The detachment was destined to remain there until 1971, although the personnel changed on an annual basis.

So, a slight diversion . . . Neil Johnstone – 'one of the most decent blokes in the SBS' said everyone interviewed – came into the Royal Marines for his National Service, moved quickly into the SBS and became one of its longest-serving officers. When I arrived to talk to him at his home overlooking some spectacular countryside in January 1997, a hawk sitting comfortably on its perch on the front lawn eyed me cautiously and a beautiful white barn owl fluttered into its hide nearby.

The hunting dogs barked and the ferrets peered through their cages as Neil ushered me inside for a most entertaining five-hour briefing on his life and times in the SBS, recollections that are included at various sections of this work:

> I joined for National Service and wanted to be a frogman and eventually took an SBS course and went out to join 6SBS in Malta under 'Sticks' Dodds. He was a flamboyant character and in fact created the motto that exists today. We were in his office one day and he said: 'Let's think of a motto.' I came up with one or two suggestions, and he eventually arrived at his own NOT BY STRENGTH, BUT BY GUILE. The 'but' was eventually edited out, but that became the motto and was eventually adopted when we all withdrew back to the UK.
>
> Kuwait was being threatened and 2SBS in Singapore was extended by an officer and four men to cover the Middle East. I was sent to open up our first base for a permanent detachment in Bahrain. The building had two doors swinging in the wind. We looked inside and it was empty, so we painted our colours on it and drew a padlock and that's how we started in Bahrain.
>
> The beaches had to be checked. We were going around all the beaches up there, updating previous intelligence. In December 1961 we were ordered to pack our kit because Kuwait was threatened again. The Iraqis had massed their troops on the border. We were embarked on HMS *Empire*, a war department LST [Landing Ships, Tanks] with 17/21 Lancers and sent up to Kuwait. We stood by off Kuwait, but nothing happened; the Iraqis withdrew and we weren't required operationally. From then on we were deployed with the AW [Amphibious Warfare] Squadron, largely on beach reconnaissance during my time there, and taking part in major training exercises along the coast and around Aden.

Exercises were also a show of strength, and the beaches of the Middle East presented a particular problem, especially for landing or withdrawal of heavy-duty vehicles. The beaches generally had very long, shallow gradients, as if the tide were permanently out, and could often be reached only by the flat-bottomed Gemini inflatables.

For their crucial plotting measurements, Johnstone and his team pioneered a new kind of reel and distance line, used for their precise calculations. They also developed a new format for signalling beach recce check results, which was believed to be the precursor to a system later adopted by NATO forces.

Neil Johnstone had purchased his own wetsuit for swimming and diving while in Singapore, and as a future SBS training officer was instrumental in opening up a long-running debate and trials on the type of suit the SBS should adopt. He is credited with the description of SBS operatives coming ashore and having to discard their wetsuits, displaying the rather noticeable targets of 'white arses in the moonlight'. More about that later, when we catch up with Neil back in the UK.

The SBS also established a good working relationship with C Company of 2 Parachute Regiment, which was also based in Bahrain. They worked together on a number of exercises and projects – in and around the vital Trucial States, which abutted the Strait of Hormuz.

The Bahrain detachment continued with its recces and exercises and led by Rupert Van der Horst, went to Aden again in 1965 in support of 3 Commando Brigade on two major exercises – another show of strength at a particularly difficult time. British troops in Aden, recently reinforced after the decapitation of two soldiers captured by the Yemeni forces, were operating in a vacuum. Everyone knew that the British under a new Labour government would pull out soon. The politicians insisted that British military responses to attacks were to be defensive, almost to the point of turning the other cheek. Hence, many exercises were staged to display the British fire power and provide the basis for a hearts and minds campaign among the local population.

Into this vacuum stepped the founder of the SAS, Colonel David Stirling – by then freelance – who had realised that royal families and heads of state in the wealthy Arab world required more than just personal bodyguards. They needed force commanders with British contacts capable of organising counter-revolutionary forces, training local armies and acquiring decent equipment. The last part of the equation provided no difficulty. The British government and international arms dealers were heavily courting the Arabs. Many fortunes were made, especially among entrepreneurs like Adnan Kashoggi.

Stirling's principal involvement was in the supply of men and in tactical skills. Former SAS and SBS men, mostly of Second World War vintage, had been freelancing for years without much attention, but lately 'mercenary' had become a dirty word. That the man who founded the SAS regiment should resort to it curiously enough had the ring of British approval. Stirling, after 12 years in Rhodesia, was financially at a low ebb at the time and was trying various business schemes. He was introduced to the prospect of taking a key position in the Middle East through a Scottish Member of Parliament, former veteran Special Operations Executive Lieutenant Colonel Billy McLean, who regularly visited the region, and who in turn had the ear of the previous Tory Prime Minister, Alec Douglas-Home.

The idea appealed, and Stirling was fixed up with a contract to aid the deposed Imam run his guerrilla campaign from the mountains. Six former SAS members were flown to Yemen and onwards to the Imam's stronghold, although three of them were eventually murdered at a road-block. Soon, Stirling had persuaded the former commanding officer of 21 SAS (Artists) TA to join him, and a little later Colonel David Smiley, also recruited by his old SOE associate Billy McLean, arrived on the scene to make reports and assessments from battle areas for the Saudi royal family. He later became the Yemeni mercenaries' commanding officer before being succeeded by two former SAS commanding officers. They controlled a mercenary force of around 50 men, leading the royalist army.

Smiley himself was very impressed by their operations:

> The royalists had set an ambush in a valley between sand-dunes and rocks . . . The grim relics of the battle littered the sand on either side of the track. There was a wrecked Russian T34 tank and the burned-out shells of several armoured personnel carriers. I counted – with my handkerchief to my nose – more than 50 decomposing bodies, half-buried by sand and

half-eaten by jackals. I saw, also, six decapitated corpses – executed republicans, they told me.

Some have alluded to external connections among the mercenaries, noting that they and the royalists had kept around 70,000 of Nasser's troops and many MiG fighters occupied in Yemen at the time of the Six-Day War. It is implausible that the mercenaries alone were capable of gathering such numbers of troops and obtaining such equipment. It is possible, however, that David Stirling and company, with the tacit approval of the British, formed a bridgehead while the bulk of the British force was withdrawn from Aden in 1967. By fighting on, the royalists secured and held the territory that became North Yemen. But in spite of the hired guns of the ex-SAS, the royalists were never a match for the Nasser fire power that supported the republicans, and after eight years of fighting a political and military stalemate was reached.

Around Yemen and beyond, through Oman, into the Trucial States and the Gulf, many other odd things were happening. The mercenaries were assisting in the supply of arms and weapons, often parachuted at night from aircraft by the Rhodesian Air Service and the Iranian Air Force into drop zones manned largely by ex-SAS personnel. By the mid-1960s the bodyguard and mercenary business, along with other lucrative arms sidelines, were such big business – in the Middle East, Africa and other war zones – that David Stirling had set up a Jersey-based company to exploit it.

The Arab world remained, as ever, a patchwork of delicate alliances and bitter hatreds. The British were attempting to steer a path that would ensure the best trading potential of what was emerging as one of the most valuable markets in the world, while securing its oil interests and providing a positive basis for future stability. At the same time the CIA and American government analysts, whose reading of the Middle East complexities were seldom more than naive, thought the whole problem could be solved by the recognition and acceptance of the Pan-Arabia of Nasser's dream, a view too simplistic by half, as they would learn at considerable cost.

Britain's future position relied heavily on the mass of intelligence its military and political advisers were receiving; in three years this had developed into a veritable mountain of paper, including a good deal through the activities of the SBS. The interconnections were multi-dimensional, still deeply classified and beyond the scope of this book. A few explanations and clues are available as they involved the SBS.

Oman became a particular focus as the Yemeni troubles subsided. This vast sultanate in many ways provided a cross-sectional slice of the Middle East as a whole – a place of wild extremes in its landscape, its climate and the management of its people. It was an absolute monarchy, a barbarous closed society and, until the late 1960s, its people were largely poverty-stricken, disease-ridden and uneducated. The climate is horrendous. Supper could be cooked on the volcanic rocks. Summer temperatures reached 120 degrees Fahrenheit, while in the northern mountains the winters were so cold that a water-bottle would freeze solid in minutes. In the wilds of Dhofar, there was no shelter from the vertical rain of the monsoons.

Sultan Sa'id of Oman was a small, ageing recluse with white whiskers who spoke perfect English and ran his country by fear and violence, guarded by a coterie of young men of African descent whom he openly described as slaves. With a pistol always to hand on his desk, he communicated with the outside world by radio telephone from his room and through British expatriates on his staff. He and he alone ruled, and would not permit the social improvements so desperately needed, such as in health and education, because he believed his nation was not ready for development.

British interest in this unwelcoming and forbidding country focused on two key elements. First, oil was discovered in 1964 which made the country ripe for exploitation; but to the British, and indeed the whole Western world, that was really a side issue. Political sway in Oman and the Trucial States was linked to control of the west bank of the vital Strait of Hormuz, a slender waterway linking the Persian Gulf to the Gulf of Oman, and out into the Indian Ocean. On the east bank lay Iran.

Through that liquid Z-bend passed more than 55 per cent of the oil used by the free world. If the flow were halted, hindered or

Exit and re-entry of SBS raiders and their equipment from dived submarines to provide greater security for night-time clandestine operations became the subject of many trials from the early 1960s onwards. After personnel had exited in a risky manoeuvre, weapons and stores were floated to the surface in waterproof packaging, along with an inflatable craft visible in the photograph above. Although phased out by the SBS in the 1970s, it is still used by the South African Special Forces today.

Tight squeeze: looking down upon a diver rigged for exiting a submarine with single escape chamber.

Fast pick-ups of swimmer-canoeists from the water without the parent craft having to stop, while possibly under fire from the enemy, were rehearsed with many devices. This ring connector had to be grasped by the swimmer while the craft was passing at speed.

SBS underwater activity increased dramatically through the decades as new operational tasks came into view, especially in the area of maritime counter-terrorism training. A typical suited operative in the 1970s looked a bulky soul.

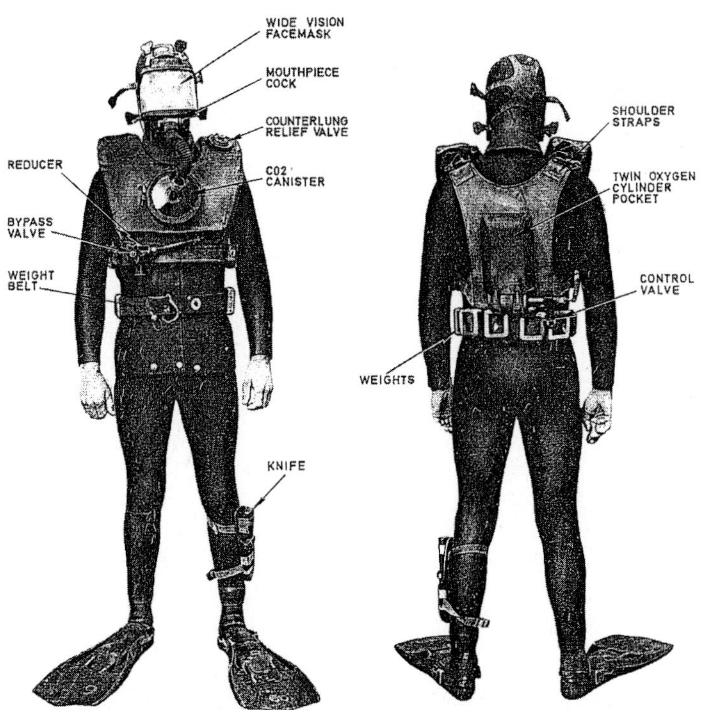

SWIMMER CANOEIST DRESSED IN SCBA

Paddy Ashdown was one of the test drivers of an early underwater swimmer-delivery tug based upon a converted torpedo, designed by a submarine commander and built by Royal Navy engineers in Singapore. Various Swimmer-Delivery Vehicles were later built and trialled specifically for SBS operations from the late 1960s onwards.

An American-built Swimmer Delivery Vehicle on trial to meet the needs of the 1990s.

Another crucial SBS underwater tool for reconnaissance tasks – a beach profile recorder, first used in the 1960s.

Air drops of men, craft and stores to the target area were also the subject of many SBS trials. The stores came first followed by the men.

Similarly, air drops of SBS personnel with inflatables were also trialled. The craft is packaged and attached to the man's body to be inflated upon hitting the water. This technique was used to drop men and equipment to the threatened *QE2* in mid-Atlantic

Meanwhile, canoes were also becoming faster, although there would be no replacement for the original manually paddled type on some clandestine missions.

After aircraft drops and submarine refinements, SBS added one more delivery system to its repertoire, using helicopters with RIBs (Rigid Inflatable Boats equipped with substantial outboard power) slung below and dropped close to the target, with operatives roping into their craft.

disrupted in any way, national economies could collapse, and Britain's in that pre-North Sea oil era more than most. That is why the Trucial States became a place of regular training and exercise for the SBS, and why British intelligence was so pleased when SBS Major H. B. Emslie, MC, left the service and turned up in a key role on the staff of the Sultan of Oman.

Emslie's knowledge of the Middle East and its territories was excellent. He was involved, it will be recalled, in the Alexandria mission at the time of King Farouk's departure and had kept in close touch since. Despite his departure from the British military, Emslie's position had obvious advantages, and there remained a fair degree of consultation and cooperation between the British government and the Sultan of Oman through the offices of Emslie himself.

It was he who tasked and coordinated yet another SBS recce of Kuwaiti beaches during further sabre-rattling from Iraq. Lieutenant Pentland and Sergeant Michie were dispatched to Kuwait in civilian clothes, made their way to the beach areas to make an up-to-date report of the situation, and produced brand-new charts and calculations taken entirely in a covert operation.

British expatriates in Oman were, by then, openly in collusion with a group of Omani sheikhs and aristocrats who were plotting a coup against the old sultan if he would not abdicate in favour of his son Qaboos. In July 1970 one of them walked into the sultan's office and demanded his retirement. Sa'id picked up the pistol from his desk and opened fire, wounding the rebellious sheikh, killing a palace servant and shooting himself in the stomach in the process. However, that night the sultan agreed to go and, with SAS protection, he was put on a RAF plane for England, where he died two years later.

It was around that time that military intelligence reconnaissance photographs appeared to show a group of terrorists in training in a remote region populated by primitive tribespeople bordering the Musandam Peninsula, close enough to the Strait of Hormuz to become a problem. The terrorists were thought to be Iraqi-trained guerrillas. Britain, anxious to shows its support for the new sultan, Qaboos, agreed to investigate and deal with the nest. The SBS Bahrain detachment was at the time engaged in beach recces on the east coast of the Trucial States, working from minesweepers not far from where the terrorists were thought to be encamped.

They received a signal from base commander in Bahrain instructing them to link up with an SAS squadron. The SBS, with its knowledge of the coast and inland terrain through its exercises in the region with 2 Para, were to carry out a beach recce before putting the SAS ashore and covering their backs. The rules of engagement were such that the officer commanding the SBS had orders to shoot anyone confronting his patrol.

Having completed the recces, the SBS detachment took the SAS ashore by Gemini inflatables. One suspect was shot during the landing and a member of the SAS squadron was killed soon afterwards during a night-time parachute drop into a valley surrounded by mountainous peaks. Once the SBS detachment had completed that phase it returned to Bahrain, although later Lieutenant Bagshaw and Sergeant Grant were called back to the Musandam Peninsula and spent several weeks with the SAS squadron patrolling the area, resupplying patrols by Gemini operating from Diba.

Oman was the scene of a further SBS deployment some time later during Operation Storm, which was conducted in association with the SAS at the opposite end of Oman's rambling terrain in the regions of Dhofar butting on to South Yemen at the coast and stretching up into indistinguishable borders with Saudi Arabia. The SBS detachment was deployed under the command of SAS B Squadron and, although initially brought in for beach landings, later joined fighting patrols and ambushes. In the same region the SBS joined the SAS on hearts and minds patrols, with two- and three-man teams travelling through the plains dispensing medical and other aid to villages and settlements.

But undoubtedly, throughout its time conducting operations off the coast of Oman, the most delicate tasks confronting the SBS were those concerning the Strait of Hormuz and a group of small islands at its mouth, which in the early 1970s were again under threat of disturbance. The British were playing piggy in the middle over the disputed ownership of the islands of Tunb and Musa, sited in a strategic position close to the Iran side of the strait. Iran and the Trucial States laid claim to them; Britain was courting both.

The SBS detachment was brought in for a recce, operating from a minesweeper patrolling the waters. Over several nights, SBS swimmers paddled to the islands and went ashore. Their orders restricted them to a recce; they were not to go inland, nor engage the occupants of the islands. The SBS men scrambled ashore; they collected their intelligence; they even heard voices in the close vicinity but did not investigate.

Three weeks later Iranian Special Forces occupied the two islands and, with the country still under the control of the Shah in those pre-Khomeini days, Britain had seemingly secured this vital route by proxy. Behind that manoeuvre lay another intriguing tale which would ultimately fall into the growing Middle East catalogue of lost causes.

The SBS association with Iran stemmed from a 1959 visit to Britain by the then Iranian defence minister. Britain continued to support the Shah of Iran, whose succession it had engineered, through thick and thin, in spite of mounting and widespread opposition to his regime. SBS links were destined to last for almost two decades, continuing on through the traumas of political upheaval in Iran and eventually ending in dramatic fashion. During his tour in 1959, the Iranian minister was brought to the SBS headquarters at Poole and was so impressed that he decided there and then that Iran should have a similar unit. Under British government policy of providing training packages for the military or police forces of friendly nations, SBS instructors went to Iran for five months in 1965.

From then until 1971, SBS teams were deployed to Iran twice a year for several months at a time, either to the diving school at Bandar-e Pahlavi on the Caspian Sea, or Bandar-e Abbas on the Gulf coast. The British team was tasked with selecting men from the ranks of the Imperial Iranian Navy for their Special Operations Group. They took them through a training routine similar to that established for British SBS courses, including exercises at Kharg Island for instruction on parachuting into water. In December 1969 30 Iranians were taken to Cyprus by SBS Lieutenant Richard Clifford, then the officer commanding 3SBD for additional training. That year, the Iranian government had formally approached the

British government to establish an armed forces training package, because the scheme provided by the Americans was not sufficient for their needs.

A British military assessment team visited Iran during one of the SBS training missions and agreed to formalise the arrangement. Among their needs was the formation of a commando unit with a Special Boat Section attached. In 1973 the SBS sent a team to help select officers and men for SBS and commando training in the UK. At the same time the Royal Marines Advisory Team helped form its new force. Iranian personnel who were to become the nucleus of the Iranian instructors were brought to Britain for training. SBS Colour-Sergeant Jonah Jones was given a two-year assignment in Iran as part of the Royal Marines Advisory Team, working at a new Iranian training camp at Bushehr on the Gulf coast of Iran.

Come the revolution, the association ended abruptly. Ayatollah Khomeini returned to Teheran in February 1979 and exiled the Shah. The British-trained Iranian SBS was, however, credited with rescuing and evacuating one of the Iranian princes. It was probably its last act. The Iranian SBS was identified with the shah and his political associates and allies. The SBS men were all thought to have been arrested after he fled the country, their fate unknown.

Within a year, Iran was in the grip of the Islamic revolution. A hundred hostages were trapped inside the American embassy in Teheran and became pawns in a long-drawn-out cat and mouse game that saw a disastrous rescue attempt by the crack US Delta Force crash-land in the desert. In London a month later, the SAS put its name in lights for ever with its spectacular assault on the Iranian embassy in Knightsbridge, killing four of the five gunmen who had held nineteen hostages for six days.

Back in the Gulf, in 1969, Lieutenant Clifford kept the detachment up to mettle with instructional sorties to Malta for training in deep diving, to Cyprus for parachuting into the sea and trials on dropping Gemini inflatables from aircraft, and to Singapore for jungle training.

Then, activity in the Middle East was all over. In 1971 the Conservative government of Edward Heath, continuing the policy laid down by his Labour predecessors, pulled the British out of the region. The Bahrain SBS detachment was tasked to cover the withdrawal from Bahrain based on the aircraft-carrier HMS *Albion* in November 1971.

It had barely left the Gulf, however, when India and East Pakistan began shouting at each other. HMS *Albion* was detached from the fleet to assist with the evacuation of British nationals from the Pakistan regions under threat of conflict with India. A large Union Jack was painted on the flight-deck as the aircraft-carrier arrived at speed, sailing the east coast of India. A cease-fire was negotiated in the meantime and an evacuation was not necessary. The SBS flew home . . . the end of an era, for them and the nation.

And also the beginning of a new phase.

PART THREE

A New Kind of War

1970 to the Present

Black September, 1970. Special Forces are on standby to make a storming entrance, but it is too late and perhaps, anyway, an impossible task without heavy loss of civilian life. Six days of tortuous negotiations and appalling conditions for 250 very frightened men, women and children trapped in hijacked aircraft climax in spectacular fashion . . . a huge pall of smoke and flames rises into the baking atmosphere as three airliners – British, Swiss and American – forced to land on a disused RAF airstrip in the Jordanian desert, are blown to bits by Palestinian terrorists. A fourth, a Pan American jumbo, is blown up in Cairo. The planes were taken in mass hijackings over northern Europe; 200 of the passengers were released before the explosions . . . Now frantic international efforts are being made to free the remaining 56 hostages still held by the terrorists. One of the gang, Leila Khaled, who was arrested on an El Al plane when it landed at Heathrow after another failed hijack attempt, is being held in London pending talks for an exchange.

The era of the terrorist . . .

CHAPTER FOURTEEN

To save a queen

First a brief look at events leading up to it. In the early months of 1971 the SBS began to take on a new shape, chameleon-like, to meet the current trends. It was forced into doing so. SBS attachment to colonialist battles that had one foot in the past and one in the future ended with almost shocking abruptness.

At the turn of the 1970s the face of the British military map changed beyond recognition, and for ever. Suez, Aden, Bahrain, Singapore . . . the withdrawals were all virtually complete, and soon Malta, too, under its new Socialist leader, Dom Mintoff, would scrap the defence pact with its old ally and look towards Libya and Colonel Gaddafi for friendship.

Most of the great military and naval associations with territories that formed part of the old empire were at an end, swiftly and determinedly and rightly severed during the six years of Harold Wilson's Labour government. All the classic areas of maritime and commando action, the backdrop to these pages so far, were consigned to history. Only Hong Kong and a few minor and far-flung outposts of colonialism remained, along with Gibraltar, which had also been the cause of perplexing moments in Whitehall in recent times: the borders with Spain were still closed; the Fascist dictator General Franco slammed the gates in June 1969 and offered all Gibraltar citizens Spanish nationality.

The locals, by and large, had no wish to give up their long and fruitful association with Britain: what would they do without Marks

& Spencer? Nor could Britain contemplate losing that most strategic and handy place at the entrance to the Mediterranean, and port of call to hundreds of thousands of matelots and tommies over the years. It also held a place of special significance for the SBS as the launch-pad of so many Second World War and post-war operations.

So 6SBS was deployed in its usual soft-footed fashion to hold the fort and generally have a good look around the coast to make sure Franco wasn't planning any other surprises, such as a sea-borne invasion or, perhaps, a blockade. This niggling dispute over Gibraltar had rumbled on intermittently for years and would continue until Franco died, and still occasionally resurfaces in the Spanish Parliament. The SBS connection with Gibraltar continues to this day. A large piece of rock was brought back to England by Richard Clifford to stand as a memorial to SBS men who lost their lives in action. Today, it is positioned at the entrance to the headquarters building at Poole.

Meanwhile, the unremitting chill of the Cold War and Soviet repression of any Eastern European nation that stepped out of line ensured the continued employment of the mass of British armed forces. Cuts would still be necessary. The declared policy of the Chiefs of Defence Staff in 1961 – 'Britain must be prepared to intervene in Asia and Africa . . . Her major military role over the next decade' – was dead and buried. The review of defence in the 1970s focused on the forces' commitments to Europe and NATO, defence against the Soviets, and what was termed a policy of strategic mobility – military or naval intervention if, when and where needed – to which the politicians would add, only when absolutely necessary. Cuts and more cuts were demanded as the troops piled home after that final splurge of 1960s activity.

Everything's changing, they were saying. Air power – that's the future. The foot-soldiers will be ambulance chasers, mopping up local difficulties. Fewer men, fewer ships, and the army mustn't go looking for trouble. It's all changing fast. And do we really need Special Forces? Both SAS and SBS found themselves in a tricky situation. They had nowhere "active" to do their stuff, no arena in which to score points or collect gongs. Not a single conflagration anywhere that might require the services of upfront raiders, saboteurs and beach recce experts. Or, at least, that's how matters appeared for a while – until terrorists and the IRA turned up the heat.

The SBS brought its sections home from the Far East and Bahrain and regrouped in Poole in new accommodation that had been designed to hold fewer sections. It found itself squeezed by a most unsatisfactory chain of command that ran through various levels of the Royal Marines and ended at a desk in the Ministry of Defence in London. If they wanted work they had to go and find it.

The SAS was promoting itself fiercely. Its last piece of action was in Dhofar in 1970, and when it ended there was nothing on the stocks, so it invented a new role for itself.

Back at its Hereford headquarters it drew up a list of important VIPs and heads of state around the world whose assassination would be against British interests. This the SAS took to London, to offer the Foreign Office, through the MoD, a unique service: it would train and equip bodyguards for these people, and Britain would be rewarded by the protected VIP with political or economic favours. In certain special or urgent cases, the SAS would itself provide the bodyguards until such time as local cover could be trained. A special house was built at headquarters for training purposes.

On a wider brief, the SAS could continue to offer training and instruction for Special Forces for the likes of the Sultan of Brunei, the Sultan of Oman or the Royal Family of Saudi Arabia, or wherever they might be needed – just as the SBS was already doing for the Shah of Iran. There were dozens of countries that would hire the SAS's services, given the opportunity, though it would become a matter of government policy as to who would be eligible for such a service.

Such training would be called Team Tasking, and it consisted of training packages devised by the Special Forces for the security forces or police forces of other friendly nations, generally to be carried out in these countries. Team Tasks were usually at the request of a foreign government and were subject to approval by the Ministry of Defence and ultimately the Cabinet. Nor were the SAS and the SBS the only forces offering this service. From the early 1970s it became a competitive business, with Special Forces of several Western countries competing for the business and more often than not managing to undercut the British charges.

Once government approval had been obtained, an advisory team would visit the host country to map out its needs. SBS training was sought by a number of countries prior to 1979, but by definition the only true team tasks were setting up the Australian commandos, creating the Malay Special Services Regiment in 1965, and training the Iranian SBS, which went on from 1965 to 1979. The SBS was not backward in looking for mainstream tasks either; it had to, or it wouldn't have survived. Successive officers commanding SBS secured operational work in the early 1970s largely through their own efforts and contacts rather than by way of orders from above.

They did, however, have a friend in a higher place or, as one who was there at the time put it, on the right hand of God. Colonel John Mottram, OBE, who had been in the SBS early in his career with Pat Troy, was by then in a senior position on the staff of the Commandant General, Royal Marines. He was in a position to influence the future of his former outfit.

This he would do by writing the SBS into a paper drumming up support for a counter-terrorist force (although that was some way into the future; at the beginning of the new decade, it was not even on the drawing-board, and no one guessed or contemplated the carnage that lay ahead). For the time being the SBS found itself taking on tasks that were different from anything it had tackled before; a wider brief took it into both civilian and military areas. The basic premise was the same, but the *modus operandi* was very different.

The first task that fell into the civilian category was a fairly small operation. The Bahamas police force had discovered evidence of a Cuban-based drugs- and arms-running ring operating from a remote part of the island of Andros. Britain was still responsible for the defence of the islands, which were just achieving independence from colonial rule. The approach to the area was such that it was beyond a safe landing for the ill-equipped policemen. An SBS detachment was sent to search the island. They discovered evidence of a shooting-range and also the skeleton of a US pilot who had crashed there. But no Cubans were found. On a second deployment to the Caribbean, in support of the Royal Barbados Police, 13 sacks of drugs, worth a considerable street value, were uncovered.

Next came an operation that would be tackled with the true panache, style and daring of an SBS pair, an SAS sergeant and a very courageous bomb-disposal expert, the story can now be told with the benefit of previously unpublished detail.

On 17 May 1972 the switchboard at the New York office of the British-owned Cunard Line received a telephone call at around 3.15 in the afternoon from an American, a mature male with a New York accent, asking to be put through to someone in charge. After explaining that he had vital information relating to the company's flagship and pride of Britain, the *QE2* – at that moment sailing across the Atlantic towards Britain – he was put through to Mr Charlie Dickson, Cunard's finance and operations director for North America.

The caller stated quickly and calmly that a series of six bombs had been placed aboard the ship, hidden in places that would never be found, on various deck levels. They would be exploded while the ship was at sea unless the sum of $350,000 in cash was paid by the following day.

He claimed to have two accomplices aboard the ship who did not care if they lived or died. One was an ex-convict and the other a terminal cancer case. They would detonate the explosives at a given time if the ransom demand were not met. He would make contact again later to make arrangements for the delivery of the money and warned Dickson not to go to the police. If the demand were not met, be assured the *QE2* would be blown out of the water. Then he rang off.

Dickson, a normally quiet and unflappable 58-year-old, was shaking slightly and his mouth was dry as he checked his watch. The *QE2* would be somewhere east of Newfoundland, heading for Cherbourg and then on to her home port of Southampton. There were 1,438 passengers aboard and around 850 crew. Immediately, he called Richard Patton, president of Cunard North America, and together they worked out a plan of action. New York City police were informed; they in turn brought in the FBI. Their advice was to treat the call seriously.

Bomb scares and security alerts in Britain were already becoming commonplace as IRA violence flared in Northern Ireland. Most were hoaxes and, at that time, the bombers had not yet struck on mainland Britain. Cunard themselves had already received a number of hoax calls concerning the *QE2*; nothing was ever found. This one was different – a New York voice that seemed to have nothing to do with politics or Ireland, and a ransom was being demanded, which was not normally the case in bomb scares. It could be a hoaxer, an almighty confidence trick, or it might be for real.

The FBI advised that the latter possibility should be taken as most probable and suggested the company arrange an immediate search of the ship without alerting passengers. Staff and crew should work on the basis that there were bombs on board which would be exploded if the money was not paid. Furthermore, the FBI advised, the money should be drawn in cash immediately and be available for the drop, as instructed by the caller.

The search of the ship was already under way. Charlie Dickson had wired the *QE2*'s master, Captain William Law, a cool-headed, gruff 60-year-old veteran, by coded message, briefly explaining the alert and ordering a search of the ship without alarming passengers. However, the task was virtually impossible in terms of speed or thoroughness – 13 decks, over 1,000 passenger cabins, miles of corridors, hundreds of nooks and crannies.

Scotland Yard was informed and began combing the passenger list for any suspicious names. Special Branch joined the inquiry, as did the Yard's bomb investigations specialists. The list was also wired to the FBI. All shore-to-ship calls were monitored for any coded message from the New Yorker to his supposed accomplices on board. But the bands played on, the games of bridge and the chat in the bar were uninterrupted, and in the evening the gala dinners went ahead as usual. Life remained apparently undisturbed on board, the passengers unaware of the drama unfolding around them.

Throughout the night, *QE2* staff continued their search. The following morning, Victor Matthews, chairman of Cunard, called an emergency meeting of his directors in London, and they agreed to follow the FBI's advice. The ransom money would be drawn from a New York bank ready for payment. Cunard also contacted the

Ministry of Defence, and the alert went all the way to the top: Prime Minister Edward Heath was informed.

The MoD put the SBS and the SAS on standby, along with the Royal Army Ordnance Corps (RAOC) bomb-disposal unit. Somehow, a team of experts had to be flown out to the *QE2*, equipped to deal with the bombs. There was no point in waiting to see if the continuing search of the ship turned up any or not. There could be an explosion at any minute. No one really knew for sure. By then, the *QE2* was around 1,500 miles from home. The only way to reach her was by air and a parachute drop of men and equipment into the sea – exactly the kind of operation the SBS had been training for in recent times.

At the Poole headquarters, SBS officer commanding, Major S. L. Syrad MC, RM, took the MoD call at around 11.35 on the morning of the eighteenth. It so happened that Lieutenant Richard Clifford, officer commanding 2SBS, was outside his door at the time. Syrad gave him brief orders: prepare to send two men by air to jump to a ship at sea. No name or location was given. Clifford decided he should go himself and collected as his number two Corporal Tom Jones. Dry diving-suits and parachuting equipment were prepared quickly by them, with a set for the explosives expert who would be joining them from the RAOC.

A Wasp helicopter was commandeered from the Royal Naval Air Service at Portland – not without some toing and froing, because operational codewords did not then exist for unscheduled covert movements in those days. In due course, however, the helicopter arrived at 1 p.m. and ferried the SBS team to RAF Lyneham. Flight Sergeant Terry Allen AFM, the SBS parachute jump instructor, was already at the air base preparing for the flight.

Back in New York, Charlie Dickson was in his office at first light waiting for the call. Like Richard Clifford, he had decided he would go himself, personally taking the cash to the blackmailer when he was told where to drop it. He sat back for a long wait . . .

The *QE2* sailed on . . . breakfast . . . elevenses . . . lunch . . . a quiet snooze in the library . . . a walk on the deck.. a bit of clay-pigeon shooting off the stern . . . and the officers and engineers were still searching.

At Lyneham, Richard Clifford and Tom Jones linked up with the demolitions officer, Captain Robert Williams, and Sergeant Cliff Oliver from the SAS. The four men still had no idea where they were going or which ship was involved – not an uncommon aspect of SBS tasking, as already seen. After a short delay, probably for ministerial clearance, the team boarded an RAF C130 Hercules and took off for what would be a four-hour flight to reach the ship. After 15 minutes aloft, the men were told their destination and what would be required of them. The Hercules was tracked by a Nimrod maritime reconnaissance aircraft.

One other member of the team on the sidelines was Flight Sergeant Geoff Bald, another parachute instructor. He had a particular mission: to give advice to Captain Williams, who never in his life had done any military parachuting, let alone into water – which, as any SBS man knows, is not a pleasant experience first time down, and especially into cold, rough and windswept Atlantic waters. Williams had previously completed only three static line jumps in freefall mode, which he hated.

They had around three hours of flying time to drill Captain Williams in parachuting without his actually doing it. It did not augur well for the operation when Williams announced that he did not feel too good. Geoff Bald tried to reassure him: 'Not to worry. You'll be all right by the time you reach the target.'

In New York Charlie Dickson was looking at his watch every five minutes. It was now 2.15 p.m. (local time) and he had not received a phone call. He was beginning to think the whole thing was an absurd hoax when his office door burst open and he was brought a hand-written letter that had just arrived by special delivery – 28 cents postage due! The letter instructed Mr Dickson to place the $350,000 in $10 and $20 bills in a blue canvas bag and proceed to a certain telephone booth on Route 299, two hours north of New York City, where he would receive a call giving him further directions. 'You will be watched,' the note read. 'Be alone. Any sign of police and you will have a catastrophe on your hands. Remember Hong Kong [an apparent reference to the old *QE* which had burned out in Hong Kong harbour the previous year].'

Dickson was instructed to arrive at the telephone box at 9.30 p.m.

If anything went wrong, the ship would blow within the hour. The FBI wanted to send an agent to make the drop. Dickson insisted that he went himself; he dare not, he said, risk the lives of 2,300 people.

The Hercules was half an hour off the target when the four men began final preparations for their drop. They had pulled on their dry suits. Captain Williams was still feeling decidedly unwell.

The plan was that the two NCOs would carry the bulk of the equipment, and Lieutenant Clifford would carry one smaller pack attached to his body by a line with a breaking point of 1,500 pounds (680 kilogrammes). His main task would be to talk Captain Williams through the drills in the air and to make sure he did not drown when they hit the water. The parachute used was a PX, whereby the parachutist has to remove his reserve, release the main buckle and clear his leg straps when 200 feet above the sea, so that he does not get dragged in the water.

'*Attention, please . . . attention . . . this is your captain speaking . . .*'

After-lunch snoozes and the games of bridge were halted as *QE2* master Captain Law ordered 'Stop engines!' and made his announcement to the passengers at 2.20 p.m. ship's time. 'We will shortly be taking procedures to check a report that there may be a bomb on board. We have already conducted a search of the ship and found nothing. The likelihood is fairly remote . . . However, we have to be certain. Very shortly we will be receiving the assistance of British bomb-disposal experts, who will be circling by RAF aircraft very shortly. They will be dropped into the sea and will be brought aboard. In the meantime, please try not to alarm yourselves . . .'

Crowds rushed back to their cabins to grab their cameras and line the deck railings. The games of bridge were abandoned, although one stubborn foursome at a crucial point in the game carried on with their hands. For the moment they could see nothing . . . the team had hit problems.

The cloud base was down to a variable 300 to 400 feet (90 to 120 metres) when the Hercules reached the *QE2*. The ship was not even visible from the safety of 1,000 feet (300 metres). The Nimrod, with all its radar and tracking communications, was close by, acting as the eyes and the link between the Hercules, the *QE2* and London. It was raining and the *QE2* reported a 20-knot (37-kilometre-per-hour) wind, with a long 5-foot (1.5-metre) swell running in the sea. Every one of those statistics – cloud base, wind and swell – were well outside the safety limits for jumps over water. Training manuals put cloud at a very minimum of 1,200 feet (365 metres). Their situation was not even half that safety margin; a jump from their height without clear sight below was not only unsafe but an impossibility; 1,000 feet (300 metres) was the minimum height allowed to ensure the operation of the reserve parachute in case of malfunction. This was especially important in the case of an inexperienced jumper – and their key man was one of those!

A brief conflab as the aircraft circled, flying blind through the cloud, and Flight Sergeant Terry Allen suggested a possible solution: if they first got underneath the cloud, the pilot could then open the throttle and climb rapidly, disgorging the para-drop team at the point of extra gravitational pull. Flight Sergeant Bald agreed that it could work; difficult, perhaps, and dangerous, but the only way to get them down into the water. The others agreed.

The huge plane was buffeting and banging in the turbulence. Captain Williams felt 'jolly sick', visibly green and 'scared to death'. He tried his best to look calm as the aircraft dipped below the cloud at around 350 feet (100 metres), a highly dangerous manoeuvre. Williams was barely able to look down when the expanse of water below him finally came into view.

The pilot made several dummy runs to test the plan before the first drop. The two NCOs, Tom Jones and Cliff Oliver, would go first, carrying the bulk of the bomb-disposal gear, parachuting blind in the cloud. They positioned themselves by the port door, with Flight Sergeants Allen and Bald standing by. The aircraft came around again to the drop zone, eased up to around 500 feet (150 metres), and then . . . nose up and throttle hard to climb to 800 feet (240 metres). As he did so – and only Tom Jones's words can describe the moment – 'on Sergeant Allen's command we forced ourselves through the port door against an exceptionally high gravitational force which I am positive lifted all four of us off the flight-deck. During descent we carried out the necessary drills and quickly hit the water, too damn near the bows of the ship for my liking. Although the sea was running a heavy swell, it was refreshing after so long in the plane.'

A *QE2* lifeboat set off to collect them, cameras whirring and clicking among the crowds lining the deck rails. Not an inch of viewing space was to spare.

Now, back again for the second drop, and as the Hercules pilot dipped low again Captain Williams threw up, every morsel of his stomach contents heaving forth. The Flight Sergeants were yelling last-minute instructions above the roar of the plane and the turbulence, and then . . . Go!

They made their jump on the next pass by the same process. Watching from the bridge of the *QE2*, Captain Law saw Williams land awkwardly and disappear under the water. Law was sure he had been injured. He bobbed back to the surface and appeared to be giving a signal. Lieutenant Clifford swam quickly to his side and held him afloat until the ship's lifeboat recovered them. The NCOs and their equipment were then hauled aboard, having been in the water for about ten minutes waiting for the other two to join them.

The team was taken aboard the *QE2*. Williams was not injured, explaining that he just felt bloody sick. They immediately reported to Captain Law on the bridge, who briefed them on what he had done so far. Captain Williams then took charge of the team and the situation. Before starting a search, Lieutenant Clifford presented Captain Law with the day's newspaper, which he had picked up on the way out of the SBS base.

The search was continued and a suspicious-looking case was blown open by Captain Williams. False alarm. Several passengers were also questioned, and two large and very heavy suitcases opened and examined. They were found to be crammed with books.

Charlie Dickson was now heading out on Route 299 to the telephone box where he was to receive further instruction on where to leave the $350,000. He reached it ten minutes before the appointed time. He waited. Disguised FBI agents were doing drive-bys. The phone rang at 9.40 p.m. and Dickson recognised the voice as the previous caller. He obviously knew that the police had been called in, and asked Dickson why he had done so – he had now put the lives of everyone on board the ship at risk.

Dickson said he had had no choice; his board of directors was involved, Cunard was a public company and he had to do it to get the money. The caller gave him further instructions. He was to drive to a small diner nearby and go straight to the washroom. There he would find a message taped underneath the washbasin. And, by the way, there would be three guns trained on him.

Dickson did as instructed. He found the message, which directed him to one more place, a deserted area further down the road. He would there discover a marker where he should leave the bag. Once the money had been received without incident, the message said, then a call would be made to the *QE2* enabling the bombs to be disarmed.

The instructions were followed to the letter. Dickson dropped the bag by the marker and drove off. The FBI remained on hand, discreetly and clandestinely.

On the *QE2*, Captain Williams and his team had found no trace of bombs, and by the early hours of the morning they were given a meal and a stiff drink, provided with cabins and began the two-day journey to Cherbourg in first-class order. *En route* they continued their checks and searches, and when that was done were entertained lavishly by grateful passengers. 'Their hospitality was embarrassing at times,' said Tom Jones, 'especially the Americans. But it was nice to see how much our efforts had been appreciated.'

The FBI was still not convinced that the call was a hoax and suggested that the ship be evacuated immediately it reached Cherbourg. In the event, that was not enacted. Twenty-four hours later the bag containing the cash was still where Charlie Dickson had left it, watched by the FBI. All shore-to-ship calls were blocked until the *QE2* docked.

She sailed on to Southampton. No bombs or any devices were ever found, and Charlie Dickson never heard from the extortionist again. The bag was picked up as soon as the *QE2* reached Cherbourg. No bombs were ever found but the caller's threat had caused a four-man team to display considerable courage in jumping into the sea to get to the ship. Each of them was awarded the Queen's

Commendation for Brave Conduct. Lieutenant Clifford was also nominated the Royal Navy Man of the Year for both the *QE2* affair and his first successful crossings of the Atlantic in his own 26-foot (7.9-metre) yacht.

As for Captain Williams: 'I never want to go through anything like that ever again.' For the SBS, however, the exercise proved to be merely a prelude to another alert aboard the *QE2* – one that would require a force of 30 of its top men to handle.

Chapter Fifteen

And again . . .

Terrorists and extremists were already a reality in the United Kingdom and their activities spread across the world. Bombs and bullets soon began to shatter the lives of ordinary folk, far from any theatre of war or place of conflict, pursuing their daily lives in all innocence. And now terrorism blazes out from the television in the corner of the living-room: war on the doorstep, watched in the home.

The irony of this new twist for the military and the intelligence gurus to wrestle with was nowhere more plain than in Britain itself, and they were at last confronting it, if tenuously, by using the Special Forces. The *QE2* mission became an operational model for the future. It was dissected, and lessons were noted and redrawn into a contingency plan which would be activated for any future attacks on ships or in coastal waters by terrorists or other insurgents. It was a prophetic move. Variations on the same theme would soon be much in demand for anti-ship attacks and, more especially, for counter-terrorist activity when the oil-rigs began to mushroom in the North Sea. And if any doubts remained as to the need for Special Forces and rapid-action teams, ready to respond to any situation, anywhere in the world, the *QE2* operation and the events of the next few months would dispel them once and for all.

Urban guerrillas and bands of extremists were in their embryonic formation across Europe and the Middle East: Black September, Bader-Meinhoff, Red Brigades, IRA and PLO to name but a few. It was almost two years since the four airliners were blown up in Jordan and, in the aftermath, all Palestinians were expelled by King Hussein. Anniversary trouble was anticipated, but the Germans were not adequately prepared for the way it was to be marked – by Palestinians causing death and mayhem among the 10,000 international athletes at the 1972 Munich Olympic Games. As an exercise in how *not* to handle such a situation, this one, supervised by German security forces with politicians in close direction, was a classic.

At dawn on 5 September a group of eight Black September Arab guerrillas broke into the Israeli building in the Olympic Village. The Germans had been tipped off in advance to expect some form of attack and had 250 plain-clothes police patrolling the area. None of them saw the Arab invaders dressed in black scale the fence.

They burst into the Israeli building with sub-machine-guns blazing at 5.10 a.m. Moshe Weinberg, a wrestling coach, was killed instantly; Yosef Romano, a weightlifter, was fatally wounded as he held a door shut while two of his team-mates escaped through the window. Another 15 also escaped through the windows and side-doors. Ten were taken hostage, but one of them, Gad Tsabari, suddenly made a dash for freedom, weaving in and out and dodging bullets to escape.

The guerrillas remained holed up in the building with their nine remaining hostages. They demanded the release of 200 Palestinians held in Israeli jails and a safe passage out of Germany. Within hours the Olympic Village was surrounded by 12,000 police. The games were suspended and the remaining Israeli team members prepared to leave Munich because security measures were blatantly inadequate. With the world looking on through intense television coverage, West German Chancellor Willy Brandt arrived to take personal charge of negotiations with the terrorists. There were dramatic televised pictures of German officials talking to the guerrilla leader, who was wagging his finger at them while dictating terms.

Brandt and his advisers agreed that the terrorists would be allowed to leave Germany with their hostages and fly to an Arab country. They were taken by helicopter to the Fürstenfeld military airport 25 miles from Munich. Just before midnight the guerrillas and their nine remaining Israeli athletes began to walk across the tarmac to a waiting Boeing 727 aircraft. They had walked about half-way when suddenly all the airport lights were turned out and German police marksmen opened fire.

The rescue attempt went tragically wrong. In the ensuing gun battle all nine hostages were killed, along with four Arabs and one German policeman. Three Arabs were captured, and the other just ran away and escaped. Just over a month later the Black September group struck again, two of them armed with pistols and grenades hijacking a Lufthansa Boeing 727 over Turkey. The terrorists demanded the release of their three comrades held after the Olympic Games débâcle. Germany gave in and did as requested to avoid further bloodshed and another disaster like the one at Munich, about which they were roundly criticised.

Everyone, from governments to airlines and any organisations involving the gathering of large numbers of people, had the jitters as a world-wide terrorist campaign gained momentum, joined eventually by other groups, other extremists, and a supporting cast which included Colonel Gaddafi and assorted Arab leaders based in Beirut.

For Black September, another possible target was already moving into view – the *QE2*, with perhaps as many as 1,500 Jews on board. On 19 October 1972 it became known that the ship had been chartered by Mr Oscar Rudnick, president of Assured Travel, Worcester, Massachusetts, specifically to carry Jews from America and Europe to Israel for the celebrations of the twenty-fifth anniversary of the Jewish state the following April.

Originally billed in low-key fashion as an 'Easter and Passover' cruise, the trip provided the opportunity of joining the *QE2* at Southampton, sailing to Haifa for a ten-day stop, then returning to Southampton. Alternatively, passengers could join the ship in Haifa. The population of the ship would be almost entirely Jewish. In fact, the trip was just one of a number of international cruises being organised from various countries.

The cruise received a large number of bookings, substantially from the US, and Rudnick was anticipating that the ship would be full when she eventually sailed. However, after the Black September attack on the Olympics, a particularly active union convenor for *QE2* workers, Joe Allan, went public over a situation that Cunard had hoped to keep the lid on, at least for the time being. He made a press statement claiming that the intended Jewish cruise posed a threat to his members, who were likely to be killed in the event of a terrorist attack, and said that in view of Munich his workers would want danger money – or they would not go aboard.

Cunard made it clear that it had thought things through and had decided to go ahead with the cruise. The fact was that since all *QE2* sailings were planned and scheduled well in advance, the company had long ago contacted the Ministry of Defence for discussions. These had reached ministerial level and were put in the hands of a committee led by the Commandant General's Chief of Staff, Royal Marines, who in turn reported to the Joint Operations Committee chaired by Prime Minister Edward Heath.

It was with the Munich disaster fresh in public focus that security arrangements for the *QE2* and her passengers was planned. Assessments of the likelihood of terrorist action presented a gloomy scenario – that Black September, specifically, was planning to infiltrate the cruise for an on-board attack or, possibly, to raid the ship by sea or air. To this threat was added a later interjection by Colonel Gaddafi, who stated bluntly that the *QE2* would be blown out of the water.

Edward Heath and his ministers laid down the policy that became the adopted stance throughout the coming decade of terrorist attacks and on into the 1980s and the IRA atrocities: that British life, institutions and commerce would not be cowed by such threats or even attacks. Cunard's chairman Victor Matthews (later Lord Matthews from a life peerage awarded during Margaret Thatcher's premiership) agreed, but obviously needed more protection than he could muster from his own security resources or private organisations.

Although Cunard had themselves introduced sophisticated security screening since the bomb threat a year earlier, only the military could mount an adequate defence or deterrent against possible terrorist attack or action by Gaddafi-backed raiders. Cunard therefore formally asked the MoD to arrange the cover, for which the shipping line would make a payment towards costs.

An operations officer from the security service and Major D. A.

Pentland, the officer commanding the Special Boat Company – as it was then called – set about planning the operation. It was significant in one other major and sensitive area: it would bring the Special Forces under the media microscope for the first time and in a manner that was totally new to them. Lessons and precautions would be learned in that direction, too, leading quite quickly to what became the established code of secrecy surrounding all future SBS and SAS operations, and about the forces themselves.

In the months leading up to the cruise, a plan was devised and rehearsed. Apart from discreet naval and air cover to accompany the *QE2* when she sailed out of Southampton, there would also be a large covert contingent of SBS personnel aboard the ship. The planning and the nature of that presence was, as one might expect, governed by strict security. It would entail 30 well-armed and well-equipped SBS travelling on the ship throughout the cruise to provide continual on-board, surface and underwater surveillance. Their cover story was that they were trainee Cunard travel agents, a device which in the face of media scrutiny was later accepted as being a touch naive.

Sending any group of Special Forces into operations where they were supposed to fade unobtrusively into the civilian population was quite new. To achieve that objective, the men had to adopt the appearance of ordinary everyday citizens, with long 1970s-style hair and stylish civilian clothes. True enough, in covert beach recces in Cyprus and the Middle East SBS operatives had often disguised their military origins, but never in their home base or in this manner. The sudden appearance of SBS ranks wandering around with shoulder-length hair, coloured sweatshirts, flared trousers and sneakers caused a stir among the Royal Marines at Poole. In fact, it became the uniform of the future.

The operational plans were submitted to the Chiefs of Staff and finally approved on 30 March 1973, two weeks before the cruise began. The force commander, Major Pentland, was himself under direct command of the MoD's Director of Operations, Central. Each member of the team would carry a pistol at all times, generally a Browning 0.38 automatic. This was to be hidden in their clothing, with each carrying an underarm holster. The SBS also devised a crotch holster made of suede leather for use when the men were wearing shorts.

Their general equipment – always a feature of any SBS operation – included Sterling sub-machine carbines, rocket-launchers, explosives, their own communications radio for secure signals, and their diving gear. They would be going over the side at regular intervals to check the hull of the ship for bombs. Finally, the briefing gave Major Pentland open-ended rules of engagement – to take whatever measures were necessary in the event of an attack.

On 15 April the planes carrying American Jews who were to join the cruise began arriving at Heathrow. By then, their numbers had been dramatically reduced by cancellations. The original anticipated 1,500 passengers was now down to around 650, and the organisers stood to lose a fortune. They were ferried by coaches under strict security and police escort to Southampton to join the British passengers. The Ocean Terminal was surrounded by police and soldiers. The media focused on the new phenomenon of the security checks that would soon become a way of life in Britain, whether in airport terminals, department stores or theatres. All luggage was searched, hand baggage checked and passengers frisked with electronic scanners.

Very little had passed into public domain about the extent of the military cover involved other than the statement that the *QE2* would be shadowed by an RAF Nimrod and other long-range aircraft along with escort ships of the Royal Navy, including one capable of launching guided missiles.

John Penrose was among the small army of Fleet Street journalists who joined the cruise. He reported:

> It was a curious feeling. After all the drama of getting aboard, and passing through nine separate security checks, the ship itself was eerily silent, a virtual ghost ship. With so few passengers, corridors and bars were deserted. Bands played to almost empty rooms. Waiters stood about idly. And the ironic line in the brochure promising "excitement and adventure" had taken on a rather sinister meaning. Apart from that, we knew that there were men of the Royal Marines on board, and

that frogmen had been diving underneath to check for explosives, but their presence was especially unnoticeable.

The *QE2* sailed away with an escort of small craft seeing her off, including Prime Minister Heath in his newly launched ocean racer, *Morning Cloud*. As for the SBS, they performed their drills and recces according to plan, while up above the Nimrod appeared at critical points for overhead surveillance. The ship made one call at Lisbon, where the SBS divers once again checked for limpet mines, and then sailed into the Mediterranean, where the American 6th Fleet joined the watch. As she neared Haifa, security was tightened again. The SBS men were on permanent watch, and the Israelis provided two heavily armed escort ships at the 50-nautical-mile limit from their coast.

The journey, with its subdued and rather nervous passengers, passed without incident, and the *QE2* sailed into Haifa, where she remained berthed for ten days. This period was, perhaps, the most critical of the entire journey for the SBS team, now working in cooperation with Israeli security forces under the direction of Mossad. They were prepared for every possible eventuality, all types of attack.

One Israeli general in charge of Haifa took objection to this. His complaints, recorded in an article in the *Daily Telegraph* by R. Barry O'Brien, were that security had been too tight and over the top. Many people had been scared off what had been a wonderful project, he said, all because of the 'tremendous exaggeration' of security needs by Cunard and the British government. Within a matter of months he would be eating his words as terrorist atrocities were unleashed around the world in an unprecedented manner – including a sea-borne attack on Haifa itself. There, raiders in inflatables came ashore just south of the harbour, hijacked three buses travelling along a coast road, and killed 30 passengers and wounded 80 others.

The general's outburst, however, led London journalists who stayed for the duration, and bereft of action, to take a glance at the security cover. Some indication of Special Forces on board had been leaked by a drunken marine who spoke Arabic and had been brought along only as an interpreter. The day the return voyage began, R. Barry O'Brien ran a further story, this time in the *Sunday Telegraph.* Under the headline '*QE2* Agents Uncovered', he announced that a party of 'armed British soldiers playing James Bond roles as plain-clothes marksmen are changing their cover for the return journey'. On the way out they posed as travel agents; now they were booked in as individual tourists.

The *Sunday Telegraph* editor, was prevailed on by the MoD not to publish more of O'Brien's copy, because doing so might have endangered a particular source of intelligence in Libya. This indicated that Colonel Gaddafi had drawn up plans to launch a missile attack from two motor torpedo-boats as the ship passed the north coast of Libya. The SBS informed the *QE2* master, Captain Mortimer Hare, a veteran of Second World War Atlantic convoys. He quite coolly said he would run the ship up to maximum speed, and was quite sure that he could easily outpace the MTBs if ever they appeared. A Nimrod circled overhead to keep watch, but Gaddafi's boats didn't show up. Nor, on this occasion, did Black September, although they would not be dormant for long, and any lingering doubts about 'over-the-top' security would be totally dispelled. There was no doubt that without the cover the *QE2* was a sitting duck.

The catalogue of terrorist attacks and hostage-taking beginning in the 1970s and extending into the 1990s has been written into history, including the infamous raid by a pro-Palestinian gang on OPEC oil ministers meeting in Vienna in December 1975. They seized 70 hostages, including 11 ministers and the powerful Sheikh Yamani of Saudi Arabia although they were later freed. That same month, by coincidence, the SBS was tasked to begin planning protective cover for yet another cruise on the *QE2*, again in the direction of Israel. Called The Cradle of Civilisation Cruise, it was scheduled to call at Alexandria and Haifa in March 1976, this time with many more passengers.

Taking lessons from the first cruise and, in the intervening years, intensive training on maritime counter-terrorist exercises, the SBS this time, planned a different approach. They used a two-pronged cover: an overt force, wearing Cunard uniforms, provided an obvious if discreet guard, while other SBS men went in plain clothes as tourists mingling with other passengers. All were permanently armed. There was also a careful selection of personnel, using five officers and ten NCOs. Three SBS wives even went along as part of the husbands' cover. They had with them, too, a clearance diver who made regular inspections of the hull. The operation has gone into the SBS archives as a meticulous example of planning and execution which left nothing to chance. It was, curiously enough, also regarded by some of those who took part in it as a tiring (and tiresome) engagement which required long hours of attentive surveillance which, in the end, became 'rather boring'. That could hardly be said of some of the training and operations which confronted the SBS closer to home as they prepared to meet the growing terrorist threat and IRA bomb attacks on the British mainland.

CHAPTER SIXTEEN

Counterforce

The SBS have maintained an intermittent presence in Northern Ireland since 1971 and are still there as these words are being written. Typically, they have kept a low profile and have managed to avoid the critical broadsides launched against the SAS during their time in the province. In spite of medals and commendations won, the SBS has remained out of public view and rarely mentioned in the welter of published and televised material on their counterparts of the SAS or other military and intelligence agencies in the Six Counties during the last 30 years.

Their role in Northern Ireland fell principally into two categories: first, to provide personnel for covert intelligence-gathering and for patrols on the streets, and, secondly, in their more conventional mode of sea-borne operations against gun-runners and terrorists. Admittedly, their strength there has never been high in terms of numbers, and the overwhelming media focus on the SAS was bound to follow by the very nature of the regiment's history. From its origins in desert warfare, running ahead of the charging herd, dropping in on an enemy nest, stirring up trouble behind enemy lines, and dominated by hard-man NCOs, the SAS operated in a manner once described by an American general who served with it for a time as 'soldiering turned upside-down, resembling no military organisation I had ever known'. The unit's arrival in Northern Ireland aroused both indignation and fear and was likened by one commentator as the intelligence equivalent of putting tanks on the streets.

Both SBS and SAS came to Ireland direct from their wars in faraway places. The familiar dark murderous back-streets and alleys in the Middle East and swamp battles with Communist guerrillas in Borneo were replaced with inner-city streets and ambush action in lush countryside within the United Kingdom.

SAS and SBS alike were confronted by a situation for which there was no reference section in the Special Forces handbook, i.e. confrontation from within its own civilian population. The hearts and minds of the natives of Borneo or Dhofar they could handle. Northern Ireland was a different ball game. They were unused to the disciplines of war on the streets, running side by side with the masses, going about their daily lives, surrounded by the fervour of multi-dimensional political, religious and paramilitary activists. Nor had the SAS ever faced the experience of prolonged and intense local media scrutiny that came with those disciplines. No one paid much attention to them in Oman or Sarawak!

Says one former SBS officer:

> As everyone knows, the mystique and mythology that surround the Special Forces always existed. Modern controversiality, however, really emanates from the 1970s Northern Ireland experience. Until that time, the SAS – and certainly the SBS – went about their business relatively unscrutinised by the media and largely devoid of widespread public interest. The stories then were of military prowess or unconventional attitudes, and not of trigger-happy maladroits, as the SAS have lately been portrayed. Military response to Northern Ireland and modern terrorism provided the basic ingredients for controversial insight, but a particular, underlying reason for the phenomenon which opened a window upon Special Forces is often overlooked. Here, for the first time, they would be confronted by urban terrorism and anarchy among their own people, British civilians, white English-speaking faces, armed to the hilt. For both SAS and SBS it was a completely new situation. They came to Northern Ireland from the deserts and the mountains of the Middle East. I'm not sure we were either adequately prepared or briefed, at the beginning, to handle it. One school

> of thought reckoned that coming fresh to it was just what was needed, battered, day in and day out, as the province was, by extremist outrages. No one mentioned either, incidentally, that we would also face political shenanigans and dirty tricks from our own side in those early days which we, I know, tried to steer clear of. We were sideways on to the rivalries that existed within a very crowded intelligence arena. Very dirty stuff. We were dragged in. That's not an excuse. It's a fact. What happened after that ran in with established policy of Her Majesty's Government. There were risk-takers and even renegades among us, of course, and we have always had them. But 99 per cent of the time we moved and operated within the parameters which were set for us, no more and no less, against an enemy who showed no desire for constraint.

SAS involvement and activity in the Six Counties, not undeservedly, became the subject of acres of published material. The SAS has been blamed for many things, some of which happened but not all at the hands of the SAS. The torture of terrorists arrested at the time of the introduction of internment cast the SAS as the main perpetrators, although no SAS unit was serving in Northern Ireland at the time. Their fire power remains indisputable, however, and gave rise to the rumours of shoot-to-kill rules of engagement – between 1971 and 1990 more than two dozen extremists were shot in SAS operations.

The involvement of the SBS goes back to those early terrible, turbulent times, racked with unprecedented violence and killings. Riots flared across the province after the imposition of internment under new emergency powers. In four days that summer, 5,000 Catholics and 2,000 Protestants were made homeless when their properties were burned to the ground. Daily, the death toll mounted from bomb attacks and sniper fire.

The SBS entered this unhappy place in a year that extremist action in Northern Ireland claimed 467 lives, the peak figure for any single year during the modern troubles. Its men were to join a new reconnaissance unit, which was formed on the back of a heady atmosphere of bravado and determination to tackle sectarian violence and anarchy.

The men found themselves swimming in waters muddied by confusion, myth and lies. Law and order in the province had virtually collapsed. The battle to restore them was one in which a misty blur posed as truth. It was the time of an emerging internecine warfare between the two principal non-military intelligence agencies, MI5 and MI6. Meanwhile, the Royal Ulster Constabulary's Special Branch and officers of British Military Intelligence were running their own operations and agents with little coordination between each other.

Plot and counter-plot, dirty tricks and dangerous liaisons were to become rife within a British security effort that was supposed to be fighting terrorists but spent a good deal of time setting traps for each other. Gerald Seymour wrote a novel called *Harry's Game* which was nearer the truth than any of the stories peddled and planted by MI5's media leakage department or characters on the make or with a personal axe to grind.

In the spring of 1971 the SBS was required to send a small number of men for a particular mission: to become part of the Military Reaction Force (MRF), formed as a direct response from political pressure to improve intelligence-gathering. The MRF would put soldiers on the streets of Northern Ireland in civilian clothes to carry out covert and clandestine operations against the IRA.

The MRF was not an SAS unit. It was attached to the 39th Infantry Brigade, and was created by Brigadier (later General) Frank Kitson, Commander of Land Forces, Northern Ireland, from 1970 to 1972, a veteran of the campaign against Mau Mau terrorism in Kenya in the 1950s and later one of the planners of military action involving the SAS in Oman. He attempted to apply some of the same principles used in both those operations to Northern Ireland. Principally, he was to set up a unit that would use all measures of covert activity available to track and identify the bombers and the terrorists. Kitson's most famous coup in Kenya, and copied in Oman, was to turn members of the Mau Mau and use them against their former comrades. He proposed this technique as the basis of the new unit, with soldiers in civilian clothes actively courting ex-IRA members or their supporters – known as 'freds' –

to act as spotters and informers to identify active IRA personnel.

They would be photographed by the MRF using concealed camera equipment in unmarked patrol cars. Once identified, they would be entered into the picture files for future surveillance. Among the many other schemes devised to glean intelligence was their infiltration of a massage parlour. Another base for covert operations was the Four Square Laundry, on the surface an ordinary laundry but in fact fronting a forensic laboratory in which clothes brought in were tested for traces of explosives or other incriminating material.

This method of intelligence-gathering was regarded as particularly effective. Addresses from which clothing containing suspect elements was collected were noted and filed and the occupants clandestinely photographed and monitored. Some were among those raided in Operation Motorman in the summer of 1972, when 12,000 troops moved in to smash Ulster's no-go areas, principally in Belfast, Londonderry and small towns designated by Republican leaders as Free Ulster.

The existence of the MRF remained unknown to the public at large, even when two of its members compromised it after opening fire from a moving car with a Thompson sub-machine-gun on two men standing at a bus-stop in Belfast. The two MRF soldiers were arrested and charged with attempted murder. They were later acquitted, stating that they were fired on first. The date of the shooting was 22 June 1972, the very day on which Mr William Whitelaw, Secretary of State for Northern Ireland, revealed that the government would respond favourably to the offer of a ceasefire by the Provisional IRA. MI6, which had helped set up the talks, were furious that their efforts had been jeopardised.

In any event, the ceasefire, tenuous from the outset, was abandoned within the month, on 21 July, when 11 people were killed and 130 injured in IRA bomb attacks in Belfast. The MRF, with its SBS contingent, was finally betrayed by one of its informers, who had turned back to the terrorists. On 2 October 1972 the IRA ambushed the apparently innocent-looking van from Four Square Laundry, killing the driver and wounding his companion. Both were, of course, soldiers in civilian clothes and members of the MRF forensic collection unit. The MRF was disbanded soon afterwards.

Though it had been criticised for some of its more questionable operations, its demise undoubtedly dented the intelligence capability of the security forces, especially in accumulating knowledge from the no-go areas and the so-called Republican ghettos. Towards the end of 1973 a new unit, 14 Intelligence and Security Company, was formed to fill the void, and the SBS now sent ranks to that unit. Fourteen Company also operated under cover names of 4 Field Survey Troop and Northern Ireland Training and Tactical Team.

Again this was not an SAS unit, although it was placed under the command of Captain Julian 'Tony' Ball, who had come from the ranks of the Parachute Regiment and the SAS before gaining his commission in the King's Own Scottish Borderers. His experience in covert operations in Northern Ireland was considered first class, having set up the first covert observation post in the Republican areas of Belfast.

Ball's second-in-command was Lieutenant Robert Nairac, a Grenadier Guardsman and product of Sandhurst and the army's joint intelligence college at Ashford, Kent. Nairac had volunteered for special duties and, like all members of the detachment, had joined special training in which SAS and SBS instructors were used. Operationally, the men were equipped with unmarked Q-cars and had available non-standard weapons, such as Ingram submachine-guns with silencers, folding shotguns, small arms, cameras and an array of electronic surveillance gear.

Operations were testing even for SBS and SAS veterans. They could be lying in surveillance for hours or days at a time, or following one man for weeks. They drove around in well-used cars with hidden radios, their small arms carefully out of sight. The recollections of one, operating in 1974, sets the scene:

> On my second Sunday night I went out in an old Vauxhall Viva driven by Taff, who'd been around a long time and knew the place backwards. We each had a Browning, and I put mine on my lap hidden by a copy of the *News of the World*. We stopped at traffic lights; two youths were standing in a doorway clocking traffic. They rushed forward and yanked Taff's door

> open. 'Get out of the car,' he screamed, 'or I'll blow your fucking head off.' His right hand was inside his bomber jacket. I thumbed the safety catch on my pistol and looked at him. Where was his shooter? Show me your shooter, you bastard. I couldn't do anything. If he was unarmed, I'd be up for murder. I glanced at the other, still standing there. To shoot or not to shoot? Taff took the decision for me. 'Fuck off, you wanker,' he said, and pulled the door towards him and smashed it back into the youth. Then Taff was off, screeching the car on the wrong side of the road . . . I radioed in . . . and realised I was shaking. This was a different type of fear than in Oman. This wasn't nervous tension, followed by the old adrenalin rush . . . This was sudden shock. I'd been close, very close, to appearing in the dock on a murder charge.

On 16 January 1975 the IRA ended its Christmas ceasefire. Six days earlier one of the commanders of the Provisional IRA, John Francis Green, had been shot in an isolated farmhouse in County Monaghan, where he was taking a Christmas break. The IRA blamed the SAS. Some years later Captain Fred Holroyd, an intelligence officer of the Royal Corps of Transport, and several investigative journalists would claim that Green was shot by Captain Ball and Lieutenant Nairac, accompanied by two unnamed NCOs from 14 Intelligence Company. They burst into the farmhouse and opened fire, then Ball took Polaroid pictures of the body before they left. According to Tim Pat Coogan, in his book *The Troubles*, 'MI6 had engineered the truce; MI5 wanted it broken down'.

Ball and Nairac were unable to answer this oft-disputed claim. They were both dead by then. Tony Ball returned to the SAS in 1975 and left the service two years later with the rank of lieutenant-colonel to command the Special Forces of the Sultan of Oman. He was killed in a car crash in Dhofar in 1978, at the age of 38, and was subsequently transferred to the place where most SAS end up – their own burial ground at Hereford.

Nairac, more famously, was a victim of the IRA. On 14 May 1977, by then a captain, he was kidnapped by the Provisionals while on a covert operation in South Armagh, lured from the bar of The

Three Steps public house at Drummintree. After a massive 48-hour search by troops and police discovered only his damaged and blood-stained Triumph Dolomite, the Provisional IRA announced that Nairac had been arrested, interrogated (meaning tortured) and executed. They claimed that he was an SAS man, which was untrue, although by then a number of SAS men had joined SBS in 14 Intelligence Company.

By the time of Nairac's death, the SAS were in Northern Ireland in strength. On 7 January 1976 Prime Minister Harold Wilson announced that the 22 SAS Regiment would supply a squadron for patrol and surveillance. The statement was treated with derision within Ulster and by a number of British journalists, who claimed that the SAS had 'always been there, shooting and killing at will'. In those confused days, the MRF and 14 Intelligence Company had no lines of distinction. They were all engaged in covert operations and as such were branded as SAS regardless. The demarcation lines were further blurred when 14 Intelligence Company and its SBS contingent was brought under a new joint command with the SAS, known as Intelligence and Security Group. It was this renamed unit that Robert Nairac was attached to when he was captured by the IRA.

The arrival of the SAS was meant to be a public relations exercise on Wilson's part. It was in response to a recent spate of killings, the deaths of 49 British soldiers in the South Armagh border area with the Republic of Ireland, and mounting criticism of the government's failure to curb months of anarchy. What Wilson's announcement also meant, but did not say, was that the military was changing its method of intelligence-gathering.

From then on the SAS became the subject of intense focus and criticism, which the SBS managed to avoid, although it continued to operate within the intelligence-gathering community and later jointly on operations with the SAS.

By the time the SAS arrived in force in 1976, the main body of SBS was continuing with its more traditional business off the coast of Northern Ireland. The SBS was a natural contender to beat the gun-runners. Coastline recces for possible landing-points were carried out and have been constantly updated ever since. A number of ships suspected of carrying guns and explosives were tracked and intercepted, but by far the greater activity of the SBS from the mid-1970s was focused on the area exclusively devoted to their talents – anti-terrorism at sea, which was not especially to do with the IRA.

In 1975 the SBS was written into plans for a new and, for them, exciting Maritime Counter-Terrorist Force, which was formed specifically to guard against international terrorism raging out of control across Europe and the Middle East. The emphasis everywhere was on security, intelligence and prevention. Special government committees were formed jointly with the Home Office and the Foreign Office to coordinate a combined military and civilian strategy covering everything from day-to-day security on British streets to airports, shipping terminals and sensitive installations.

The SBS would participate in providing a prompt reaction to terrorism involving ships, harbours and coastal installations. Most of all, Britain's mushrooming and lonesome oil-rigs of the North Sea were believed to be particularly vulnerable. The Royal Marines were tasked to provide a series of anti-terrorist reaction forces. These were divided initially into three groups: a detachment of marines who were on two hours' notice to move (NTM), an SBS section at four hours' NTM, and a rifle company at twenty-four hours' NTM.

The only dedicated force was the SBS section 1SBS; the others were to be raised on a rotation basis, although as the number of oil-rigs grew this was found to be an unsatisfactory arrangement as the task was extremely specialised and would require a dedicated force with its own command and control team, intelligence group and support team.

The SBS was involved in many training operations and experiments for the new force. They perfected greater efficiency of dropping to a target at sea from an RAF C130 or helicopter, parachuting teams with their Gemini inflatables as close as possible to the target zone without being spotted. The Geminis would be secured to platforms; inside would be packed their equipment, weapons, engine fuel and outboard motor, all in waterproof bags and all secured by a ring-main of rope. The team, parachuting separately, would, on landing, cut free the ring-main so that the platform and the engine packing would sink, then put the engine in place, load their weapons and set off for their target.

Fresh work was also carried out on the exit and re-entry of SBS men from submarines while at sea and while submerged. Many weeks of coordinated planning were needed to perfect the system because of the inherent dangers of releasing divers through a time-consuming system of breathing connections from the moment they moved into the five-man chamber in the submarine through which they would make their exit and, once outside, release their boats, equipment and weapons from housing units on the casing before finally making their way to the surface.

Delivering anti-terrorist forces by submarine was a favoured method in the Joint Theatre Plan for a clandestine approach of an occupied oil-rig, particularly if a huge rough swell were running in the North Sea. However, there were only three submarines in the British Navy fitted with five-man exit and re-entry chambers. SBS training officers were quick to point out that if such a task occurred, and there was no five-man-chamber boat available, how would they get the men near enough for a really clandestine method of entry? And if two of the five-man-chamber boats were otherwise engaged, only four men could be carried to the target rig.

What could four men do? Captain Neil Johnstone dreamed up a system of breathing apparatus and air-bottles on the casing that would allow the multi-release of up to 14 swimmers who then go to the surface and swim towards the target. This was so successful in rigged-up trials that the Royal Marines awarded Johnstone the princely bonus of £45, a Herbert Lott award, and the system was accepted into service within 14 months.

The scope of the counter-terrorist force soon began to expand. By the turn of the decade there would be 130 oil and gas installations around Britain's coastline and more being built. In April 1979 the Admiralty Board and the Chiefs of Staff approved the formation of a new, independent company of 300 ranks, called Comacchio Company after one of the Royal Marines' most famous victories on Lake Comacchio in Italy towards the end of the Second World War. They were based at RM Condor Arbroath in May 1980, and in addition were charged with providing a fast-reaction force for the protection of nuclear weapons in both static sites and in transit, and for counter-terrorist movements on offshore installations or ships at sea.

The SBS in Poole deployed one dedicated counter-terrorism team to Comacchio, which became 5SBS; 1SBS remained in Poole to provide the lead section to combat terrorist incidents on ships. Meanwhile, a series of exercises and rehearsals was planned aboard the oil-rigs with the cooperation of the United Kingdom Offshore Operators' Association. In top-level exercises, the Home Office, the Foreign office or possibly the Cabinet Office would lead the planning.

After several studies and papers on anti-terrorist operations, the two SBS sections were amalgamated at Poole in 1987 with two rifle troops and became M Squadron of the SBS dedicated to Maritime Counter Terrorist.

By 1990, it had three troops, Black Gold and Purple, each tasked at various levels of MCT activity and manned entirely by SBS ranks. The squadron carried out numerous operations which for reasons of security remain classified and beyond the scope of this book. Further, with a considerably greater call for underwater work in both clandestine approach to an assault target and in security investigations, a dedicated Swimmer Delivery Vehicle team was founded. They were trained specifically in the use of motorised underwater tugs and towing craft for the speedy delivery of personnel to an operation.

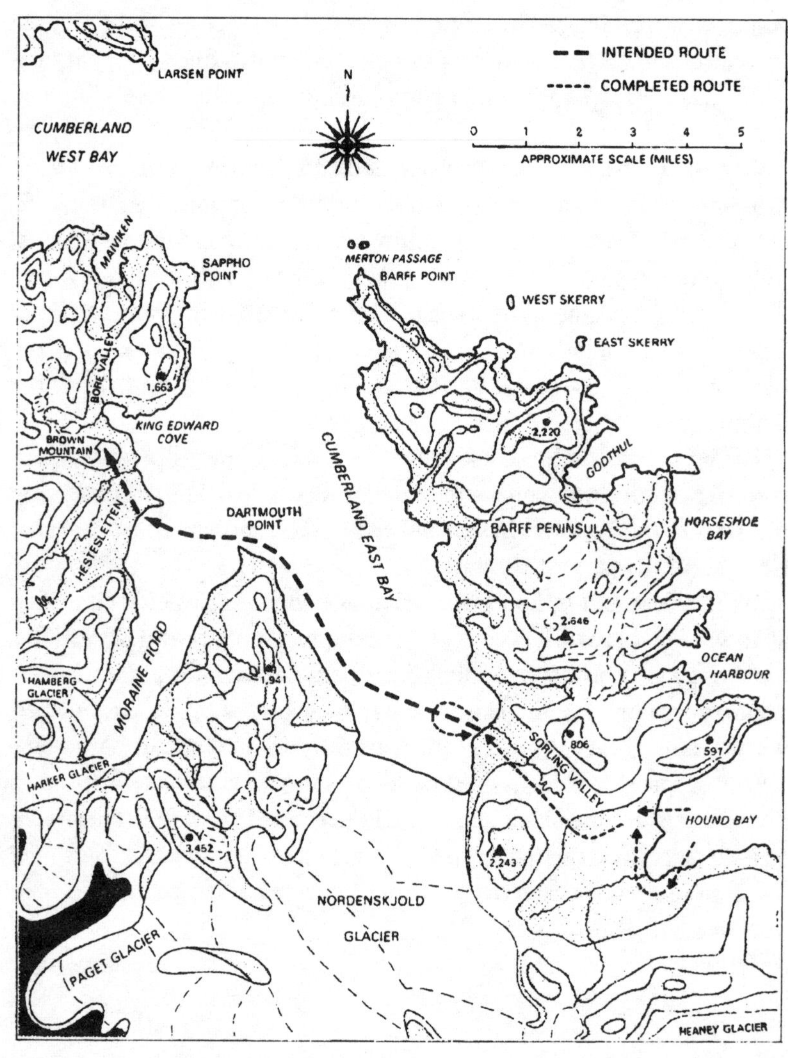

Proposed SBS reconnaissance route on South Georgia prior to taking the Argentine surrender.

Chapter Seventeen

Bring me South Georgia!

In the voluminous accounts of the Falklands War, the controversies and the reflections, the role of the SBS has regularly been overlooked. As the largest amphibious task force Britain had mounted since the Second World War headed to the South Atlantic, SBS sections were already dashing to the scene. They were the first to deploy, playing a major part in the retaking of South Georgia, and went on to open the doors for the invasion force with surveillance operations that provided gateway intelligence ahead of the Falklands landings. SBS patrols and recce teams were operating within Argentinian positions, virtually staring the enemy in the face, up to 21 days before the assault troops arrived. They led the troops ashore and then joined the offensive and became involved in some spectacular fire fights.

There was still snow on their boots when the Falklands panic blew up. Northern Norway had once again been the setting for SBS winter exercises training for its NATO role in Scandinavia. The exercises were renowned for survival techniques in appalling conditions, leading the men to the most inaccessible mountain positions – and getting them back again.

The yelling of the NCO instructors – 'It's only bloody pain!' or 'Cold? You'll know you're cold when your balls drop off' – was ringing in their ears. The limbs of the less fit ached and toes were still numb from the wet and cold let in by boots that didn't quite match the task. 42 Commando was the only unit in the Brigade to go to Norway that year because of stringent defence cost-cutting, which was so bad that several Royal Navy frigates were lying idle in their berths because there was not enough cash to pay the oil bills. 40 Commando was left to do their training in the UK, and 45 Commando went mountain-climbing in Scotland after a tough six months in Belfast, although one company was jungle training in Brunei. Two SBS sections had joined the Norwegian jaunt, on Exercise Clockwork, just as it had done every year since 1970. Few in the unit had not gone through the demanding three month annual training set in the depths of a Norwegian winter; some had been through it six or seven times.

It was just as well that they had. General Leopold Fortunato Galtieri, unstable head of the Argentinian military junta, had suddenly demonstrated his impatience to reclaim the Malvinas, as he insisted on calling the Falkland Islands. The British government and its ministerial team at the Foreign Office had shown a remarkable reluctance to accept that he would even try. Due notice had been served, well in advance. A British embassy military attaché in Buenos Aires reported to Whitehall in January predicting almost to the very day when an invasion by Argentina would happen.

No one paid much heed, with London preoccupied with cost-cutting. Almost to the last, Margaret Thatcher's Defence Secretary John Nott insisted that he would proceed with the withdrawal of the Royal Navy's sole bearer of the White Ensign in the southern hemisphere, the ice-patrol vessel HMS *Endurance*, to save £3 million a year in the defence budget.

Something of a national debate opened up over the future of the ship with letters to *The Times*. The Argentinians were listening. Galtieri took the proposed withdrawal of the ship to mean that the British government didn't care about the remote sheep-farm with its 1,950 inhabitants although *Endurance*'s commanding officer, Captain Nick Barker, RN, had been warning of increasing Argentinian radio traffic since the beginning of the year.

He and others had correctly read the signs, but Lord Carrington's last-minute request to keep *Endurance* on station, was turned down by the Cabinet. Minds were only changed at the very last minute when a gang of Argentinian scrap dealers landed on South Georgia –

which was not part of the Falklands – and hoisted their national flag.

The SBS, just returned from Norway, were about to go on leave, its stores still returning by sea. The men's departure was blocked even before the invasion. The SBS OC had been attending a conference in London the day before, 30 March. From what he learned, he made the correct assumption that there could be trouble at any second. The following morning he received confirmation and was alerted to keep all his units on standby.

What exactly could be done from 8,000 miles away if Galtieri did invade had yet to be decided. Some mad, mad schemes were being bandied about Whitehall. According to one who was there – and which astounded SBS people when they learned of it – a civil servant at an early planning meeting would suggest that the military 'make a loud bang in the South Atlantic by Friday 9 April' – seven days after the invasion took place. Whatever did he mean? No one seemed to know, and, anyway, short of dropping an A-bomb, there was no way of getting a loud bang of any sort to the region in seven days. Some very foolish people were around in those early days of the Falklands War, and they were not only somewhat inexperienced in handling such a crisis but they were panicking, and, as always happens when people in politics panic, they made some daft decisions and then tried to mislead the media.

When the Argentinians invaded, the SBS were among the first to learn of it and to be sent to action. Years of training and exercises for their arrival ahead of the troops, in what could only become a classic sea-borne assault, now came to the boil. The first signal at SBS headquarters at Poole ordering them to stand to came in the early hours of 1 April. Less than 24 hours later, they were on the move. Galtieri's troops had made their move on the Falklands and taken the token British force of Royal Marines prisoner. Argentinian photographers flashed around the world a photograph of them being marched away with hands over their heads. Prime Minister Margaret Thatcher was furious, and so she might be. In the words of Denis Healey, it had been 'an almighty cock-up'. Lord Carrington resigned, accepting full responsibility for 'this national humiliation', along with two other ministers. John Nott offered to stand down, too, but his resignation was rejected. He would, however, walk the plank later.

Thatcher responded on the day of the invasion by announcing she was sending a task force of 40 warships and 1,000 commandos to retake the islands. Suddenly, money was no object. As in Argentina, the forthcoming conflict deflected thoughts away from all other ills gripping the nation at the time, like unemployment and factory closures. The Poole headquarters was buzzing, although curiously enough without great conviction that a battle would result. Even so, over the next few days sections were mobilised one after the other.

First 2SBS, plus a strong command team, set off by air to Ascension Island to catch either HMS/M *Spartan* or HMS/M *Splendid* for a quick route south. That plan was aborted by operational headquarters, CINCFLEET, even as the men were *en route* and neither submarine was to stop at Ascension. 2SBS would join the Royal Fleet Auxiliary *Fort Austin* as soon as she arrived from Malta. *Fort Austin* was carrying urgently needed stores for HMS *Endurance*, now sailing around the Falklands with no port of call. At Ascension, the SBS were joined by SAS D Squadron to make a combined force of around 50 men. They would be joined by M Company of 42 Royal Marines under the command of Major Guy Sheridan, RM. The men were at sea aboard *Fort Austin* before they learned of their destination – to reclaim South Georgia as soon as possible and provide Mrs Thatcher and her politically embarrassed government with a face-saver.

Meanwhile, 6SBS travelled to Faslane, Scotland, to board the nuclear-powered submarine HMS *Conqueror* and set off for the South Atlantic. Politics ruled over military planning and instructions came from on high that *Conqueror* was to go direct to patrol the waters between the Falklands and Argentina. Later, *Conqueror* would be used to enforce the newly declared 12-mile exclusion zone around the Falklands, within which any Argentinian ships would be attacked. On the night of 6 May *Conqueror* sank Argentina's only cruiser, *General Belgrano*, with the loss of 362 men, although whether *Belgrano* was inside the zone would become a matter of some debate.

The last SB section to go out was 3SBS, deployed in Royal Fleet

Auxiliary *Stromness*, with a further 12 men deployed later to Ascension, taking the SBS force up to 85 men who, by the end of the first week of the campaign, were scattered over the South Atlantic. Back in Poole, SBS Rear ran the remaining section, 1SBS, to deal with any emergencies, such as a terrorist attack in the North Sea, plus the welfare and Special Forces liaison groups.

The assault on South Georgia, codenamed Operation Paraquat, was the first objective. On the way south, both the SBS and the SAS squadron began testing their equipment and practised launching their inflatable boats over the *Fort Austin*'s high sides. SBS divers also went into the ocean and joined the drills of loading their boats with equipment, with men and kit passed down scrambling-nets in a swell that tossed the inflatables up to 15 feet (4.5 metres). Having launched in rough sea, the boat troops practised motoring around the ship. Often, they had to paddle back manually because of the failure of some of the elderly outboard motors.

This was a problem that they worked on with increasing concern. The ship's engineers joined the SBS and SAS teams in trying to get the motors to work efficiently, but even as they neared their destination the motors refused to perform well, becoming a problem that was to put the men at risk when the time came for their landings.

On 12 April *Fort Austin* sighted HMS *Endurance*, which according to one recollection was 'bouncing around on the horizon like a flaming cork'. Those soldiers who suffered seasickness in the smaller ship would find no respite in *Endurance*, which on occasions rolled in an arc across 60 degrees. For the next 24 hours the SBS and SAS teams heading for South Georgia were cross-decked from *Fort Austin* to *Endurance*, along with their stores, boats, engines, weapons and equipment, plus much-needed supplies for the crew of *Endurance*. They stood watching as the load-shifting of supplies began, cradled underneath two Wessex helicopters. The first load, a supply of food, had to be ditched when the helicopter suddenly lost power. The rest of the transfer was completed without mishap, and the Paraquat force set off for the remainder of its journey, joined now by the destroyer HMS *Antrim*, the elderly frigate HMS *Plymouth* and the large Royal Fleet

Auxiliary tanker, *Tidespring*, between them carrying tons of stores and men airlifted on board while the ships were moored off Ascension.

Planning staff for the reoccupation of South Georgia had its headquarters on *Antrim*. The SBS would be put ashore from *Endurance* to reconnoitre the Grytviken and King Edward Point area. The SAS would land at Fortuna Glacier to recce Leith Harbour, Stromness and Grass Island. Their initial objective was to discover the location and strength of the Argentinian garrison, which was known to be on South Georgia, and to do so without alerting them to the imminent British assault.

Antrim and *Tidespring* sailed for a position just north of Antarctic Bay for the SAS insertion, while *Endurance* and *Plymouth* carried on towards Hound Bay carrying the SBS recce team.

The SAS team was to go in first. *Antrim* reached a position 15 miles from South Georgia expecting to see the island ahead of them, but the 'moderate' weather was nothing like the crew had been led to expect. A half-gale was gusting, with squalls of snow, visibility was low and the cloud base was around 400 feet (120 metres). They waited for an improvement, and a couple of hours later a helicopter took off for an inspection of the weather closer to shore. Slowly, through the murky morning, the island loomed up before them, a breathtaking vision of desolate beauty yet awesome in its implications. Sheer cliffs, the massive and threatening Fortuna Glacier which had to be crossed, the incredible backdrop of its mountains . . . all were fantastic, if you were a tourist or the film-makers from Anglia television who happened to be filming on the island at the time of the invasion.

The helicopter pilot judged that there was a sufficient break in the weather to get the team ashore. Boats were out of the question. He returned to *Antrim* and within the hour the three helicopters of the two ships were ferrying the team towards Possession Bay. But as they flew towards landfall, the weather deteriorated and they hit a wall of snow. To continue would have been foolhardy, so they returned to *Antrim* to await an improvement.

By midday, they tried again, and this time made a successful landing, buffeted horrendously by wind gusting at 80 miles an hour through poor visibility and on ground that contained hidden traps. One helicopter, landing partly on a crevasse covered with new, soft snow, almost toppled over. As the 16 men clambered out, carrying their stores and three pulks – preloaded sleds weighing up to 200 pounds (90 kilogrammes) for pulling behind them – the lead helicopter pilot radioed to all: 'I'm glad we won't have to come back to this place.'

It was the kind of remark that tempts fate.

The team roped themselves together in fours and set off towards the high rim of the glacier, hauling their sleds behind them. The terrain was toothily rough and dangerous, with deep crevasses filled with snow that collapsed when trodden upon, creating a trap to break anyone's leg. Another problem became obvious immediately: their general-purpose lightweight machine-guns froze up in spite of being heavily oiled. Worse was to come. They travelled little more than half a mile before nightfall when the troop leader, Sergeant Lofty Arthy, a climber of the Himalayas with vast mountaineering experience, decided that the journey was too dangerous for them to continue. They decided to settle in for the night as best they could.

The hard surface of the glacier made it impossible to dig any form of deep cover. They could merely hack out shallow trenches with their ice-axes into which they would bed down in their sleeping-bags. A few of the small two-man tents were pitched, but half of them just blew off into the night in the high winds.

Out at sea, *Antrim*, still anchored 15 miles offshore, had a similarly unpleasant night. A force 12 was blowing, and the ship was tossed around like a matchstick. All stores had to be lashed down, and attempts to show a movie to the off-watch officers in the wardroom proceeded only with the operator holding the projector between his knees.

On Fortuna Glacier, the weather tumbled to disaster point. The katabatic winds hurling snow at 100 miles an hour made progress virtually impossible. The men would not have survived another day of it, and finally they had to give up. At 1000 hours the team leader instructed his signaller to call *Antrim* for help. They needed to be lifted off pronto! Was it even possible? As the signaller removed his gloves to operate his set, his hands went completely numb. *Antrim* command agreed to abort the attempt.

Once more, the three helicopter pilots were forced to return to the hazardous icy slopes to pick up the team, which had switched on its search-and-rescue beacon and would release green smoke indicators as soon as the helicopters came close.

It was well past midday before a break in the weather allowed the pilots to make the attempt. In spite of still-gusting winds, the three aircraft managed to locate the men, who set off their smoke when they heard the engines. Lieutenant Mike Tidd, RN, pilot of *Yankee Foxtrot*, one of the two Wessex 5 helicopters from *Tidespring*, with an aircrewman coincidentally named Tug Wilson led the flight convoy down and settled first on the glacier amid a swirl of blown snow. The SAS men trundled forwards and threw their gear through the open doors and scrambled aboard.

Tidd, first down, was first off. He lifted safely and headed north with mountains on either side of him. Within minutes he was hit by a white-out, a snow squall that totally obliterated his vision, and he knew there was sheer rock rising all around him. The altimeter was unwinding fast as he lost sight of both ground and horizon. He shouted to Tug, who was already giving hot drinks to the six men in the back: 'We've got a problem . . .'

The words were hardly out when the helicopter hit the glacier surface at about 30 knots (55 kilometres per hour) and went crashing on across the craggy ice, tearing off the left side of the undercarriage, bits of metal flying all over the place. The left side of the cockpit where the second pilot would have been sitting was smashed to bits. The pilots of the other two helicopters, about to take off, watched in horror. They quickly flew to the crash site and discovered with disbelief that not one of the men on board was seriously hurt.

The men from the crashed chopper were loaded on to the other two helicopters, although much of their kit was dumped. The twin-engined Wessex 5 took the larger number of men with weapons and stores. Within ten minutes the two helicopters lifted off together to head back to *Antrim*, with the ship's own single-engined, rather ancient Wessex 3 (nicknamed *Humphrey*), piloted by Lieutenant Ian Stanley, RN, leading; Lieutenant Ian Georgeson in the larger Wessex 5 from *Tidespring* followed.

Within three minutes of take-off they hit another white-out. Ian Stanley managed to navigate through it and Georgeson followed behind using Stanley as his guide. Ahead was an obstacle neither could have foreseen, a high ridge of ice on the edge of the glacier and invisible in the white-out. Stanley went up and over without any problems. As he passed over and dipped down the other side, Georgeson lost sight of him.

He glanced at his altimeter. The ground was heading up towards him fast. The white-out had him in its grip, and he reduced speed ready for 'an involuntary landing which proceeded towards me with a certain inevitability'. He almost got away with it. The wheels touched the ground, the craft rumbled and shook and for a moment seemed to rise until it was caught in a strong gusting wind of around 50 knots (92 kilometres per hour) which swung it around and sent it crashing across the ice, ending up in a tangled mass of rotorblades and crunched metal, with the overloaded bodycount inside on top of each other.

Ian Stanley had picked up the running commentary of Georgeson and his number two in his headphones. His own second pilot was now watching from the port cockpit side window . . . 'Steady, steady . . . Yeah, he's made it . . . No! Oh God . . . He's gone.' There was nothing Stanley could do but carry on to *Antrim*. He was fully loaded already and dare not risk the lives of the men aboard. As the last of the helicopters made its way back to *Antrim*, the signaller radioed in: 'We're on our way home. ETA 15 minutes. Regret we've lost two of our chicks.' The news was received with great disappointment in London.

Back on the ice ridge, the bodies lay on top of each other, stunned by a second crash within 15 minutes. They quickly stirred and extricated themselves from the wreckage. Incredibly, there was not one fatality, or even serious injury. Georgeson himself was trapped in the cockpit, and, in spite of the risk of fire, the SAS clambered back aboard to rescue him. The troops set off to the first wreck to recover some of their kit, including a radio and their inflatable boats, which they used to build a shelter.

On *Antrim*, Ian Stanley was watching the weather, waiting for permission to go back to see what he could find. Two attempts were aborted. Then, at 1600, there was a window in the weather for another try. There would have to be at least two rescue flights because the Wessex 3 could not carry 16 men with kit through a gusting wind. Stanley was given permission to go ahead, and by 1645 was once again heading close to the ice cliff on Fortuna Glacier, intending to bring the men home in two parties of eight.

Conditions had worsened even as he left and progressively deteriorated as he went inshore. On the ground the crashed party's radio was now working, and Ian Georgeson made contact, ready to guide Stanley in if he ever got to see the helicopter. The weather was worsening by the minute. Stanley came down towards them through a gap in the cloud and realised instantly that he would have no chance of making two trips that night. All gear and kit would have to be abandoned and the men crammed into the back.

Stanley wasn't so much concerned about take-off; he had enough power for that. The landing might be a problem on a moving ship with slightly warmer air and less wind.

Antrim command anxiously tracked the helicopter back and watched *Humphrey* hover and come in to land. The aircraft hit the deck with a mighty thump but did no damage to itself or to those aboard. The first part of the mission to recce South Georgia was over, with two dead helicopters and a quarter of a ton of stores lost.

The SBS had reached their destination, Hound Bay on the north coast of the island, where they were to be put ashore in three recce parties by the two little Wasp helicopters from HMS *Endurance*, once again with stores and equipment making a heavy load. They were to find and estimate the number of Argentinians in that area of the island in preparation for a landing by the Royal Marines. The Wasp managed to get only a third of their numbers ashore before the weather closed in. The men on the ground waited for more than two hours, then realised that the rest of their group would not be joining them. They began to reconnoitre the area.

Moving through the now pitch-black night the SBS patrol

stumbled inadvertently into a half-asleep colony of penguins remonstrating loudly for the disturbance. A little further on the patrol leader swung around, gun at the ready, when something dark reared up beside him. He had trodden on the tail of a slumbering elephant seal, which was just about to put its wide-open mouth around his ears when he made a dash for safety.

The journey became progressively worse. By midnight there had been no let-up in the weather, and the other two-thirds of the SBS patrols were still aboard *Endurance*, anchored offshore. At 0300 the Wasp pilot tried to make another attempt to land the remainder, but he was literally blown back, twice almost dropping into the sea. Heavy snow finally put paid to the attempts, layering four inches (ten centimetres) thick on the windscreen, with frozen chunks flying off and hitting the canopy and the engine.

The SBS men on board decided to attempt to land on the island by taking their inflatables through the heavy swell, a manoeuvre entirely dependent on efficient outboard motors. Manpower alone would not have been sufficient: the boats were heavily laden, six men and stores in each. They also had a longer route to follow, as landing was impossible close to where the Wasp had dropped their colleagues because of a mass accumulation of ice which would have split the rubber boats.

Captain Nick Barker took *Endurance* as close as he dare and remained while the SBS dropped over the side. Finally, they got under way, the aged 40-horsepower outboards spluttered into life, and at around 0330 they headed for shore. The swell was huge and the wind howling; by the time they reached the shore they were all very wet and cold.

The new bunch unloaded their gear while two of their number set off in search for the remainder of the section lying up around the other side of the bay, a couple of miles away. They made their way cautiously around the curve of the bay, over rocks and ice and into another area thick with angry seals and penguins. They made contact 40 minutes later and all returned to the landing-site.

The plan now was for the three patrols to make their way across the bays and inlets, through a fiord and on towards their charted position for an observation post looking down at King Edward

Point, where the Argentinians were thought to be building their troop numbers on the island. To reach this observation post they would need boats to carry the three sections across Cumberland East Bay, an eight-mile stretch of water.

It was planned that they would rendezvous with the *Endurance* helicopter the following morning to accept delivery of two Geminis for the water crossing. Before first light the SBS party moved off, each carrying their 80-pound (36-kilogramme) Bergen rucksacks. They made their way over the treacherous terrain of the Soirling Valley, which normally would have presented no difficulties but now covered with ice and filled with snow-topped hazards and invisible crevasses. By mid-morning they had reached the foot of Nordenskjold Glacier, which looked on their charts a possible launching-place for the Geminis.

It turned out to be a great creaking, frozen mass disgorging icicles the size of an Exocet missile into a bay filled with growlers and icebergs. Dangerous shards filled the water. A Gemini wouldn't have lasted five minutes, and nor would they. They moved on and prepared to meet the *Endurance* Wasp at the agreed RV site. The recollections of one who was there provide an insight into the remainder of the operation:

> The helicopter arrived in mid-afternoon with the two boats and their engines slung in a net beneath the undercarriage. We saw him coming in low so as to avoid being seen by the Argentinian troops over the other side of the bay. In doing so, he probably hit the front tube of one of them on the ice. When we blew it up to full strength, it leaked badly and could not be used. We decided that we would have to split up, half remaining where they were, the others taking the second Gemini across the bay.
>
> We laid up until nightfall, making ourselves as comfortable as possible in freezing winds, with half of us still wet from the journey across. We loaded the boat and made ready for the crossing under darkness. In those couple of hours, the weather changed dramatically. A force seven was blowing and packice was on the move – you could hear it crunching and banging.

> The change of wind direction was blowing it back into the bay, and it was hitting the shore-line and just stacking up. By the time we came to launch the Gemini, there was just one small channel free of ice, less than 50 yards wide and closing. Well, the others decided to make a dash for it before the ice closed up completely and headed out in pitch darkness; you couldn't see a bloody thing, and the waters were grey and impossible. Within 800 yards, they were in trouble. You could hear the motor was overworking and hitting chunks of ice; it was like a food mixer with too much to tackle. It faded and stopped several times. The ice was piling towards them – huge chunks of the bloody stuff – and they needed engine power to avoid being hit and sunk. They had to turn back and rejoin the rest of us on the shore. It was decided we would lay up for the night and make another attempt the next day.

First light showed no improvement. The ice by then had filled the bay and to attempt a crossing in a rubber boat was impossible. They radioed the Operation Paraquat planning team on board HMS *Antrim* for instructions but could not make contact. They assumed they were out of range and climbed to a higher point; still no reply. Unknown to them, there was nobody there! All British ships in coastal waters had been ordered out to sea after the Argentinian submarine *Santa Fe* was reported to be patrolling the coast, and in the dash to get out *Antrim* command had overlooked the SBS party.

They finally restored radio contact later that night, 24 April, after three very cold days ashore. The SBS asked to be taken off but there was some dissension on *Antrim*. Ought they not to make another try? Eventually, the SBS mission was aborted and the men were recovered by the two Wasps and taken back aboard HMS *Endurance*.

There was a curiously fortuitous result to the SBS's difficulties at Cumberland East Bay, which was just ten miles from the Argentinians' own base. The coded radio traffic between the SBS and *Antrim*, and then with *Endurance*, alerted the Argentinians that something was afoot. They already knew of the presence of British ships in the area, and were certain an invasion party was about to be put ashore. The submarine *Santa Fe* had been summoned to patrol that section of South Georgia and was in fact very close to where the SBS operation was aborted.

On 25 April another SBS team was mustered aboard HMS *Antrim* to be flown ashore for a further attempt. The men were landed a few miles away from the original team's insertion point, once again by Lieutenant Ian Stanley flying the *Antrim* helicopter *Humphrey*. On the way back Stanley spotted *Santa Fe* sitting temptingly on the surface on the edge of Cumberland East Bay. Stanley swooped low over the vessel, her casing gunners began firing at him, and he loosed his entire stock of depth-charges around her. They did enough damage to prevent the craft from diving and, alerted by Stanley, the Wasps from *Endurance* and a Lynx from the frigate *Brilliant* darted to the scene and blasted the submarine with a salvo of missiles and machine-gun fire.

Santa Fe limped off, oil flooding the surface, towards the British Antarctic Survey Station at Grytviken. The planners aboard *Antrim* decided the attack must be followed up immediately, but the Royal Marines in *Tidespring* were still hours away. A force was pulled together from the ships in the area, including SAS, SBS and *Antrim*'s own Royal Marines detachment of 10 – in total, just 75 men, fewer than half the size of the Argentinian garrison.

They were landed at various points, now without any thought of clandestine movement, and headed for Grytviken, where *Santa Fe* had berthed. When they arrived, the whole place was decked with white sheets, and as soon as the British force turned up the Argentinians formed up beside their flag and surrendered. Later, 2SBS joined D Squadron of SAS and flew into Leith Harbour, where Captain Alfredo Astiz, the renowned torturer of Argentinian political prisoners, saluted the team leader and handed him his pistol in surrender. Not a shot was fired. In London the newspapers were already preparing their headlines: SOUTH GEORGIA RECAPTURED.

Margaret Thatcher had been given her face-saver. She came out of 10 Downing Street and made that memorable, jingoistic little speech to waiting television cameras and, waving aside questions from the assembled journalists, screeched into the microphones: 'Rejoice! Rejoice!' Whether we should rejoice for her and her government or for the troops who had performed these death-defying first efforts of the Falklands adventure was not immediately clear.

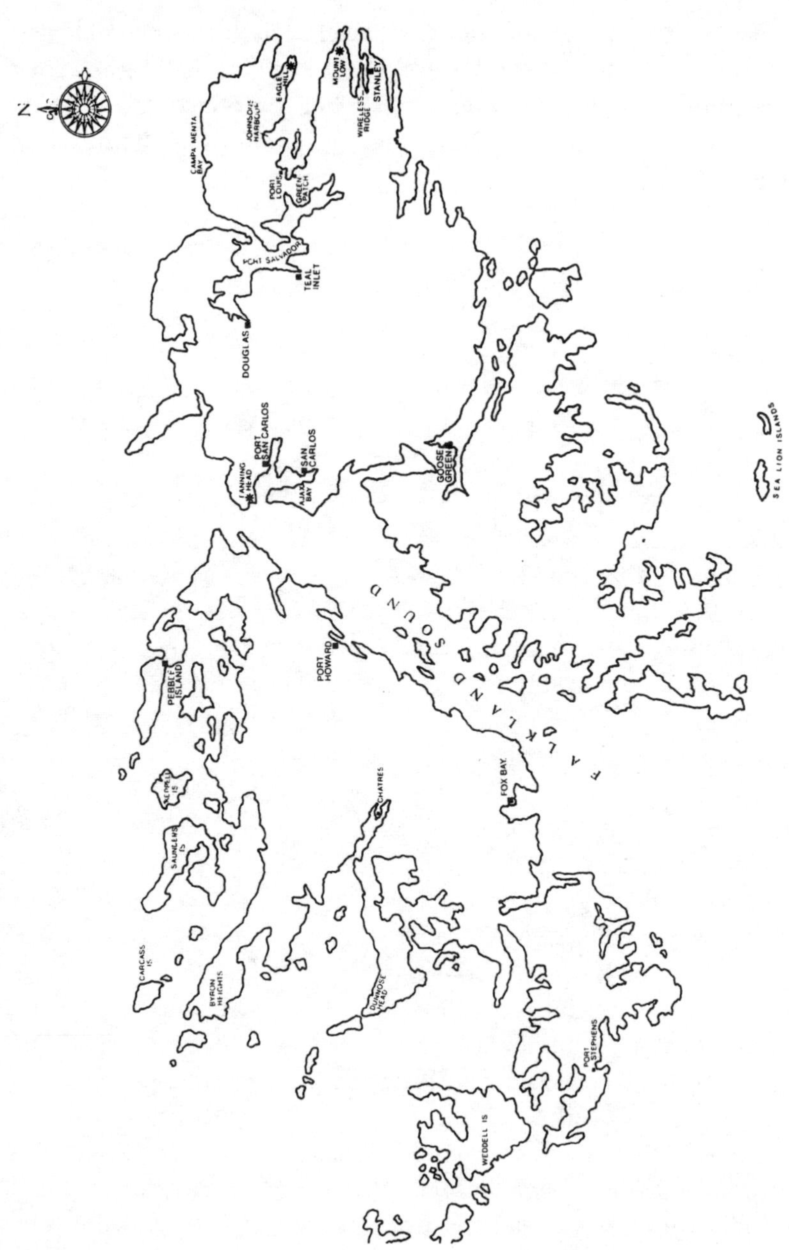

Falkland Islands.

Chapter Eighteen

Finest hours

South Georgia secured, the SBS went off to join the advance force fleet in preparations for the main task: Operation Corporate – the recapture of the Falkland Islands. 3SBS was already aboard HMS *Hermes* sailing from Ascension, and 6SBS joined the advance force as soon as it was released from Operation Paraquat. The bulk of SBS work now would be to go ashore at crucial points around the Falklands to recce landing-sites and to report on enemy positions and on the going, terrain and beaches and possibly to clear landing-site obstacles. Three separate areas of the Falklands were to be reconnoitred and patrolled, stretching the meagre resources of the SBS to the limit. But SBS men were the first British troops to go ashore in the Falklands and were there behind enemy lines a full three weeks before Royal Marines and paratroopers stormed ashore at San Carlos Bay on 21 May.

The most crucial reconnaissance of the Falklands conflict was placed in the hands of the SBS. The task was the Trojan Horse equivalent of penetrating well behind enemy lines to provide the gateway intelligence for the major troop landings that were to follow. Without them and their intelligence reports, casualties would undoubtedly have been far higher. The British government naturally declined to confirm that any British troops had landed prior to the first major assault, and so the SBS men were once again vulnerable to the whim of the enemy if they were captured. The grey area of being treated as prisoners of war had, historically, been a bugbear ever since Hitler declared that the secret raiders should be interrogated and shot.

Their wide brief and the equally wide area to be covered meant they also had to move around the theatre of potential conflict much more than they would normally be inclined to do for recce work, so that each site could be covered. An additional discomfort for the patrols was that they could not send their reports by radio for fear of interception and had to use the slow hand-speed Morse for general communication. The more complicated beach recce reports and charts were too long and involved for transmission by any other means than personal delivery, and often the men had to go back to base or ship to report direct to their controllers and then return ashore.

The SBS patrols were flown in generally by Sea King Mark 4 helicopters, although occasionally they went ashore by more traditional method, delivered by Geminis. They were moved only at night by pilots flying on Passive Night Goggles, a brand new technique they had mastered only at Ascension on the way south with equipment borrowed at the last moment from Farnborough. The helicopters flew from up to 180 nautical miles offshore at 50 feet (15 metres) above sea-level into enemy-held territory. As soon as they were landed with weapons and stores, the SBS dug into the rolling, coverless hillsides and remained hidden for days at a time while the enemy searched for them with small aircraft, helicopters and ground troops.

As the most crucial period of the conflict approached, the SBS had observation teams scattered throughout the Falklands, watching Argentinian positions and carrying out beach recces. Patrols were deployed to Campa Menta Bay, Eagle Hill (twice), Johnson's Harbour, Ajax Bay, San Carlos and Port San Carlos for up to a week at a time before being withdrawn to report their findings and for insertion elsewhere. The stretched resources of its limited manpower also showed up the importance of the SBS in intelligence-gathering: when no patrol was available to cover Port San Carlos for a vital five days, the Argentinians moved an entire company into the area unseen.

Key Argentinian positions were under constant observation. One patrol established a post at the proposed main British invasion site, in a refrigeration plant at Ajax Bay. Another was dug in across San Carlos Water on the Inner Verde Mountains, while the recce team at Port San Carlos observed troop movements for seven days without a break.

The procedures were well established and rehearsed through years of SBS exercises and operations. The men usually worked in teams of four, although sometimes more. They would clear the landing-area quickly, one of them watching to give covering fire, then make their way under darkness across open country towards their selected observation site, often having to set up temporary bases *en route*, and lying up during daylight.

One would keep watch while the others built the hides and covered the stores. If the lookout had to stray from the lying-up site, they used the old SBS fishing-line trick: with one end attached to a Bergen rucksack in the hide, the lookout would give a pull on the line to warn of approaching danger.

Well aware that they were being hunted, the men took enormous care to ensure that the hides were virtually invisible, even if they were to be used for only a few hours. They knew that care in that direction could save their lives. The Falklands earth, when not frozen solid, was of a consistency that could be carved into small bunkers, perhaps on the side of an incline, of about six or eight feet (1.8 or 2.4 metres) square. The turves from the top were cut and saved to be used later as a roof. The men dug down to about two feet (0.6 metres), lining the sides of the bunker with waterproof sheets. The soil from the hole was placed around the hide and covered with turf. Chicken wire and netting were slung across the top, and the turves placed back with an easily removed access point and spy-holes for observation.

If the job were done properly, the hides would be completely invisible from the air, and even Argentinian ground troops were known to have walked by without noticing them. Two other hides, for food and equipment, would be built nearby, where possible in a straight line for easy access during darkness and within ten feet (three metres). The stores – always a problem in their movement from place to place – were substantial, especially for a seven-day recce. Equipment included binoculars, night-sights and a tripod-mounted telescope.

The men each carried sleeping-bags and duvet trousers, a change of clothes, high-protein ration packs and tinned food that required cooking on hexamine stoves. They carried emergency rations and were well armed. Each man would be equipped with an M-16 Armalite rifle, one M-203 grenade launcher, six high-explosive grenades, one 66-millimetre (2.6-inch) anti-tank missile, 300 rounds of ammunition, smoke and phosphorous grenades, a 9-millimetre Browning pistol and a hunting knife. The hides would be used for lying up during the daytime, using the cover of darkness for recce, although that was not always possible. Food for the day had to be drawn before first light, and the men who went outside the hides for whatever reason would brush their tracks as they went back so as not to leave any footprints or flattened grass. By dawn they had to be under cover and hidden away for another long stint, taking it in turns to go on watch and often in situations where matters of personal hygiene and the call of nature had to be dealt with as best they could be.

The routine was similar, often almost identical, to the procedures described by Captain Len Holmes in the observation posts of the Borneo campaign. By day they each took a two-hour watch while the others rested, made tea or prepared their rations; cooking a meal took perhaps 40 minutes or more, each man preparing his own. The daily intake of sustenance, particularly in a cold climate, could never be ignored. At night they took one hour on watch and three hours off, and under darkness they would venture out to get a more precise view of the local situation. Making sure the hides were carefully concealed, they moved stealthily around the area, noting all that was required of them for full recce reports with charts and drawings, especially those assigned to potential landing-sites.

As usual, these all had to be checked for gradients and underwater obstacles, such as rocks and shelving. They also had to be largely free of kelp – a major problem throughout the islands and which choked motors – so that landing-craft carrying troops could make a swift, unhindered entry. The surrounding terrain had to be mapped out, and beach profiles drawn and checked for easy

International terrorism of the 1970s brought new tasks for the SBS, especially around the coastline of the United Kingdom, dotted with oil and gas rigs. SBS was earmarked for maritime counter-terrorist measures, rehearsed here on an actual oil rig.

Ship protection became another area of SBS training, here boarding and taking the initiative in a counter-terrorist exercise.

Arctic training is an annual event for the SBS. Apart from hazardous mountaineering and rock-climbing expeditions, immersion in sub-zero temperatures is one of the obligatory trials. Many a canoe has also been punctured by razor-sharp ice flows.

Arctic training stood the SBS in good stead when they were sent to the Falklands ahead of the British Task Force to gather pre-invasion intelligence. Their first port of call was this formidable glacier on South Georgia, providing a dramatic backdrop to the tiny SBS craft heading towards the shore.

In hugely unpredictable seas, the SBS inflatables were at times hopelessly out-manoeuvred by the forces of nature.

Ahead of the task force: SBS teams were first ashore in the Falkland Islands, often landing in exceedingly rough conditions under the cover of darkness and hiding up in observation posts close to Argentine positions for up to a week at a time.

FRIDAY MARCH 1, 1991 ★★ 25p (Republic of Ireland 35p)

VICTORY **Today** SOUVENIR

KUWAIT CITY, FEB 28 1991

BACK IN THE LAND OF THE FREE

PICTURE : Steve Back

THE LAST ACT: A British Commando slides down a rope from his helicopter to reclaim our embassy in Kuwait City. For 75 days it was part of a desecrated country where a tyrant swept away all semblance of justice. Now its liberation heralds a victory for the freedom of all mankind.

The reclaiming of the British embassy during the Gulf War made headline news. The SBS team which carried out the mission were as anonymous as ever, described universally at 'British commandos'. *(Courtesy of News International)*

The raid on the ship *Fox Trot Five* at Greenwich after its alleged drug-running voyage across the Atlantic bearing a multi-million haul of Colombian cocaine. With one SBS black-garbed team on board, another can be seen in the background about to board the ship. *(Courtesy of Dr Joyce Lowman)*

Dedication of the permanent memorial to fallen SBS personnel at the Royal Marines base at Poole. It is in the form of an inscribed plinth bearing a rock brought from Gibraltar, staging post of so many SBS operations and exercises. The dedication was made by the Reverend Donald Peyton-Jones DSC, himself a former commanding officer of the SBS.

approaches from the landing-zones to inland positions for the massed troops. Cliffs and steep gradients were out of the question. Equally important were the inland approaches, so that the advancing troops did not become trapped by natural barriers. At Sandy Bay, for example, the SBS recce team discovered that behind the headland of one possible landing-site leading to a settlement containing Argentinian troops lay a secondary beach in which the British invasion force would have become sitting ducks.

There were many near-misses of discovery of SBS patrols, and at the most sensitive place of Ajax Bay, where they kept up a 16-day watch, it seemed that they were being specifically hunted.

Once, an Argentinian helicopter landed less than 150 metres from the hide. The pilot got out, strolled around and then stopped for a quick pee. 'A few more yards further on and he would have been pissing into our hide,' one of their number recalled. Later, another helicopter hovered virtually on top of the hide and the downdraught blew away some of the camouflage. Even then the pilot did not see the gang of four hidden just a few feet below him.

By now, the amphibious battle was hotting up. After *Belgrano* was sunk, the Argentinians began hitting the newly arrived task force with French-built Exocet missiles. The destroyer HMS *Sheffield* was sunk on 4 May with the loss of 21 lives, and the *QE2* was about to set sail with infantry reinforcements.

At the time other complications were arising from political sources in London and the United States as the US tried to intervene with a peace plan being brokered by General Alexander Haig, a plan that almost led to a ceasefire. Contingency schemes were made to withdraw the bulk of SBS and SAS, leaving stay-behind patrols. But the ceasefire proposals came to naught and the SBS was back in business.

One incident caused a good deal of concern for different reasons at SBS control: two of their corporals went missing. Apart from worries about their safety, the possibility arose that SBS operations might be compromised. The trouble hit a patrol led by Sergeant KJ as it made for a mist-shrouded hilltop to find a position for its operations. By coincidence, the same spot had been chosen by an Argentinian patrol, which was approaching from the other side of the hill at exactly the same time. The two corporals, who had gone on ahead to recce the position, crept forward in fog and heard voices. The British patrol had to make a choice: open a fire fight with the Argentinians and alert them to their position or stealthily retreat, allow the Argentinian patrol to occupy the position and be none the wiser of British presence. The British chose the latter and pulled back. The rules of engagement were clear: no fire fights unless absolutely unavoidable. This left the two corporals with the Argentinian patrol advancing on the hilltop and cutting off their route to the rest of the SBS team.

The pair made a quick retreat and went to ground, unavoidably losing contact with their comrades. They had no radio or other form of communications, and very little else. One of the corporals, TWM, was an old hand at SBS practices, although both knew the procedures. They pursued the emergency drill of moving through a list of pre-arranged rendezvous points on their map and waiting for a specified time. If the RV was not met, they would move on to the next, and follow that procedure until contact was hopefully made.

The patrol made several sorties to look for the missing pair without success. Sergeant KJ was now confronted by his own difficult decision: he had to pull the rest of the team out to meet his own RV for the helicopter pick-up, which would mean leaving the other two behind. It had to be done. The team flew back to the base ship, leaving the corporals to their own devices.

The sergeant asked to be allowed back on the ground to carry out a further search. Several days passed and no contact was made. There was a chance that the missing men had died of exposure or had been taken prisoner. Their SBS comrades were pretty certain that neither was the case. The corporals were well used to rough weather and had a good eye for self-preservation. More than likely they were following the manual to the letter, hiding up in the day and moving around at night. What they would not have done was to make contact with locals unless absolutely necessary.

It was seven days after the two were separated when the sergeant took a team back to the area and painstakingly retraced the pre-arranged rendezvous positions, a task made all the more difficult by the darkness of the night. And they would be well hidden because there were Argentinian patrols all around. But looking for an SBS hide that was built and skilfully camouflaged with the specific object of *not* being found was a needle in a haystack job. The search now concentrated on the final RV on the list, and there finally the rescuers came upon the two corporals. A barrage of expletives was exchanged by both sides, and they headed off back to base. They had a good meal, half a bottle of medicinal brandy and a good sleep before being debriefed. Within three days they were back on patrol.

Meanwhile, other issues had to be resolved. During the advance force phase, 2 and 6SBS were held in the battle group for anti-shipping tasks. In one such operation, 2SBS was dispatched aboard two Sea King Mark 4 helicopters to board and apprehend the 1,300-ton Argentinian fish factory-ship, *Narwal*, which was discovered in the British exclusion zone. Before the men reached their target, however, the ship was bombed and strafed by two Harrier jets. The vessel was already listing badly when 2SBS arrived. With the helicopters hovering above the ship, the men roped down to board her, using the procedures they had practised during their Maritime Counter-terrorist training.

The section managed to rescue the crew, some of whom were badly injured (one was dead). They also took possession of charts and operation orders before setting charges and blowing up the ship. In spite of claims by Argentina that she was an innocent vessel, the orders showed she had been shadowing the fleet and, presumably, signalling intelligence.

By now, the SBS teams were working through the most crucial stages of the reconnaissance operation. Several of the recce teams had come close to being discovered, the Argentinians were clearly attempting to root them out as the possible invasion of British troops edged closer. The main amphibious force was nearing the Falklands, carrying the major body of troops and fire power. HMS *Hermes*, the anti-submarine carrier and parent ship to the Sea Kings, headed south to accompany the task force.

With few helicopters now available, the SBS had to join the queue for use of the two Wessex 5s flying off HMS *Antrim* at the very time they needed to put recce teams back into Ajax Bay and Fanning Head to monitor Argentinian movements around Port San Carlos. The SBS had less than four days before the beginning of the biggest amphibious assault since the Second World War.

The countdown to that assault saw some frantic activity: on 16 May an SBS recce team was landed by rubber craft from the frigate HMS *Alacrity* south of Ajax Bay and set up an observation post overlooking the vital San Carlos Water. On the same day another team was reinserted to its former operations site on Ajax Bay. On the next day a third team was launched from the frigate HMS *Brilliant* to take up an observation position overlooking Port San Carlos. As this last approached the target area, however, the men saw lights and heard voices. Evidently, there was an enemy company close by, and they returned to *Brilliant* without landing.

It now became imperative to get a team into the area of Port San Carlos and in particular to that feature of it known as Fanning Head, a hill dominating the entrances to both North Falkland Sound and San Carlos Water. The exact enemy positions were not known, but if the SBS could insert its teams now, the intelligence would be covered well in advance of the troop landings.

The SBS managed to get hold of the two Wessex helicopters from *Antrim*, and 2SBS, with a half-section from 3SBS along with an SAS mortar detachment were tasked with locating and dislodging the Argentinians from its Fanning Head position in the hours running up to the landing. For this, the SBS had acquired a useful piece of equipment never previously used in any military operation. It was a thermal imager (TI), at the time in experimental use among police forces in Britain for tracking escapees from justice who were being tailed by bobbies in helicopters. The imager, now familiar to television viewers of police action programmes, could pick the presence of bodies, live or recently dead, simply from the heat they generated.

The TI was fitted to *Antrim*'s ancient Wessex and began flying the area in square patterns. Sure enough, a company of Argentinians was picked up on the screen, from which their exact position could be calculated. This was radioed from the Wessex and for the next two hours HMS *Antrim* bombarded the target with its 4.5-inch

(11.4-centimetre) guns. In the meantime the Wessex made five trips back and forth to collect the remainder of the assault team, a task fraught with danger since the landing-lights of the helicopter could be seen from some distance. Then the SBS moved in. One of their number who spoke Argentinian Spanish called for the surrender of the Argentinians. The reply was a burst of gunfire which hit the rucksack of one of the team. The SBS gave them one more chance to give up and then moved forwards. They shot and killed twelve, wounded three and took nine prisoners.

The Argentinians had been on Fanning Head manning anti-tank guns and mortars covering the straits and would have had British ships in their direct line of fire. The remainder of the company, around 60 men, were sheltering in houses in Port San Carlos area. They did not see an SBS beach reception party as it crept into position two hours before the first troop landings, by the Parachute Regiment, but the SBS did not see them either. The Argentinians moved out when the Fanning Head fire fight started. They were still in the area as the first troops went ashore and were able to shoot down two Royal Marine Gazelles which were escorting a Sea King carrying a Rapier missile battery ashore. Three of the four Gazelle crew were killed.

The landing itself was unopposed and, with the essential beach-head now in British hands, the invasion force moved ahead for the final assault and the recapture of East Falkland.

On the north coast, by Port Salvador Water, 6SBS was inserted from HMS *Fearless* to clear up ahead of the arrival of the Commandos. The section faced a long journey by water at night, with three raiding craft, before establishing a forward base on the tussock-covered Green Island, four days before the Commando Brigade began its advance from San Carlos. The section carried out close recces of Port Louis and Green Patch settlements, reported them clear of enemy, and conducted one beach recce. 2SBS inserted from HMS *Intrepid* joined them, operating in the Teal area, ultimately guiding 3 Para into Teal before moving on to establish an observation post over an enemy company on Long Island Mountain.

This was followed by a small operation by the SBS to winkle out an enemy observation post. Their only casualty to date, Sergeant

Hunt, was killed here on the hill forward of Teal in a blue-on-blue incident, hit by SAS fire. The SAS pointed out that the SBS team leader, an experienced Commando, had strayed into their Green Patch operational zone. There were no recriminations despite the death; indeed, the incident led to closer cooperation between the two units. As we will see, they came together for one of the last, and spectacularly difficult, operations involving the Special Forces in the Falklands campaign.

By now the advance force in East Falkland was reaching its bloody but successful conclusion. The SBS continued its covert operations to the last and from 10 June began scouring the string of islands of West Falkland for enemy positions and airstrips. Teams were deployed to Port Stephens, Weddel Island, Chartres, Dunnose Head, Byron Heights, Caracass Island, Keppel Island, Saunders Island and Pebble Island, and one team went to Sea Lion Island off Laffonia.

Enemy were found on Pebble Island, estimated to number 30 to 50. The SBS planned to attack this garrison with 36 men and two Harriers, but they were overtaken by the surrender of the Argentinians at Port Stanley. An SBS major took the surrender of Pebble Island and discovered that had the SBS taken it on they would have confronted a well-armed garrison of 112 men.

Three pockets of stubborn resistance were cleared up on the west island with the SBS directing naval bombardment, one on Fox Bay and two on Port Howard. The operations were one-night stands in which the SBS teams were inserted by small boat from a supporting frigate to a point within 1,000 metres of the target.

The final deployment of the SBS in the campaign, its one remaining piece of action, was shared between a joint force of SAS and SBS as part of the battle for Port Stanley. While the main action took the credits, this little piece of activity was barely noticed by historians, though it should have been. On 12 June 2 Para began its attack on Wireless Ridge, five miles west of Port Stanley. A six-man team from 3SBS formed a volunteer raiding-party with D and G Squadrons, SAS, with the object of creating a diversionary assault from the sea to deflect some of the hostile fire from the paratroopers. The task was unplanned, spur of the moment, dreamed up by the Special Forces, who could not possibly stand around looking on as the massed guns came blazing out.

After a day in an observation post, the SBS team was to swim across to Wireless Ridge and move forwards. In the event this was impractical, and on 12 June the team, with a troop from SAS D Squadron, were to move across the Murrell River by four fast power-boats, RRCs (rigid raider craft) brought round during the night by the trawler *Cordella* and driven by men from the Royal Marines 1st Raiding Squadron. They were hidden off Kidney Island until they were ready to launch their assault.

The next night, 13–14 June and the last day of the war, the men began their approach towards their target area. On the way they had to pass the Argentinian hospital-ship *Bahia Paraiso*, berthed in Port Stanley harbour. As they did so, the crew switched on their search-lights, drawing them in an arc across the water. The boat raiders were sitting targets. Argentinians on both sides of the water, certain they faced a full-scale sea-borne assault, turned everything they had on the SBS/SAS teams: mortars, artillery, anti-aircraft cannon, even small arms. The skies were filled with metal, hot and gleaming.

The raiders had no option but to withdraw. One of the RRCs was badly damaged and limped back on hardly any power. The coxswain steered her by the hospital-ship for a shield and the boat died on them just as they reached the water's edge. Another sank just offshore, but close enough for the team to swim to safety. Good luck and poor shooting by the enemy – plus a lot of guts on the part of the coxswains – saved the men from disaster. An SBS corporal and two SAS troopers were wounded. The RRCs were riddled with holes and had to be destroyed. This time, the combined unit of SBS and SAS admitted they had broken the first rule of raiding-parties: don't do kamikaze missions. But to be fair, they weren't anticipating the hospital ship to get involved. Even so, the exercise provided a 'terrific diversion' for 2 Para on the other end of Wireless Ridge and doubtless saved a few lives at that end.

There remains, as we come to the close of this glimpse at SBS activity in the Falklands, one other area that was a subject of controversy in the aftermath: the raiding of the Argentinian main-land. This has never been admitted by the Ministry of Defence. This book has attempted to deal only in certainties and fact and to avoid speculation, but most of the reporters of the campaign and several television documentaries would suggest that the Special Forces were involved in raids on Argentinian mainland positions before the campaign ended. The BBC's James Fox provided an account that claimed they had entered through Chile, landing in a Sea King helicopter which was then dumped.

Chapter Nineteen

Footsteps to the Gulf

The Falklands experience focused military minds – as all wars do in the aftermath and the inquests – on the future. The Special Forces, whose contribution to that campaign remained oblique and guarded for many years, became the subject of numerous internal papers. An ongoing debate into their role was not fully resolved until 1987, when the present Special Forces Group command was formed. It became a brokerage for all tasks and special projects that were the speciality of Special Forces units, predominantly SBS and SAS, with support from other units from the army and the RAF.

If there were any remaining doubts as to their effectiveness, they were countermanded by the analysis of the Falklands. What Operation Corporate highlighted – and the Gulf War of 1990–91 would re-emphasise – was that where there was no contingency plan for the conflict, the specialised skills of the SAS and SBS were vital. It was perhaps significant that the SBS was chosen to join a Special Forces contingency study. Plans to counter any future attack or invasion of the Falklands by the Argentinians were drawn up. The SBS carried out a detailed recce of the islands and all the proposals were rehearsed in 1985.

To make sure that a similar problem might be averted in Belize, that other outpost of Britain's colonial past on the eastern coast of central South America, an SBS detachment was posted there in 1983. Belize, with its population of 175,000, was granted independence from Britain in 1981 and became a member of the

Commonwealth. But it was also the subject of a long-running territorial dispute with Guatemala, which had periodically threatened to invade and, like Argentina, had been making rumblings in that direction around the time of independence. Britain remained responsible for defence of the country, and a contingency plan against invasion or other incursions was prepared. The SBS sent a team to join two SAS patrols, based in a military compound 6 miles from Belize City. They were to remain there until 1987.

At home, with a dramatic increase in the size and impact of the IRA's mainland bombing campaign, the SBS role in the Maritime Counter-Terrorist Force activity was also consolidated and extended. As we have seen, it had previously been under the control of the Comacchio Company of the Royal Marines. Soon after their return from the Falklands, the two SBS sections involved with maritime counter-terrorism were amalgamated, and command of the group switched from Scotland to Poole. After several studies and papers on anti-terrorist operations, the group was expanded further in 1987 with two rifle troops and became M Squadron of the SBS, dedicated to maritime counter-terrorism.

By 1990 it had three troops, Black, Gold and Purple, each tasked at various levels of counter-terrorist activity and manned entirely by SBS personnel. The squadron has carried out numerous operations although for reasons of security details remain scarce. By then, new areas of operations were being included in the SBS brief. These included working with anti-organised crime units within police and Customs and Excise, focusing especially on drug trafficking, and other projects that are today on-going and remain ultra-secret, including a continued presence in Northern Ireland.

Changes in the whole concept of Special Forces were under way, and not merely or in relation to their deployment and control. A lot of baggage, transported from a previous age, was being discarded. The SBS was also undergoing a significant change in its man management. In the 1950s and 1960s officers came and went after a two-or three-year stint; it was not considered a good career move to linger too long. The original theories of the likes of Nigel Willmott and Blondie Hasler of a unit with a higher proportion of officers were, in those times of crisis and austerity, diluted.

The change began falteringly when the SBS switched from its post-war role as a predominantly instructional group to an operations-led force. It remained a training ground, especially for upwardly mobile officers in the Royal Marines, and NCOs still formed the backbone of the SBS, as they do today. As the SBS raised its profile, so too did the standards of entry and selection of men. Former SBS training officer Captain Neil Johnstone confirmed:

> People just couldn't understand the failure rate, and challenged it. We can now see that, historically, it has never been any different, except that it hardened on the side of rejection. It's got to be like it is. The summer and winter courses, which were adopted in the 1970s, for example, proved another factor that people couldn't understand. Why have two? The answer was simple. One man may not be able to withstand the extremes of the wet and the cold in winter, and conversely others might not manage the heat of summer training or operational activity. We need people who can operate in both. We always found that when you dropped one of these training situations for economy, the unit suffered later. We kept going, hardening up the selection process, and ended up with a lot of super, intelligent blokes who were very good indeed.

The point was emphasised by his story of a young marine who almost did not stay the course. 'S' was a 'ghastly corporal'. His officers constantly moaned about his attitude – 'It's S being difficult again' – and they were wondering what to do with him. He took a sergeant's course and went on to become a training colour-sergeant and was 'magic, very good indeed'. He was still reluctant to go on. His officer advised him to go for his commission: 'There's everything in the SBS now. Why don't you go for it? The alternative is to go back to the Corps and work up from there.' S stayed the course, won his commission, and later served with distinction.

Extensive training, the opportunity to learn specialist skills, from demolition to languages, and forced situations of endurance are the similarities shared between SAS and SBS. The common thread is that the men are called on to do things that they would never do voluntarily. They may look at a particular challenge, from rock-climbing to endurance swimming, and say to themselves 'I can't do that', but they do it anyway, driven by a combination of macho bravado within the group, personal challenge or plain and simple survival. At that point, the SAS and SBS reach a fork in the road.

They differ in both philosophy and objectivity. The SBS was more likely to consider the consequences of its actions and to weigh up the alternatives to brute force and fire power. It is, perhaps, no better typified than by comparison between the two mottoes, a comparison I was repeatedly invited to consider during interviews for this work: WHO DARES WINS and NOT BY STRENGTH, BY GUILE. The end result may well be the same, once the troops under either banner have reached their target, except that with the SBS the body-count may not be as high.

The basic philosophy may not have changed, but the whole context of SBS activity has itself undergone a total overhaul in the decade or so since the post-Falklands studies began.

The Iraq v. Iran, Iran v. Salman Rushdie, Israelis v. Palestinians and others, Iraq v. Kurds, bombing them with mustard gas, Iraq massing troops on the Kuwaiti border. To veterans of the SBS, those headlines were decidedly déjà vu. On 2 August 1990 Iraq invaded Kuwait and, in the words of Senator Donald W. Reigle, who chaired a 1994 Senate Committee investigating pre-Gulf War exports to Iraq from the US, panic gripped those nations that had kept up their trade with Saddam Hussein virtually to the day of the invasion.

As Reigle recalled: 'Suddenly it dawned on people that we were going to have a real problem facing off against weapons that we had helped create . . . because [Saddam Hussein] had not been on the bad-guy list at the time.' By then, anyway, it was too late. Ill-judged assessments that Saddam would not invade, or, if he did, that it would be a temporary incursion, proved disastrously wrong. Pentagon military planners produced a stark assessment of what confronted them. William Webster, director of the CIA, said: 'The Iraqis are within eight-tenths of a mile of the Saudi border. If Saddam stays where he is, he'll own 20 per cent of the world's oil reserves, and he's within a few miles of seizing another 20 per cent.

Jordan and Yemen will probably tilt towards him. We can expect Arab states to start cutting deals. Iran will be at Iraq's feet. Israel will be threatened.'

It was at this point that two of the key elements of Allied action against Iraq that could involve the Special Forces began to emerge, and for which contingency planning began by the end of the month:

1) A rescue attempt to bring out as many as possible of hundreds of Western expatriates living and working in Iraq and Kuwait whom Saddam infamously declared he would use as a human shield against air raids from the West.

2) To stop the Scuds which, in the case of all-out war, would almost certainly be used against Israel. By the end of August the pre-war options had attracted a crowded arena of Special Forces from the US, led by the American Special Operations Central Command with 5 Special Forces Group, the US Sea Air Land (SEAL) units; US Air Force Special Force and other smaller groups. They were the initial component parts of a planning effort that would proceed under the title Operation Desert Shield.

British Special Forces were standing by at the early stages but were soon to be diverted by the plight of the hostages in which Britain had a large interest, with around 800 expatriates in Kuwait and slightly more in Iraq. Saddam was threatening to herd them into his airfields and chain them to military installations, and indeed did so at the end of October, placing 661 of them at key economic and military sites. By September SAS and SBS planners were working with US Special Forces frantically trying to produce viable plans to get them out. The options were incredibly limited and fraught with danger, both to the rescuers and to those being rescued. There was no central focus because the hostages were dispersed over a wide area. The operational planning began from the standpoint that perhaps fewer than half might be reached, and even then the prospect of heavy casualties could not be ruled out.

Historically, there were three particular experiences on which to draw: the evacuation of US expatriates from the roof of the American embassy in Saigon in 1975; the successful Israeli raid on Entebbe in 1976 in which 100 hostages were freed; and, more disconcerting, President Jimmy Carter's disastrous attempt to free the Iranian hostages in 1980 which ended in disaster when the helicopter carrying America's crack Delta Force crashed in the desert.

With political pressure mounting and civilian concerns for relatives and friends making the headlines, General Sir Peter de la Billière asked the Special Forces planners to look at a possible mass rescue. His idea was that teams would drop into Iraq by parachute or helicopter, gather up the hostages, call back the helicopters, load them aboard and ferry them to a collection point somewhere in the desert. The problem of location remained. A good deal of work was done by the Foreign Office and the Ministry of Defence, who helped to build a map of the highest concentration of Britons. The Britons trapped in Kuwait might be more easily contacted and reached, since an underground communications network was established quickly among them; some were still contactable by telephone. The BBC World Service was available for bulletins and was already broadcasting messages from friends and relatives. A seaborne infiltration of Kuwait by the SBS was one possible option. The SBS would hopefully gather the Britons at a central point, perhaps the grounds of the British embassy, and airlift them by helicopter to safety, either to a desert rendezvous or to a ship in the Persian Gulf. The risk factor occurred in all deliberations, especially when the Americans began talking about diversionary raids to cover the evacuation. The British Special Forces were not at all happy.

By mid-November the British Special Forces command had assembled a force of around 800 men, including SBS, SAS and an RAF Special Forces section to join the Americans for the evacuation raids, although still no formal plan had been approved. At the same time, the prospect of them actually going in was diminishing daily. Amid diplomatic efforts to get the expatriates released, the Iraqi hostages were being moved around constantly, and no single human being in Iraq provided intelligence on their whereabouts. The best information came from watching CNN, and intelligence officials videoed and watched every frame of the news items. The chances of an effective round-up seemed slight. Even so, Special Forces were directed to press on and advance their plans to operational level so that, even if an all-out war did not develop, they might still be required to go in and bring out the hostages, by force if necessary.

Suddenly, that particular crisis was over. On 6 December Saddam Hussein released the hostages and said they would no longer be needed. This, in turn, gave the British Special Forces freedom to concentrate on a strategy for their own involvement in the war, if and when it came. They returned to their maps and intelligence to carve out a role for themselves, although few tasks were actually perceptible.

The US Special Forces had commandeered front-line reconnaissance as the Allied armies were arriving daily, by every means of transport available, until the Saudi Arabian desert was crammed with three-quarters of a million troops, kicking their heels and waiting for the off.

The style of the campaign was also not one that fitted the pattern of classic Special Forces operations, at least not in the beginning. It would be a high-tech, computer-controlled, satellite-directed air and missile attack, and there was no point in any Allied forces getting in the way of that. However, at the British Special Forces training base on the Arabian peninsula, planners went to work on surveying all possible objectives for an offensive role for their groups, listing attacks on military air bases to hit Saddam's supposed stock of 700 warplanes, deep infiltration to pinpoint likely targets for the Allied bombers, severing vital lines of communication and generally causing trouble.

There was, however, one other hurdle for them to overcome if they were to go to work at all. Overall commander of the Allied forces in the Gulf, General Norman Schwarzkopf, was not fond of Special Operations. He told journalists as much during one of his briefings, admitting that Vietnam border operations had left scars. He had also been let down in more recent times: the US commando tactics in the invasions of Grenada and Panama were both severely flawed, the Delta Force disaster in Iran was seared in American memories, and the aid-for-Contras scandal caused more bother than it was worth.

Then, all changed overnight. Apprehension vanished as Saddam Hussein began launching test flights of his Scud missiles from a site near Basra, day after day, test after test. US satellites tracked the missile flights and produced rapid predictions of their capability, damage and range. The last was an impossible equation because with mobile Scud launchers, Israel and Saudi Arabia were easy targets. There was also the unknown factor of his warheads. Was he bluffing or would he use them?

The CIA NonProliferation Center in Washington had a mass of data on that painful topic. The CIA had established that Saddam had been manufacturing his own Scud warheads, filled with gas and biological agents. This intelligence was to be proved entirely correct, if understated. UN teams after the war found 13,000 shells filled with mustard gas, 6,200 rockets loaded with nerve gas, 800 nerve agent aerial bombs, 28 Scud warheads loaded with nerve gas, and a stockpile of 75 tons of nerve agent – not counting that which was blown up during the war or squirreled away for future use.

On 17 January the air war began 12 days ahead of schedule with a spectacularly televised precision blitz on Baghdad by the Coalition. The Iraqi Scuds started flying before the day was out, and with them came fear of what the warheads would contain. The chemical and biological threat is fully explored in my earlier book, *The Killing Factory*, and has since been aired fully and controversially. My opening paragraph set the scene as the Coalition prepared for Scud attacks:

> 'Gas! It's gas . . .! Level four, level four. Not a drill. Repeat, not a drill.' The words were shouted often as thousands of chemical detectors and alarm systems positioned across the Saudi Arabian desert among the tented cities of the Coalition forces screamed the alert and sent the troops diving for cover. Sweating buckets in their protective suits, drugged with a cocktail of 13 separate vaccines and tablets, breathing air heavily polluted by sand, dust, diesel fumes, jet fuel, pesticides, bug sprays and depleted uranium tips of armour-piercing shells, the massed armies of Desert Storm were on the very edge of their nerves . . . The tension could be sliced with a blunt bayonet.

On the second day of the war a dozen Iraqi Scuds hit the suburbs of

Tel Aviv, bringing an immediate demand from Israel for air clearance to strike back. Schwarzkopf knew full well that doing so may well have compromised Arab support for the Coalition, support that was at times threatened but always vital. Apart from the sensitive political implications of allowing Israeli jets over Arab air space, an Israeli air intervention, possibly followed by a full-scale invasion, would also disturb the pre-planned and computer-programmed air attacks, with Coalition sorties running to hundreds a day. The Scud factor had to be met. The untried and hugely expensive Patriot surface-to-air missile response would not provide an absolute deterrent, and in any event they were still in short supply.

According to General Sir Peter de la Billière, he 'steamrollered' Norman Schwarzkopf into agreeing to use the British Special Forces; having done so, they now had to be adequately tasked. At the start of the air war the Special Forces were still at their training base on the Arabian peninsula. They had to move in double-quick time to get their men, vehicles and equipment to a forward holding base 1,200 miles (1,930 kilometres) away, located 650 miles (1,045 kilometres) north-west of Riyadh. With RAF Special Forces Hercules transporters making return trips, they completed the movement within 24 hours with the help of the US Tactical Aircraft Control Centre, which guided them through every mile of air space, alive with the hundreds of Allied warplanes heading north on their bombing raids.

The role of the Special Forces now crystallised into the anti-Scud effort. With no amphibious role for the SBS, a line was drawn through the map of anticipated operations across southern Iraq. The SAS was to cover the western territory, SBS to the east. Their principal tasks would be to scout Scud launch-sites, mobile Scud traffic and any other targets that eluded the air strikes. Road-watch teams were to be inserted by helicopter 140 to 180 miles (225 to 290 kilometres) behind the enemy border.

In the SBS sector of operations lay one other crucial installation that was to become the first target of the British Special Forces, and an operation exclusively planned and executed by the SBS. It consisted of a vast and complex communications network which, among other things, linked Saddam Hussein to his Iraqi forward positions. The SBS task was to locate and destroy the heavily concealed mass of fibre-optic cable buried well below ground, identified by US satellite intelligence.

The execution of the task was not a problem with SBS expertise; the dangers lay in the location – just 32 miles west of Baghdad. With barely time for their customary work-up, the SBS team of 36, led by Lieutenant 'S', prepared for their journey. Under cover of darkness on the night of 22 January, the men clambered aboard two Boeing Vertol Chinook helicopters from No. 7 Squadron's Special Forces Flight and flew north deep into Iraq to the site close to a road.

Nomadic Arabs and desert spies abounded in the area, so close to Iraq air and ground resources that a counter-attack force could have been launched rapidly. The team, heavily armed and equipped, carried 400 pounds (180 kilogrammes) of explosives. They flew direct to the site, leaped from the helicopters and sprinted to the target a short distance from the main road. The helicopter pilots kept their engines running but disengaged the rotors to cut down on the noise and to be certain of a swift exit should it become necessary. As they landed, the night sky was ablaze with Coalition bombardment of Baghdad.

The SBS team quickly located the communications cables and dug down, taking out a length to bring home for analysis, and placed explosive charges along the exposed area. Then they retreated and detonated their charges, blowing up a 40-yard (36-metre) section. The mission was described by Sir Peter as a high-risk operation carried out with great skill, determination and courage in a most hostile environment; it was a total success. The SBS party completed the task with no casualties in 90 minutes flat.

Before they left, Lieutenant 'S' grabbed one of the cable-route markers that, on his return, he presented as a souvenir to General Norman Schwarzkopf, who was so impressed by the success of the mission that he reported it immediately to General Colin Powell in Washington. Powell in turn passed the news and US congratulations back to London.

The SAS, meanwhile, was inserting three eight-man road-watch patrols to scout the Scud box and watch for traffic along three roads deep in the desert and 20 miles (32 kilometres) apart. Their exploits and the tragic compromise of one of the teams have been vividly described in various books, most notably *Bravo Two Zero*, by team member 'Andy McNab', and *The One That Got Away*, by Chris Ryan. This latter team was discovered when an enemy camp was set up almost on top of the men, three of whom died in their frantic efforts to escape – two from enemy fire and one from exposure. Four, including McNab, were captured, while Ryan made his epic journey to Syria.

Suffice to say that the mixed fortunes of the Special Forces group were perhaps most poignantly demonstrated in the command headquarters, when the success of the SBS operation was being analysed while the commander of the SAS, Colonel Andrew Massey, was in tears over the plight of his own lost patrol.

Another mission for the SBS came towards the end of the war. They were tasked with reclaiming possession of the British Embassy in Kuwait. They were personally chosen by General de la Billière, who was anxious to re-establish a British presence as soon as possible so that the nation's interests were well represented when the reconstruction of Kuwait was up for grabs.

The SBS went into action on 27 February 1991 when the men flew into Kuwait in their helicopters and set up a temporary base at the wrecked Kuwait airport. The next day, General de la Billière ordered the launch of the operation. The SBS worked on the assumption that the embassy buildings and grounds might be booby trapped, or perhaps still be harbouring a kamikaze group of Iraqi troops. Two Chinooks took off from the airport and hovered over the building. The SBS team roped down from the helicopters on to the roof of the embassy.

They had plans and a description of the building from staff who had been the last there but, when they discovered discrepancies, quickly withdrew to plan an explosive entrance, as mandated by their operational instructions. They threw stun-grenades through the windows and blasted down the huge and famous front door, designed by Edwin Lutyens. In fact, the precautions turned out to be unnecessary. The building had never been occupied by the Iraqis, and a Kuwaiti janitor who was still living nearby could have let them in with a key.

As it was, the British Ambassador, who flew in that night to take possession of his little haven among the devastation, was dismayed that the Lutyens door had been blown up.

There were other operations carried out by the Special Forces during the Gulf War, but at the time of writing they remain classified.

Chapter Twenty

No licence to kill

The creation of a central command for British Special Forces had, by the early 1990s, developed a strategy of tasking that has brought new dimensions to the role of the SBS. No longer do they hang around waiting for wars or fill their time portraying the enemy in NATO exercises, although as an élite military group both remain their prime reason for being. Their commitment to maritime counter-terrorism also demands that they remain at peak readiness for any eventuality through training and exercises. But, just as MI5 began to diversify into other areas of civilian intelligence as the Cold War ended, SBS approaches the end of the century with one eye on the future – ready to work with other Government agencies.

The National Crime Intelligence Service (NCIS) may well become one of the organisations increasingly seeking SBS support. Launched in 1992, it targets the higher echelons of crime. It was one of the first services to be set up in Europe to deal with the development of criminal intelligence on a national scale, with approximately 500 staff drawn from the police, Customs and Excise and the Home Office. Its international division manages a network of European Drugs Liaison Officers and is linked up with the world-wide DLO group managed by Customs and Excise. The UK Bureau of Interpol is also based within this division, providing NCIS with direct access to Interpol's 176 member countries.

Although all projects in which the SBS is involved are security sensitive and remain well away from public view, modern tasking is leading them towards longer-term involvement in what may be regarded as ultra-secret activity. The SBS is never glimpsed by the media and especially not by cameramen, although one of its earliest 'civilian' tasks in the drugs arena did make the headlines, simply because of the size of the target: a ton of pure cocaine worth £160 million, the largest quantity ever seized in Britain.

Months of monitoring the movements of a ship, *Fox Trot Five*, and its largely British crew, culminated with a spectacular raid at Greenwich, London, with an SBS team swarming all over the vessel as she tied up on the Thames. The boat, which had been bought in America, had sailed to an island off Colombia and was tracked across the Atlantic. On 23 November 1992, she was sailing towards a mooring beside a warehouse on the edge of the Thames.

The vessel sailed on along the South Coast and back up into the Thames, where she was once again moored at Greenwich. There, in an operation that had so far included Customs and Excise, Interpol, the US Drugs Enforcement Administration and Scotland Yard and now the SBS, the trap was sprung. The members of the crew were watched as they unloaded a ton of cocaine wrapped in black polythene bags and carried it into a warehouse. At a given signal, two RIBS carrying the SBS teams, in their black gear with balaclavas over their faces, stormed across the Thames from a nearby hiding-place; the first group, armed with Heckler and Koch MP5 sub-machine-guns and stun-grenades, clambered aboard, followed by a second group in support. Meanwhile, a large contingent of armed police and customs men on the shore followed on behind a police-driven JCB as it broke down the doors to the warehouse. The job was done.

Five men were arrested at the warehouse, and later two hundred policemen raided eighteen addresses in the South-East of England. The SBS faded quietly and quickly into the background, disappearing whence it came. But for one sharp-eyed woman named Joyce Lowman, who took a picture of the SBS team as it boarded the boat, its presence would not have been revealed.

Is this the future or part future role of the SBS? It is certainly an area in which the SBS are likely to be used, but they are basically Royal Marines, in other words soldiers, commandos, complemented by a specialisation in maritime skills. They can provide skills that are unique. It is recognised now, in the mid-1990s, that they are able to deliver a capability that no one else has. Clearly, they have been involved in a wide diversity of operational activity. It is, however, only within the last decade that they have moved into a completely different environment. Their tasking has become substantially more positive and indeed the threatening possibilities on the international horizon have become more intense. At the same time, their reason for being is not now in accord with the popular image of the special forces, which is one of apparent personal glorification and self-satisfaction.

Survival? They are past masters of the art. And so when, in March 1994, a British army expedition from Hong Kong went missing, a joint SAS/SBS team went in to find the men and plucked them out within 48 hours of the team's arrival, a fact never publicised at the time. Lieutenant-Colonel Robert Neil of the Royal Logistics Corps led his party of ten on an army expedition from Hong Kong to the 13,455-foot (4,101-metre) Mount Kinabalu on the island of Borneo. It included himself, a fellow officer, five young soldiers and three Chinese military officers.

The region was well known to members of the Special Forces from their past involvement in this place of dense jungle and difficult terrain, which needs exceptional skills if trouble is to be avoided. Several SBS men had themselves tackled the mountain following an exercise the previous year. Its infamous attraction to adventurers, Low's Gully, so called because colonial officer William Low toasted the British Empire in port when he became the first man to conquer the mountain in 1851. The gully is a 2,000-foot (610-metre) long, steep jungle gorge that offers virtually every possible challenge to expeditions such as theirs – sheer, vertical rock to be abseiled, a 400-foot (120-metre) waterfall to be negotiated, a rock-hopping section across deep plunge-pools, dense jungle through which it took them four days to hack through a mile, and so on. It is said that a full descent of the gully, from the top to its absolute floor, has never been achieved.

The expedition split into two for the descent from the mountain. One team managed, with difficulty, to return to the base on 12

March. The second team which included the expedition leader Lieutenant-Colonel Neil, became long overdue. Initially, an RAF mountain team was deployed to find the men, helicopters searched, and two officers put on to Low's Gully found traces of the team – empty sardine cans. Heavy rain, however, turned the gully into a fast-moving river, and the two men were flown back to base exhausted.

On 21 March the Malaysian Army provided 400 trackers and soldiers to scour the valley – without success. On 24 March the RAF went back in with a six-man team, turning back after hitting trouble on the waterfall. On the same day it was decided in London to send a Special Forces team, including five SAS men, three SBS and seven others, to conduct a search.

The team left London and two days later it was on the edge of the jungle. The first air recce used a Malaysian Army helicopter with two Malaysian airmen, and by the end of the first day the missing men were found.

Two members of the Special Forces team, a major and a sergeant, spotted flashes of light which brought them in for a closer look. It was that, and not an SOS spelled out in pebbles on the river bank – as some have suggested – that drew them to the spot. Later, they discovered that the flashes of light were made by a camera, not a mirror.

The helicopter, not entirely suited to the job at hand, went in as low as it dared and the SF team found the men, starved and in a bad psychological condition. The team signalled its discovery and returned to base to get supplies, which were winched down, along with an SBS medic. The next day the SF team acquired a Sea King helicopter for the final rescue. So ended the drama of the five missing men, hugely reported in Britain and across the world. No mention was made of the British Special Forces who got them out.

Similarly unreported and anonymously enacted was the role of the British Special Forces, including the SBS, in the finale of the bloody conflict that engulfed the former Yugoslavia in the first half of the 1990s. The SBS was placed on alert from the early stages of the war in Bosnia, virtually from the moment the first of Britain's contingent of 3,500 troops were standing by to join the United Nations Protection Force (UNProFor). The explosion of ethnic, religious and territorial violence which was to bring daily images of unimaginable horrors on to television screens for the next five years began at the turn of the decade. Serbia, the lead nation of that unfortunate combination of states forced together in the early part of this century to form Yugoslavia, tried to impress its will on the others and retain control of the disintegrating republic after the death of Tito.

First it went to war with Slovenia, then Croatia, as both states won international recognition for independence. But those conflicts were a minor forerunner to the appalling and ferocious conflict that flared in Bosnia between the Serbs and an alliance of Croats and Muslims. In the spring of that year, as the Serbs pounded Sarejevo into the dust, the international community was finally, if reluctantly, forced to act and intervene on behalf of the millions caught in the crossfire.

The British intention was announced by Prime Minister John Major on 21 August 1992 as the British contribution 'to support the United Nations High Commission for Refugees operations in the former Yugoslavia. Time is now needed to assemble and prepare such a force. There is therefore pressure for those elements of the army likely to be involved to be at a high state of readiness so that they can react should the government's offer be accepted by the United Nations.'

The 1st Battalion of the Cheshire Regiment would form the core of Britain's initial troop deployment, along with a medium reconnaissance squadron of the 9/12 Royal Lancers, and they headed for the area around Tuzla as the winter set in. There began the British involvement in what the 1st Cheshire commander, Lieutenant-Colonel Bob Stewart, described as 'one of the most vicious wars ever'.

The British Special Forces as a group began contingency planning for possible tasks as the UN gathered its force of 20,000 men in that winter of 1992. The UN role, filled with complexities, restrictions, local opposition and with one arm tied behind its back, was chaotic and for the most part impossible from the start. The UN forces were the buffer in a seemingly unfathomable civil war. As Bob Stewart said in his autobiography, 'The Cheshire group . . . were not there to "make peace"; we were not enforcers of it . . . Helping to create conditions for peaceful resolution of disputes was one thing, but forcing a cessation of hostilities was certainly outside of our charter. Peacekeepers have to react to events while enforcement troops may have to create them.'

It was the ambiguity of the UNProFor role that put the peacekeeping force in constant danger and, at the same time, imposed restrictions on assault activity of any kind, regardless of the aim – and that included the SBS. Their initial role, therefore, was a delicate one concerning the humanitarian effort but equally for precautionary measures over the deployment of British troops. As the unforgettable pictures of the starving prisoners of war, the massacres, the mass graves, the relief efforts – stalled time and again – to get food to millions of starving people, along with the desolate faces of the Vance–Owen peace negotiators, reached television screens world-wide, the SBS was already in rehearsal.

The possibility of British forces being isolated, ambushed or captured in the conflict occurred daily. In early 1993, an SBS team conducted recces of certain areas. Rehearsals were staged in Britain for possible tasks of both an operational and a humanitarian nature. The following year the then commander of UNProFor, General Mike Rose, formally requested the presence of British Special Forces, and the SBS contributed teams for patrols and reconnaissance. They were operating within the region first designated for the establishment of British troops under UN command.

In October 1995, the Dayton Peace Initiative, supported by all the major Western powers under the NATO alliance, began to set in motion the groundwork for a total cessation of hostilities. In December the SBS joined a large deployment of British Special Forces, who were to become part of NATO's Operation Joint Endeavour and the British component, Operation Resolute.

In a combined and determined effort, NATO would provide 60,000 troops, including 20,000 Americans and 10,000 British to police the ceasefire and enforce it if necessary. Optimism that this war was finally ending rose when the peace formula, eventually signed on 15 December, was accepted by all sides.

Between the beginning of December and D-Day, nominated as 18 January 1996, when the zone of separation between the various 'entities' was to be vacated, a great deal of delicate negotiation was required on the ground, particularly in the flashpoints where peace was most likely to be threatened. On that day UNProFor troops would join the incoming reinforcements under the command of NATO's Allied Command Europe Rapid Reaction Corps (ARRC).

It was in this area that the British Special Forces team of SBS and SAS was operating, linked to the complicated demarcation line, hundreds of miles of the ceasefire front, along with territory swaps and evacuations.

An SBS squadron provided important advance intelligence for the incoming US 1st Armoured Division. The American force was designated to make a tactical deployment based on a forced crossing of the River Sava. The advance was, however, significantly amended in the light of SBS contacts and reconnaissance within the region.

As a direct result of SBS recommendations, the Americans made the crossing, unforced and in relative calm, by bridge. The epic building of a new 370-metre pontoon bridge over the Sava, and another 240-metre span over its flooded surrounds – the largest undertaking of its kind since they crossed the Rhine at Remagen in the same fashion 50 years earlier – was completed by 1 January 1996. The Americans moved unhindered into position.

ARRC commanders recognised that the 'initiative, judgement and creativity of the SBS' were fundamental in allowing the US1AD to adapt to the local situation and meet deadlines set by the Dayton Peace Agreement. The SBS remained until August 1996, when the peace agreements they had helped nudge into place appeared to be holding. Then it left, as usual, without a trace of its having been there in the first place, as ever a tiny cog that helped the big wheels to keep on turning. The only clue to SBS involvement were unidentifiable mentions in the *London Gazette*, when several members of its team won commendations and medals for service in Bosnia.

Epilogue

So you still want to join . . . ?

We are nearing the end of the story, and the Bosnia deployment demonstrated one more string to the SBS bow, a mission successfully completed in a place fraught with difficulties and requiring not only pre-planning but instant initiative and methods of persuasion that were never to reach the stage of fire power. The SBS has always shown a remarkable cool-headedness in this regard; it has seldom opened up an assault situation unless absolutely necessary. The lightness of casualties in operations filled with disastrous potential will have been evident throughout this account, even though SBS operational activity has largely been behind enemy lines and always close to fire power. Yet even accounting for those missions that have remained from public view, losses of men have been few.

Since the Second World War, casualties in action have been outnumbered by losses incurred during exercises and training. Even during the last war, after initial sorties, which saw a hefty toll in those killed or captured, the numbers were kept significantly light. This was in part due to good fortune but largely because of the insistence of commanding officers, the founders of the SBS, RMBPD, COPPs and SRU, that every member of those units should not only be willing volunteers but should be fully and expertly trained, be adequately equipped and undergo a full and realistic rehearsal of any intended operation. Additionally, the men were to be coordinated at all times by an effective command, control and administration structure fully conversant with SBS needs and demands, however eccentric they might appear at the time. This, as has been seen, was not always appreciated by conventional force commanders.

Those wartime traditions continued in the post-war formation of the SBS and remain at the very heart of its operations today. In short, training and planning have built-in survival factors – and survival is not just about armed combat or having sufficient rations to last a delayed stay behind the lines.

Survival is in the planning and in the training. As both Blondie Hasler in the 1940s and current CO said, the SBS and the Special Forces groups are not about sending men on suicide missions. An inadequately trained man would face certain death, and a badly planned operation spells disaster. The guidelines drawn up long ago – in 1958, in fact – have barely changed in that regard. In the manual entitled *The Organisation and Employment of Special Boat Sections* produced by the Commandant General's Office of the Royal Marines, the ground rules were specific and clear:

> It is important that SBS or sub-units should avoid being engaged by superior forces. Success depends on their skill and thorough and detailed planning and rehearsals. It is essential therefore that all intelligence is made available and that adequate time is allowed for preparation before an operation is launched . . .
>
> In accordance with the Supreme Allied Commander's policy governing Special Operations . . . directives for Special Boat Sections will be broad so far as carrying out the operations is concerned but precise in defining its object and in imposing any limitations on the operation . . .
>
> The success of a small-scale amphibious operation depends mainly upon a carefully prepared and feasible plan in which sufficient time must be allowed for delays and taking alternative action if a turn of events or deterioration of the weather makes this necessary. The plan must be simple yet flexible, with every possible contingency thought through at planning stage. This will ensure that alternative courses of action are decided upon at planning stage . . .

> The detailed plan will contain specific information and timings that are of paramount importance to each individual man taking part and which in fact must be committed to memory . . .
>
> Planning requirements: Up-to-date Intelligence reports, large-scale maps, all available charts, detailed interpretation report; Tide tables and Atlas of Tidal Streams, the Nautical Almanac for obtaining bearing and timings of Sun, Moon, etc. Appropriate list of Lights . . .
>
> SB operations may be considered in progressive stages of planning, preparation and rehearsal: 1) approach in parent vessel or aircraft to operational area, 2) the final approach by raiding-craft or by swimming or combination of both, 3) carrying out the task, 4) recovery and withdrawal 5) debriefing, 6) report writing.
>
> In execution of the above and especially where a reconnaissance raid is a prelude to a larger operation, the following measures are essential: a) Time must be allowed for at least one alternative method of recovery, b) alternative swimmer recovery-positions must be laid down, c) an alternative craft homing position must be arranged, d) a suitable lying-up position ashore should be pre-located, e) recovery on a subsequent night at an emergency rendezvous, f) if all else fails, escape overland.

The above provides a brief look at the SBS operational cycle, which in practice is vastly more detailed.

To meet those demands, the selection and training of the Special Boat Service are regularly reviewed and overhauled to meet modern trends, new technology and better, faster equipment and boats. Although one of the guiding principles that have existed since the SBS and its antecedent companions were formed in the Second World War is that all candidates must be volunteers, the last standard selection procedure was laid down in January 1994. Today, candidates wishing to join the SBS will attend a Joint Special Forces selection procedure over a tough course in the Brecon Beacons, followed by wild territory in Brunei and the ultimate test at the SAS headquarters in Hereford.

Two courses, under the supervision of a joint SBS/SAS training team, are held each year. Before the start of selection, the candidate must attend a two-week aptitude test run by the SBS training team which will determine if a man is suitable to operate in the most challenging of environments.

The aptitude test consists of the following elements:

Boating Phase (1 week). Students must:

Pass a Combat Fitness Test.

Pass the SBS Swimming Test, which demands 600 metres (656 yards) in 15 minutes, plus 50 metres (55 yards) clothed with weapon and belt, and 25 metres (27 yards) under water without diving operations.

Complete all canoe trials including carrying canoe and fully loaded Bergen rucksack for 3 miles (4.8 kilometres); and complete a 20-mile (32-kilometre) canoe-paddle.

Diving Phase (1 week). Complete a number of dives and then satisfactorily demonstrate all drills taught. Show confidence and a willingness to dive.

The first week is physically and mentally demanding, the second week is more relaxed, covering basic diving theory and drills in slow time, with the aim of instilling confidence and assisting those less adaptable. But that is only a beginning, a mere holiday camp compared to what follows.

The Selection Course itself consists of the following programme:

1. Brecon Beacons phase (3 weeks)
2. Pre-Jungle Training (2 weeks)
3. Jungle Training, Brunei (6 weeks)
4. Officer week/Signals Training (1 week)
5. Support Weapons Training (1 week)
6. Army Combat Survival Instructor Course (2 weeks).

The three-week Brecon Beacons phase begins with an initial passing-in programme, including a Combat Fitness Test and a hill-walking exercise of 23 kilometres (14 miles) with a 40-pound

(18-kilogramme) Bergen rucksack and weapon. The second week includes a series of navigational and physical training exercises, including a swimming test. The final week includes six hill-walking exercises, covering a total of 180 kilometres (112 miles) with a Bergen and weapon.

Continuation training

1. Demolitions (2 weeks)
2. Observation Post Training (1 week)
3. CQB Course (2 weeks)
4. Individual Skills Courses (8 weeks)
5. Parachute Course (3 weeks).

During the eight-week individual training period, men are trained to become Special Forces communicators or medical specialists, while officers undergo language training and attend a Special Forces commanders' course. On completion of the para course, SBS students spend eight weeks learning the specialist skills of boating and diving, which includes aspects of submarine work, coastal navigation and tactical swimming operations. In addition, a range of well over a hundred further skills and qualifications are available, ranging from medicine to veterinary training, and from welding to law – plus tuition for virtually every language under the sun, depending on the operational requirement.

The course, says RM literature, is:

> Within the capability of most marines, particularly those with the mental commitment and determination to succeed. Training is demanding, but that's the way it has to be. The rewards are most definitely worth the effort and include: a structured career; job satisfaction; realistic and challenging exercises; extra skills training work with other SF units at home and abroad; operational employment and extra pay . . . but you earn it.

And, of course, acceptance into SBS is only the beginning. Training never ceases . . . and as reflected in these pages, the physical and psychological endurance of every man, regardless of rank, will be tested to the limit time and time again.

Appendix I

Equipment list

The report of Major Hasler, commander of Operation Frankton (aka Cockleshell Heroes), detailed in Chapter Five, listed the stores drawn for the operation. This list has never been previously published in full; it is printed here exactly as it appeared in the report. It formed the basis of many similar operations in the future, and even today is not unlike the requirements of a modern SBS team setting out on a mission.

The initials at the top of each column, i.e. H S L M W E, represent the team leaders.

EQUIPMENT LIST.

Boats' Gear.	H	S	L	M	W	E	Remarks.
Cockles Mk. II	1	1	1	1	1	1	
Double Paddes Mk.II prs.	3	3	3	3	3	3	
Handgrips Mk.II prs.	1	1	1	1	1	1	
Bailers	1	1	1	1	1	1	
Sponges	1	1	1	1	1	1	
Buoyancy Bags	2	2	2	2	2	2	
Cargo Bags, sets.	1	1	1	1	1	1	set of 5.
Magnetic holders	1	1	1	1	1	1	
Codline fms.	20	20	20	20	20	20	
Sounding Reels, 16 fms.	1	1	1	1	1	1	
Repair Bags	1	1	1	1	1	1	Each containing Bostick cement, patching canvas, needle, waxed threac Oil bottle, Waste, Tyre Patch, Rubber Solution, spare split pins and copper tacks.
Sectional Charts sets	1	1	1	1	1	1 ø	
Log Pads	1	1	1	1	1	1 ø	Containing tide tables and spare paper.
P.8 Compasses	1	1	1	1	1	1 ø	
Correctors for	1	1	1	1	1	1 ø	
Monoculars	1			1	1		
Pencils	2	2	2	2	2	2	Half size, sharpened.
Dim Reading Torches	1	1	1	1	1	1	
Spare Reading Torches	1			1			
Spare bulbs for	1	1	1	1	1	1 x	
Protractors, G.S.	1	1	1	1	1	1 ø	
Camouflage Nets	1	1	1	1	1	1	Special light type.
Watches pocket, G.S.	1	1	1	1	1	1 ø	Waterproofed.
Spare Torch batteries	2	1	1	1	1	1	
Wire Cutters		1				1	

Equipment List. Page 2.

Boats' Gear.	H	S	L	M	W	E	Remarks.
Screwdrivers		1				1	
Marline Spikes		1				1	
W.T. Matches, Tins	2	2	2	2	2	2	
Camouflage Cream, Tins	1	1	1	1	1	1	
Escape Kits							
Pieces of Chalk	2	2	2	2	2	2	
Whiting line, 4 fm. lengths	2	2	2	2	2	2	
Weapons & Explosives.							
Silent Sten 9 m.m.			1		1		
Magazines for			4		4		Each filled 32 Rds.
69 Granades	2	2	2	2	2	2	Fuzed
Limpets, Rigid, 6 Magnet	8	8	8	8	8	8	Fuzed A.C. and sympathetic.
Ampoule Boxes	2	2	2	2	2	2	Each contains 4 Red, 4 Orange Ampules. 4 Soluble Plugs. 2 Tins luting.
Limpet Spanners	1	1	1	1	1	1	
Placing Rods	2	2	2	2	2	2	
Food & Medical.							
Compact rations, days	10	10	10	10	10	10	Each day contains 3 boxes, 1 Tin Meat and 1 tin Cheese.
Water cans, $\frac{1}{2}$ gallon	5	5	5	5	5	5	Filled.
Benzedrine, Boxes	1	1	1	1	1	1	Each contain 20 tablets.
Water Sterilising sets	1	1	1	1	1	1	
1st Field Dressings	2	2	2	2	2	2	
Iodine Bottles	1	1	1	1	1	1	
Toilet Paper, packets.	2	2	2	2	2	2	
Morphia Syringes	2	2	2	2	2	2	
Hexamine Cookers	5	5	5	5	5	5	Varnished.

Equipment List. Page 3.

Food & Medical.	H	S	L	M	W	E	Remarks.
Dixie, (5 pint)	1	1	1	1	1	1	With Lids.
Foot Powder (Tins)	1	1	1	1	1	1	
W.T. Ditty Boxes	1	1	1	1	1	1	
Cough Lozenges, tins	1	1	1	1	1	1	
Laxative Pills, Tins	1	1	1	1	1	1	
Cups.							

Carried in Parent Ship

Camouflage Cream, Tins	2
Mk.II Slings and Spreaders	1 set
Slip Book	1
Girder for 4" Gun	1
Purchase Tackle	1
Wire Preventer Pendant	1
Preventatives	12
Seasick Tablets, Tubes	12
Boats' Envelopes	6
Air Pumps	1
Spare P.8 Compass	1
Box of Instructional Models	1
Mineral Jelly, lbs	2
Pads for Boats	6
Needles and Twine	
Photographs	
Orders	
Intelligence Reports	

Equipment List. **Page 4.**

On the Men.	H		S		L		M		W		E		Remarks.
	1	2	1	2	1	2	1	2	1	2	1	2	
Cockle Suit Complete	1	1	1	1	1	1	1	1	1	1	1	1	
W.T. Trousers, Prs.	1						1		1				
Socks, Prs.	1	1	1	1	1	1	1	1	1	1	1	1	
Denim Trousers, Prs.	1	1	1	1	1	1	1	1	1	1	1	1	With knife sheath sewn on.
Braces Prs.	1	1	1	1	1	1	1	1	1	1	1	1	
Belts, Light	1	1	1	1	1	1	1	1	1	1	1	1	
Pants, Long Thick Prs.	1	1	1	1	1	1	1	1	1	1	1	1	
Vests, Woollen, long Sleeves.	1	1	1	1	1	1	1	1	1	1	1	1	
Seaboot Stockings, Prs.	1	1	1	1	1	1	1	1	1	1	1	1	
Blue Balaclavas	1	1	1	1	1	1	1	1	1	1	1	1	
V. Neck Sweaters	1	1	1	1	1	1	1	1	1	1	1	1	
Blue Scarfs	1	1	1	1	1	1	1	1	1	1	1	1	
Handkerchiefs	1	1	1	1	1	1	1	1	1	1	1	1	
Reliant Life Jacket.	1	1	1	1	1	1	1	1	1	1	1	1	
Gloves, 3 Compartment, Silk.	1	1	1	1	1	1	1	1	1	1	1	1	
Gloves, 3 Compartment Wool.	1	1	1	1	1	1	1	1	1	1	1	1	
Red and Green Identity Discs.	2	2	2	2	2	2	2	2	2	2	2	2	
P.T. Shoes, Brown Prs.	1	1	1	1	1	1	1	1	1	1	1	1	
Twine, 12" long pieces.	6	6	6	6	6	6	6	6	6	6	6	6	
Web Belts & Holsters	1	1	1	1	1	1	1	1	1	1	1	1	
.45 Colt	1	1	1	1	1	1	1	1	1	1	1	1	
Magazines for	3	3	3	3	3	3	3	3	3	3	3	3	Includes one in gun Each loaded 7 rds.
Knives Fighting	1	1	1	1	1	1	1	1	1	1	1	1	
Bird Calls	1		2		2		1		2		2		On lanyards.
Clasp Knives	1	1	1	1	1	1	1	1	1	1	1	1	
Sheet of Paper	1	1	1	1	1	1	1	1	1	1	1	1	Lining Ditty Box.

Equipment List. Page 5.

In the Bags.	H		S		L		M		W		E		Remarks.
	1	2	1	2	1	2	1	2	1	2	1	2	
Short Pants Prs.	1	1	1	1	1	1	1	1	1	1	1	1	
Toothbrush & Paste	1	1	1	1	1	1	1	1	1	1	1	1	
Towel	1	1	1	1	1	1	1	1	1	1	1	1	
Handkerchiefs	1	1	1	1	1	1	1	1	1	1	1	1	
Sea Water Soap Pieces	1	1	1	1	1	1	1	1	1	1	1	1	
Razor and Blades	1	1	1	1	1	1	1	1	1	1	1	1	
Shaving Brush	1		1		1		1		1		1		
Felt-Soled Boots prs	1	1	1	1	1	1	1	1	1	1	1	1	
Spare laces for, prs.	1	1	1	1	1	1	1	1	1	1	1	1	
Socks, prs.	1	1	1	1	1	1	1	1	1	1	1	1	
Roll Neck Sweater	1	1	1	1	1	1	1	1	1	1	1	1	
Spare Woollen Gloves prs.	1	1	1	1	1	1	1	1	1	1	1	1	
Cigarettes	20	20	20	20	20	20	20	20	20	20	20	20	If required.
Extra Matches, Bos.	1	1	1	1	1	1	1	1	1	1	1	1	If required.

ESCAPE GEAR.

Binoculars	1	Additional reading torch	1
Dim reading torch	1	Matches (From W.T.T.)	1
Matches (From W.T.T.)	1	Escape Kits (complete)	1
Escape Kits (complete)	1	Spare Compact Rations	
Watch	1	First Field Dressing	1
Spare Compact Rations		Iodine Bottles	1
Benzedrine Boxes	1	Morphia Syringe	1
First Field Dressing	1	Tin, Water	1
Morphia Syringe	1	Pills Boxes	1
Foot Powder (tin)	1	Pencils	1
Tin Water	1	Camouflage Cream	1
Pills Boxes	1	String, of, peices, fms.	4
Needle and Thread	1	Toilet Paper, Pkts.	1
Oil Bottle	1		
Pencils	1		
String, of, Pieces, fms.	4		
Water Sterilising Set	1		
Toilet Paper Pkts.	1		

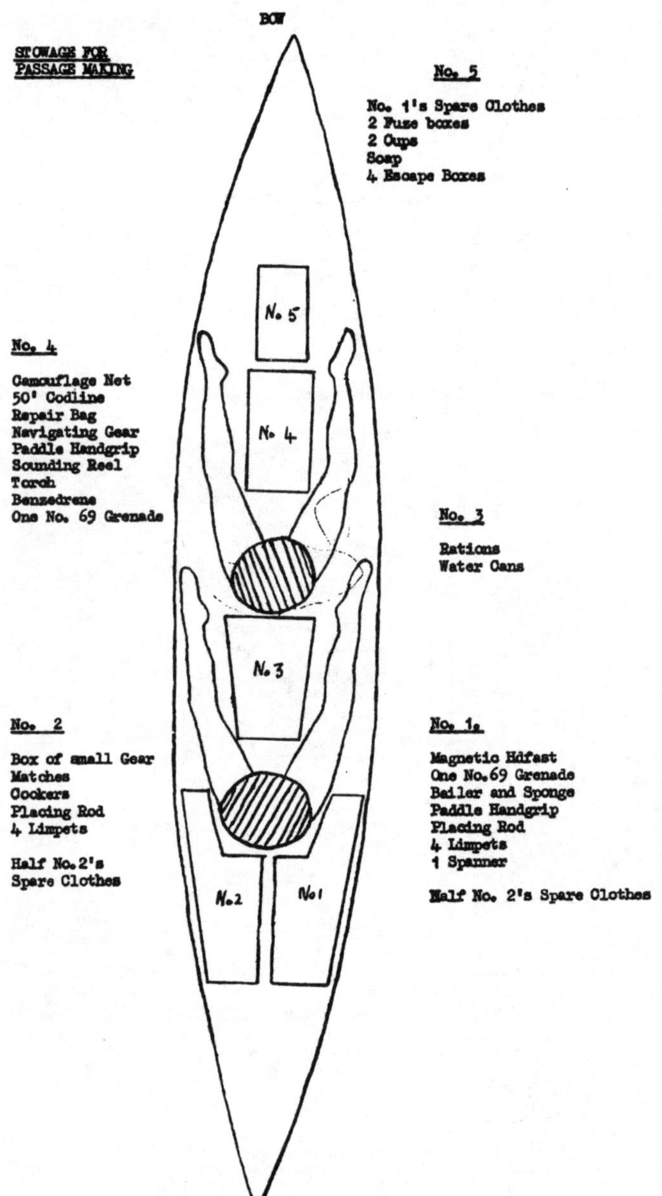
BOW
STOWAGE FOR
PASSAGE MAKING
No. 5
No. 1's Spare Clothes
2 Fuse boxes
2 Cups
Soap
4 Escape Boxes
No. 4
Camouflage Net
50' Codline
Repair Bag
Navigating Gear
Paddle Handgrip
Sounding Reel
Torch
Benzedrene
One No. 69 Grenade
No. 3
Rations
Water Cans
No. 2
Box of small Gear
Matches
Cookers
Placing Rod
4 Limpets
Half No. 2's
Spare Clothes
No. 1.
Magnetic Hdfast
One No. 69 Grenade
Bailer and Sponge
Paddle Handgrip
Placing Rod
4 Limpets
1 Spanner
Half No. 2's Spare Clothes
No. 5
No. 4
No. 3
No. 2
No 1

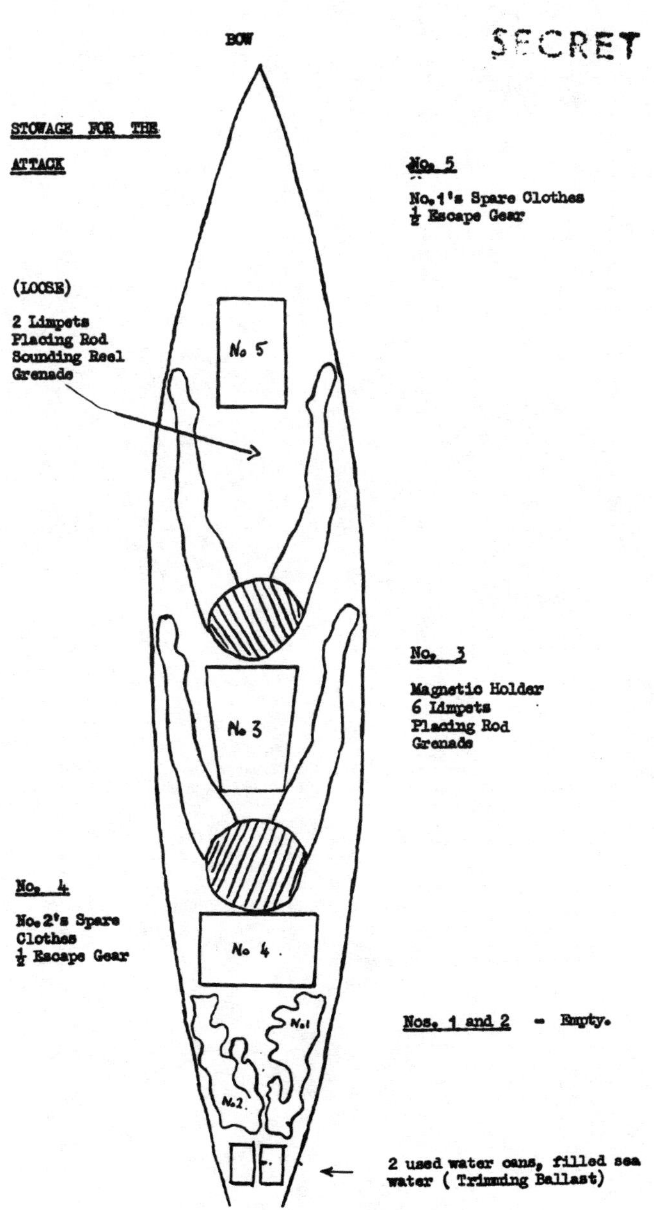
BOW
SECRET
STOWAGE FOR THE
ATTACK
No. 5
No.1's Spare Clothes
½ Escape Gear
(LOOSE)
2 Limpets
Placing Rod
Sounding Reel
Grenade
No 5
No. 3
Magnetic Holder
6 Limpets
Placing Rod
Grenade
No 3
No. 4
No.2's Spare
Clothes
½ Escape Gear
No 4
No.1
No.2
Nos. 1 and 2 - Empty.
2 used water cans, filled sea
water (Trimming Ballast)

APPENDIX II

Beach reconnaissance report

This is an early example of a beach reconnaissance report of the style devised by COPPs during the Second World War. It became standard procedure in the post-war activities of the SBS, and indeed employed a great deal of its manpower until the 1970s. Modern techniques and satellite imaging has lightened the task, but the basic requirements for a full and detailed reconnoitre of beach and location sites for major troop landings and deployment remains paramount.

EXAMPLE OF AMPHIBIOUS RECONNAISSANCE REPORT

Beach No. 35

PART I – COVERING PAPER

I. METHOD AND RESULTS

(a) The required reconnaissance was carried out by No. 4 SBS working in conjunction with H. M. 'X' Craft XE 10, by periscope by day and by swimming by night in a no-moon period on 8th and 9th April, 1953. Two swimmers were used on each night.

(b) The Pilotage Directions contained in Part III are written so as to be given as they stand (if approved) to the navigational leader, accompanied by the relevant sketches.

2. Reliability of Results

In order to show the probable reliability of the observed results the approximate route of the greatest penetration by the operators is shown on the shore-line sketch. The positions of the lines of soundings are also shown.

3. Recommended Alterations to the Provisional Plan

The beach is not one which can be approached directly, and consequently it is essential that the landing craft navigational leader is brought on to the least mistakable leading line as early as possible. It is therefore recommended that a marker beacon be set up in position Cape Gremlini 027° M. 6 miles, from which position the navigational landmarks can be identified.

4. Chance of Compromise

Neither of the swimmers attracted any enemy attention and it is considered that it can be fairly presumed that the reconnaissance was carried out without leaving any trace.

5. Form of this Report

This report covers only the matters concerning Beach No. 35.

Part II contains the Beach Report and the Beach Data Form.

Part III contains the Pilotage directions and the Pilotage Approach Plan.

Appendix 'F': Surf Report

PART II – BEACH REPORT

Beach No: 35	Name: BONDI BEACH
Classification: B	Refs:
Lat.: 45° 32′ N.	Chart Nos.: Admty. 20002
Long: 6° 18′ W.	40007
	Ruritan Y493
	X755
	Map No.: Series 3005
	Air Mosaic Series

Location: 3 miles North of CAPE GREMLINI on western shore of BAY.

SEA

(a) Anchorage and Holding Ground

A good anchorage exists in 8 fathoms of water about 1½ miles N. of the beach. The bottom of this position is shingle and appears to provide good holding ground.

(b) Navigational Difficulties and Hazards

Several areas of off-lying rocks, some of which are awash at low water exist to the South and East of the beach. These obstructions which are shown on the Pilotage Directions sketch, prevent a direct approach to the beach from seaward. North and inshore of these there are no obstructions.

(c) Conspicuous Objects and Landmarks

During the approach from seaward the following landmarks are useful for the purposes of navigation. (*See* Pilotage Approach Plan.)

(i) Capes Gremlini and Goblino.
(ii) The Saddle: a dip in the land at the head of the bay.
(iii) Conical Hill: conspicuous and conical shaped.
(iv) Tower: on the rising ground between Gremlini Cape and Conical Hill.

(d) Tidal Sets

Tidal sets in Comforto Bay were found to be inconsiderable. They appear to depend on the previous night's wind. The maximum set which was encountered inside the bay was less than 1 knot.

(e) Tides

The maximum vertical effect of the tide is 13½ feet at springs. However, a wind effect is also likely which may have a varying effect on the depth of water over the bar as shown on the attached beach data form.

SHORE

(a) Extent of Beach

The extent of the beach is 600 yards.

(b) Approach and Landing Marks

On the final approach to the beach the conspicuous white tower on the rising ground behind provides a good leading mark. Even at night this can be located, since it will be clearly skylined. A bearing of 225° M. Will take a vessel clear of all obstructions. Full details of the recommended approach are given in the Pilotage Directions.

(c) Protection from Weather and Surf Conditions

Several small fishing boats were anchored close inshore off the beach, which suggests that the shelter is good from the prevailing south or S.W. winds. Little surf may be expected. A surf report is attached.

(d) Nature of the Shore below HW Mark

The beach close inshore below the HW line has a good average gradient of 1/20 up to a depth of 3½ feet where the gradient becomes less and more variable. The eastern 300 yards is not suitable for most major L/C owing to the presence of a sand-bar about 50 yards off shore. At low water the bar dries. It is considered that LST and LCT could beach on the western half one hour on either side of H.W., but the gradient sketches on the Beach Data Form should be referred to.

(e) Soundings as observed 9th April, 1953

Yards	10	20	30	40	50	60	70	80	90	100	110	120	130	140	150	Time
Line A	3	6	5	4	4	5	6	7	7	8	8	10	12	14	14	0045
Line B	3	5	5	4	4	5	7	8	9	10	10	11	14	14	15	0130
Line C	4	6	6	5	6	8	9	11	11	11	12	13	15	15	15	0205

(f) Nature of the Shore above HW Mark

The surface of the beach from the water line consisted of sand mixed with boulders for 25x at a gradient of about 1/20. This gave way to a 50x wide stretch of shingle which was large and unlikely to jam tracked vehicles. The average total width of the beach was 75x.

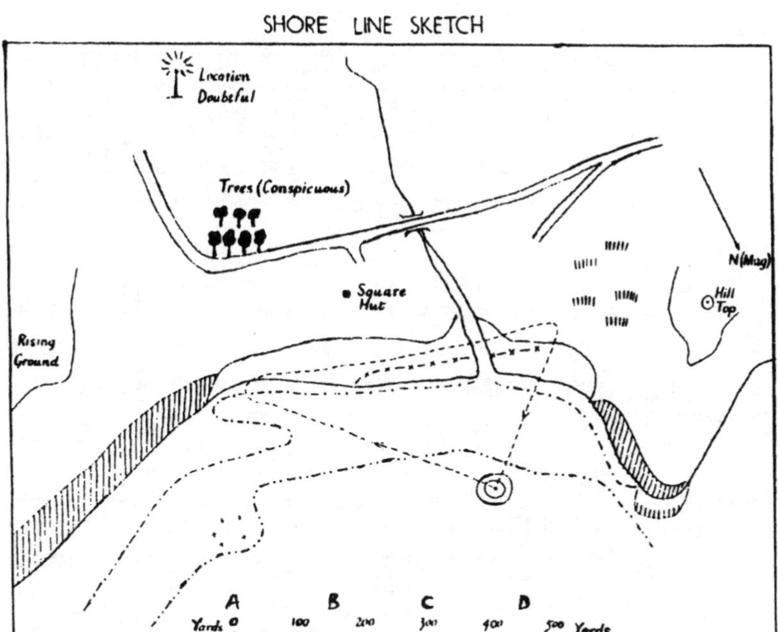

SCALE —— OR 1 INCHES TO 100 Yds

LEGEND

	Cliffs		Air Beacon
	Scrub		1 Fathom Line
	Wire fence		2 Fathom Line
	Rocky Shore		Route of Operator
	Rocks Awash		Swimmer Rel & Rec. Posns

HEIGHTS ABOVE DATUM				
PLACE	MHW SPRINGS	MHW NEAPS	MLW SPRINGS	MLW NEAPS
Bondi Beach	14·0	10·6	2·1	0·5

MARGINAL INFORMATION

SOURCES	Traced From Mosaic B564 8.4.53		
DATE	26th April 1953	LAT	45°32' N.
PLACE	Bondi Beach	LONG	6°18' W.
MAP REFERENCE	GSOS 1" Sheet N° 206 594327		
LOCATION	2 Miles North Comforto Harbour.		
MADE BY	OC N° 16 SBS RM.		

Shoreline sketch.

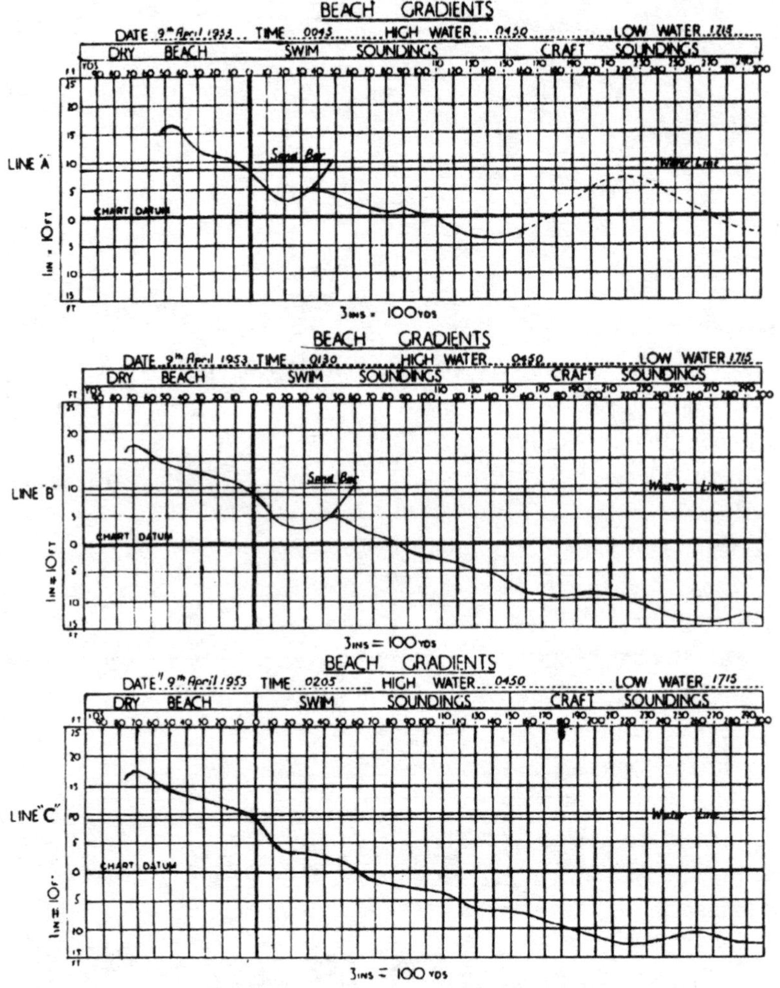

Beach gradients.

Bibliography

Billière, General Sir Peter de la, *Storm Command: A Personal Account of the Gulf War*, HarperCollins, 1992

Coogan, Tim Pat, *The Troubles*, Arrow Books, 1995

Courtney, G. B., *SBS In World War Two*, Robert Hale, 1983

Elliott, Peter, *The Cross and the Ensign: A Naval History of Malta*, PSC Books, 1980

Geraghty, Tony, *Who Dares Wins*, Little, Brown and Co, 1992 (revised edition)

Gilchrist, Donald, *The Commandos: D-Day and After*, Robert Hale, 1992

Holden-White, Vere, *Goodbye to Old Hat*, private memoirs

Holmes, Captain Len, private memoirs

Jellison Charles, *Besieged: World War II Ordeal of Malta*, UPNE, USA, 1984

Ladd, James, *SBS: The Invisible Raiders*, Arms & Armour Press, 1983

Lodwick, John, *The Filibusters*, Methuen, 1947

Macksie, Kenneth, *Commando Strike*, Leo Cooper, in association with Secker and Warburg, 1985

McNab, Andy, *Bravo Two Zero*, Bantam Press, 1993

Perkins, Roger, *Operation Paraquat*, Picton Publishing, 1985

Pringle, Major Jack, *Colditz Last Stop*, William Kimber, 1988

Ramsay, Jack, *SAS: The Soldier's Story*, Macmillan, 1996

Shortt, James, *The Special Air Service*, Osprey Publishing, 1981

Thompson, Brigadier Julian, *No Picnic*, Leo Cooper, in association with Secker and Warburg, 1985

Trenowden, Ian, *Stealthily By Night*, Crecy Books, 1995

Winton, John, *Hurrah for the Life of a Sailor*, Michael Joseph, 1977

Woodward, Admiral Sir Sandy, *One Hundred Days*, HarperCollins, 1992

Public Records Office:

Layforce WO218/89-95, plus 1, 2 and 3; SBS reports WO 218/103, 104, 112, 113, 212, 252.

RMBPD DEFE 2/988; Operation Frankton ADM 202/399, ADM 202/310, DEFE 2/216-218; Operation Rimau DEFE 2/1788, DEFE 2/650B and ADM199/1882; Sleeping Beauty DEFE 2/1144, DEFE 2/1144A and 1145; X-craft DEFE 2/1145; Welman DEFE 2/1009.

Rhine Flotilla DEFE 2/1706; Limpets DEFE 2/1719; Sea Reconnaissance Unit DEFE 2/1148 and 1145.

COPPs references, 34 separate folders viewed, on formation to operational activity, collated in ADM 234/52, DEFE 2 and WO 218, WO 203, WO 206 series.

41 Independent Royal Marines/SBS in Korea ADM 202/459; other Korean reports DEFE 2/1861; SBS post-war assessment DEFE 2/1907; Special Boat Sections, a history, DEFE 2/1621; SBS/SAS title dispute DEFE 2/1621.

SBS and amphibious warfare DEFE 2/1798. Other Second World War operations studied, all listed in ADM and WO series: Anteroom, Arenal, Bowery, Baboon, Batman, Corona, Catswhisker, Camperdown, Carpenter I, II and III, Condor 1–2, Cassoway, Chimera, Etna, Frippery, Gregory, Hawthorn, Hurry, Kelso, Kingpin, Lightning, Marigold, Postage Able, Principal, Profit, Reservist, Sandbank, Stakes, Snatch, Substract, Torch.

Other general SBS-related files and reports under DEFE 2/1373, 1545, 1546, 1720, 1453, 1454, 1447, 1736; 970, 975, 1903, 1819.

Index